Restoration Prayer Ministry Manual One

*Equipping ministers of all kinds with resources
to minister effective healing and freedom and
to train others also. 2 Timothy 2:2*

Carlotta P. Waldmann, M.A.

Founder of
Cross Walk Life, Inc.
NowFaith.TV Ministry Training School Online
Cross Walk Talk Radio Online

Inquiries should be addressed to:
Carlotta Waldmann
PO Box 2334
Santa Rosa Beach, FL 32459

Most of the scriptures in this manual are from these versions.
AMP – the Amplified Bible
KJV – King James Version
NKJV – New King James Version
NAS – New American Standard
NASB – New American Standard Bible
NIV – Holy Bible, New International Version

Acknowledgments

No one has succeeded entirely on their own efforts. Father God was faithful to bring alongside inspiring leaders and behind the scenes supporters who believed in us. Years ago I was encouraged to believe a godly belief, "God will bring people alongside you who not only believe in you but are honored to invest in your vision, your training and in fulfilling your mission." I couldn't imagine it but God honored my faith declarations and decrees.

I want to express my profound appreciation to my husband, Louis F. Waldmann III, for doing everything possible to support me as a person, a woman in ministry and all that God wants to do through me.

This book is only possible because of my dear friends and excellent editing team: Kay Flowers, Dorothy Smith, Patricia Brown and Tara Wentworth, who worked tirelessly with us for the Kingdom's sake.

I cannot express how grateful I am for Chester and Betsy Kylstra who wrote *Restoring the Foundations* and John and Paula Sandford who wrote *Transformation of the Inner Man.* Their teachings and training not only restored me but are strong pillars in my life message.

We are especially grateful to Bishop Bill Hamon and all the dedicated faithful Christian International ministers and members who have poured into our lives and have interceded for us.

We want to bless all the pastors, ministry leaders and lifelong friends, who share our vision to make these insights and training available to all churches, all cultures and all nations.

We are also greatly in debt to those to whom we have ministered, our prayer receivers, who have also taught us so much about the strategies of the enemy and our triumphant deliverer, the Lord of Hosts.

Testimonies of Restoration

I have been praying the Cross Walk Prayer, ministry prayers and scriptures. *The Lord has been working with me and in me in several ways: My ability to discern the "unspoken question," the "real issue," or to see with other eyes has improved in my interactions with others. My ability to hear the prompting of the Holy Spirit for scripture or for the right next question has increased several fold. Patience, peace and calm in difficult situations has increased also. I have seen increased levels of cooperation in the lives of my friends and those I have been ministering. I have an increase in willingness to discuss without criticism in some difficult communication issues. I have a new willingness to be patient with those who are less mature in the Faith, struggling with or dealing with strongholds. Most importantly, I see and experience a greater love among the people to whom I am ministering. Praise God for His provision and answer to prayer.*

I have been getting a huge amount of healing ever since I started restoration! This week, God has been showing me over and over, how much of a loving God he really is. For the past 3 years, my wife and I were in a church, that was very biblical, and doctrinally sound, but it leaned towards the very strict side and it would make you feel that God was there, ready to pounce on you if you messed up. The part of the prayer of thanks for God's law, that states, "forgive me for the times I blamed you for being such a harsh task master," is one of the areas that I am recovering from. In my time with God, He is continually ministering love to me and showing and speaking to me that He just wants to walk with me just like He did with Adam in the garden. He is a righteous judge, but he is not sitting there waiting for me to mess up, just so he can squash me. Healing is sometimes instant and sometimes it takes time, but through it all God is there just holding me, loving me and bring healing and freedom to my life.

I thank God, Jesus and the Holy Spirit, for what they are doing not only in my life but in the lives of those around me. May we all continue to be blessed by new spiritual openness and continuing repentance, forgiveness and healing in Christ Jesus. Amen

My mother was severely depressed and didn't leave the house except to go to work. Growing up I adopted her personality and followed her in depression and isolation. I had accepted the attitude "this is me and all I will be." I have tried many methods of healing but only Restoration Prayer Ministry to the inner self has made the big difference in my healing. I see the "surface symptoms and causes" and "root symptoms and causes" now. I have confessed my parent's sins and asked God for forgiveness for my sins, my ungodly beliefs, inner vows, etc. This week, I joined a women's weight loss bible study! This is a big step for me! It is hard for me to be in a group let alone women I do not even know. I thank God for the courage to join and socialize with other people at this level. I thank God for His unconditional love and patience with me. I give God all the glory!

From Fruit to Root: I am thankful for going through Restoration Prayer Ministry. *I learned all about going back to my "roots"- ancestors, parents, family, childhood, and early adulthood. I found out that a lot of my thinking and the "why" I react to things and people was built on past hurts and wounds. The results were strongholds, inner vows and* *walls, I didn't fully realize were there or how powerful they were in running my life. I learned how to confess the sins of my family, repent of my own sins, forgive myself, recognize ungodly beliefs and how to replace them with godly truth. I learned how to renounce my sin and break the power of it and the resulting curses by the redemptive work of Christ on the Cross. I learned (and am still learning) how to release my hurts-faults-failures- with the help of the Holy Spirit. This restoration has opened my spiritual eyes and ears. It is teaching me discernment and understanding in ministering to people who need healing. I empathize with them. I am them! I have also learned that it is possible to have God's calling - His anointing – even though still have flaws, weak areas and lessons to be learned.*

I had a lot of questions about starting this training school. I had questions about things like money, health issues and a very old computer. Two days after I found about the school, I received a prophetic word saying that there were answers for all my questions and that this was going to be a year of activation into the more of God. The next week, I called my pastor and told her about the school. She went online and looked everything over she told me to go for it. She also ordered my first textbook. Every week she prints my homework assignment. I have a big God, a wonderful and caring Father. Thank you, Love and prayers

I would highly recommend this ministry training! It has been very enjoyable. I only regret that we have time limitations and that we cannot spend even more time fully digesting the information. (We have already expanded the class from the original 2 1/2 hours to 3 1/2 hours.) "A fellow teacher"

This class has made me realize the global need for prayer ministry. Through this training, Christians around the world can be taught to minister to other Christians. I had been to a secular counselor and became more confused than I was before I went. I could not only have saved money, but could have had a closer relationship with God. Now I know how to trace from the "fruit to the root" and knowing the root of the matter can start real change in one's life.

New power through praying restoration prayers: I learned that condemning judgments and dishonoring of parents can cause the problem to come back on you. Since I have learned the Cross Walk prayer, I am praying it all through the week and I am teaching it to my three children. We have already experienced real change from so many things. I now say, "I got the power!"

Thank you, Carlotta, for your love and friendship. It really means so much to me. One of the areas I am trying to develop is believing people really do care about me. Oftentimes, I succumb to the belief that I am a burden to others and that I and my concerns don't matter to anyone. Those are the times I withdraw and I become isolated. But more and more I am beginning to resist this tendency and I reach out to friends like you who have faithfully loved me and encouraged me in all things. I have never received such love and acceptance before. Thank you, Cross Walk Life

Restoration Prayer Ministry Training is a must for every Christian Counselor! *I never cease to be amazed at the new revelations that I find. I look back and wonder how I have made it this far in life without these teachings. Now, I define counseling as helping people to apply the Word of God to their individual situations so that they can line up with God's wisdom and truth. I was well practiced in many mental health modalities, but have learned that we were unintentionally leading our clients astray. Now I know that no matter how experienced and well-trained the counselor, how well the client understands their issues, how sincere the effort to modify their behavior -- patterns are not broken by re-deciding! Now that I understand the law of sowing and reaping, I realize that we are bound to reap what we sow, until we repent, no matter how well we analyze and understand the problem! We do reap what we sow, more and later, no matter what or who we believe in. How simple God's way is. We can just repent of sowing destructive patterns, judging others, dishonoring others and blaming God for the results. As we begin to sow good seed we allow Him to live His supernatural life through us!*

Coming alive after repenting of spiritual rebellion! I feel like the fog and a weight was lifted off me. I have been on a "high" that I had not experienced in quite some time. I had felt for several years, that there was a disconnection in my brain. Coming up great thoughts and plans to execute them has not been my problem. The problem has been in the follow through. Somehow, I could not get myself motivated to accomplish my plans. I feel that God has remade all the connections in my brain since I have repented of my spiritual rebellion. God has restored my energy and self-discipline. I cannot adequately express the joy that I feel in my heart at this change in myself. God is also restoring the boldness that I have always felt in my spirit, but have been unable to completely express to others. I can see myself accomplishing great things as God does them through me. There are still several things to walk out and work out, but I have found my map and I am on my way! I am finally coming alive in God! Thank you!

Licensed Counselors need healing too! *Thank you very much for allowing yourself to be Christ's instrument to help me in so many ways. I've been declaring my godly beliefs and identity in Christ in the mirror daily, as well as listening to the prophecy God gave you for me, as well as other programs on your website. Today is day 15 without any antidepressants and I am starting to feel feelings. Although I've been having many feelings coming up, I'm focusing all of my attention on what Christ can do through me. I can't praise Jesus enough for all He has done for me and I want to please Him more and more! May the Lord bless you and your family with many inner and outer blessings. In Christ Jesus our Lord*

I am very thankful for RPM!!! I can't think of how it could be improved. I really think it was overall very balanced and am very thankful for it. My thinking was most affected. I realized that most of the depression and anxiety could be changed by thinking differently. I never thought that I would get any better by changing my ungodly beliefs. I didn't even know that my beliefs were ungodly and untrue. I learned more and more of how much God really loves me and hears me! I also am very grateful for the ministry showing me that I had and have very valid opinions in certain situations in my life. I have undergone 4 years of Christian counseling and I felt RPM was like a culmination of resolving issues that could only be resolved by this ministry. I am very blessed with RPM because God reached into my heart and resolved issues and situations that I have carried as a heavy burden for years and years. I have made life decisions from that painful place in my heart -- that is now healed!!

I had been struggling with hurts my entire Christian life. *I kept suppressing my feelings and thinking that I had forgiven all because I chose to not think about them. I began experiencing very real depression along with panic and anxiety attacks. I had strong feelings of committing suicide. It seemed like my emotions were reacting to my wounded areas and I could no longer suppress them. It was almost like my emotions had a mind of their own. I would sometimes get overwhelming bouts of anger or hopelessness. I could not understand why because I had awesome promises from God that I was expecting to come to pass. Even great prophetic words about my future. But something in me wanted me to give up on life. The demonic was harassing me. Through this ministry I learned the process the enemy uses on our minds to put us into bondage. I learned that my wounded areas needed to be brought up before the Lord for forgiveness and healing. Then I had to forgive myself for living my life based on how others had hurt me. I learned what true and lasting deliverance is. I am able to finally renew my mind. I kind of feel like a new Christian all over again. The Bible is easier for me to read and understand now that all of those hurts are not blinding me anymore. So now for the first time in my nine years of being saved I am finally getting healed on the inside. Thank you so much!*

Contents

Introduction

I was highly motivated to help others find healing and freedom in Jesus because lies and deceptions had blocked me from fulfilling my own destiny for decades. After years of experience as a mental health nurse, a Bachelor's degree in theology, being ordained as a Minister of Counseling, and receiving more training in restoration prayer ministry, I thought surely I was ready to pray for people. The Bible warns us not to release a novice into ministry too quickly, but I had been doing "Christian counseling" for years and thought I was prepared. Little did I know "how little I did know" in natural knowledge or in spiritual discernment.

My first trusting friend came for several days of restoration prayer. Wanting to be a good hostess, I rented a movie to help us relax after her trip. First of all, back then, I was too green to understand the many reasons why the movie "Ghost" was not a good Christian spiritual choice. Second, early in the movie one character is shot and killed, dying in his girlfriend's arms. At this point, my friend jumped to her feet, screaming in horror and grief. Too late, I realized my mistake. Her late husband had also been shot and had died in her arms! What a mistake! Thank God, He is able to redeem everything and He brought great healing in spite of our rough start.

I hope this book will help you avoid similar rough starts. It was written to guide you in ministering to troubled believers who have different underlying patterns of behavior and just as many different reasons for those behaviors. Perhaps the person you most want to help first is yourself. Either way, as you seek the guidance and wisdom of the Holy Spirit, you will gain knowledge and discernment of these patterns. You will receive keen discernment from the Holy Spirit as you learn to hear Him, not only for the surface issues causes but also for the root issues and root causes.

Philippians 2:12 declares we are to work out our salvation with fear and trembling. One of the Greek words for salvation is *sozo*. It carries the meaning of becoming whole, or to become healed spiritually, emotionally, mentally and physically. While for many believers there may have been an amazing transformation at the point of salvation (inviting Jesus Christ to be Lord and Savior), other areas of transformation may still require a process of repenting of specific areas of unbelief and taking whole fleshly structures or selfish patterns to Jesus to crucify on the Cross.

I believe I am a partaker of "the divine nature" (2 Peter 1:4) so my nature, or essence, is the new creation in me. Romans 6 says our old nature or old man has died, just as Christ died, once and for all. Our old nature has been buried, while the new us has been raised in newness of life, as Christ has been raised. Romans 7 and 8 say our flesh is the problem. It is like a memory card that remembers that sin might be enjoyable for a moment but is not the real us. I was happy to hear that NIV has changed its interpretation of Romans 7:18 to read that our struggle is with the flesh, not with a zombie old nature that comes back to life.

The devil cannot succeed in tempting us to sin unless we have a fleshly lust or pattern for him to hook. As prayer ministers, we evangelize unbelieving areas of the heart (fleshly doubts, worries and fears) and identify the lies and deceptions that make people vulnerable to the devil's setup. Many have tried to "modify their behavior" or "re-decide" to make better choices without experiencing success, because this too was powered by self.

Wholeness and healing encompasses much more than surface assessment of current pain or relief from an obvious pattern of dysfunction. People will very often ask for prayer, hoping that God will fix their significant other(s) in the belief that "If God will just fix them, I will be fine!" This erroneous thinking does nothing to bring the believer to face personal responsibility or accountability. For a long time, the standard for ministering healing meant simply encouraging forgiveness toward others and then offering comfort. While these are important and appropriate, standing alone they are incomplete. Our own strongholds are actually made up of our own sinful reactions and behaviors, for which we have not yet asked for forgiveness. We are often guilty of "healing the wound of my people lightly, saying peace, peace when there is no peace" (Jeremiah 6:14).

If a person is hurting as a result of violating God's spiritual laws, no amount of comfort or counseling will heal and set them free until they repent and come back into agreement with God. For example, a spouse suffering from years of betrayal may need validation for feeling appropriate anger, comfort for their wounds and encouragement to enforce healthy boundaries. That same spouse may also need to identify their own sinful reactions so they can cast out a spirits of anger, resentment or unforgiveness that have hooked them into fleshly patterns of sinful reactions and behaviors.

In this book, you will learn to do active listening on several levels at once. You will learn how to listen for "roots" as troubled believers share their circumstances. You will also learn to listen to the Holy Spirit at the same time, as He shares His strategy to heal.

Surface Issues
Surface Causes
Root Issues
Root Causes

The Holy Spirit will guide you to identify not only the surface symptoms and causes, but also the root symptoms and causes. He will form your healing prayer to include faith for restoration for the "surface issues and causes" and also to break the power of the "root issues and causes."

As you learn to effectively partner with the Holy Spirit, you can expect many darts from God's enemy. Satan will throw numerous roadblocks in the pathway to healing and "hooks" which will dig into one of the biggest roadblocks, your own fleshly baggage. Your mind and your flesh will constantly resist what can only be done by the Spirit of God.

Some people will assume they haven't gotten deliverance because they haven't tried hard enough in their own strength or they just "don't have the will power." You will stand with them as they realize they must come to the end of themselves and their own struggles and be willing to rest in God's authority for deliverance. Sometimes they ask for prayer but are not "ripe" and ready to make a full surrender to the Lordship of Jesus Christ and you will prayerfully wait for the Holy Spirit to make them "ripe." The fine print is that God's agenda is to allow them to reap what they sow in order to bring their flesh to death before He can raise them up in newness of life. Most people have to die to their ability to cope and perform before they are ready to stop striving in their own strength and to try "Christ in you, your hope of glory."

Believers sometimes, for whatever reason, find themselves stalled on their journey of faith. Most people don't understand that you don't break God's laws; they break you. People need to be guided to respond according to God's spiritual principles so that He can release them to be a demonstration of His power in their individual spheres of influence. As you pray restoration prayers, you will help make it clear that God is waiting for them to choose to respond to the Spirit and to believe they can rise up over their circumstances by trusting God for supernatural power and intervention.

They will learn NOT to respond to temptations in their own fleshly strength with fear, doubt, worry, limited thinking or self-sufficient independence. Using their free will, they can choose to walk through the open doors that God provides to be transformed, to operate in His miracle-working power and to ultimately make disciples of all nations.

To experience supernatural change and freedom from sin, we must commit to being transformed, aligning with the truth of God and taking everything to the Cross that is not from Jesus. We must allow God to shake everything that can be shaken and purify our motivations, until we hunger to know Him, to know His resurrection power and to partner with Him even in His suffering. God is able to transform us when we not only identify the devil's lies and deceptions, but also effectively repent of letting them block our lives. We then replace those lies with God's truth about ourselves, others and God.

Romans 12:1-2 commands us to present ourselves as living and holy sacrifices, allowing our minds to be renewed. In Luke 9, Jesus said, "If anyone wishes to come after Me, let him deny himself, take up his cross daily, and follow Me." In Galatians, Paul teaches that those who belong to Christ are to crucify fleshly passions and lusts. Jesus died to bring flesh to death, to resurrect His life in its place and to redeem all the rewards and blessings that we missed because of our sinful reactions and behaviors. If we truly allow our minds to be renewed, presenting ourselves as living sacrifices on God's altar, Christ in us will flow through us mightily in these last days to change not only ourselves but the entire world.

In this book, you will learn how to guide believers (and yourself) into renewal of mind and heart, and how to pray for cleansing and spiritual healing. You will learn the power of forgiveness as you lead wounded lives to seek forgiveness five essential ways. Transformed by the Cross of Christ, hearts will be changed as people come to the end of trusting in themselves, in their own righteousness or in their own fleshly strength. You will learn to enter into God's rest as promised in Hebrews 4:9-10, redeeming all the rewards and blessings and missed opportunities for spiritual growth. You will witness the miracle of the influence of the Holy Spirit on believers who were once powerless and hurting, now set free for heavenly service, empowered by the grace of our amazing God.

Carlotta P. Waldman

Brief Bio: Carlotta P. Waldman is the founder of Cross Walk Life, Inc., a ministry outreach and web site that includes over 200 articles. Filled with the Holy Spirit and endowed with strong spiritual gifts, Carlotta has seen God use her as a Bible College educator, seminar speaker, former mental health nurse and an ordained Minister of Counseling. She is known for her insights on how to break strongholds in the lives of believers, setting them on fire for service to Him. NowFaith.TV is an online 4 year video / audio ministry training school that reaches thousands every month in over 175 countries. In 2005, Carlotta began hosting Cross Walk Talk, a Christian talk radio show which invites callers to call in for ministry on the air. Carlotta has a Masters in Biblical Studies with an emphasis in Christian Counseling. You can find out more about application for Restoration Prayer Ministry, mentoring, online education, training, consultation or ministry to survivors at www.RestorationPrayerMinistry.com

To apply   http://www.RestorationPrayerMinistry.com
Home site   http://www.CrossWalkLife.com
Online school   http://www.NowFaith.TV
YouTube   http://www.youtube.com/user/NowFaithTV
Radio online   http://www.blogtalkradio.com/Cross-Walk-Talk
For survivors   http://crosswalklife.com/Recovery-for-survivors-home.html

Part I:
Preparation and Comprehension

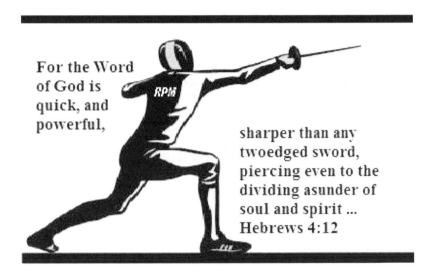

For the Word of God is quick, and powerful, sharper than any twoedged sword, piercing even to the dividing asunder of soul and spirit ... Hebrews 4:12

Understanding the Underlying Patterns

Through God's Word, we know how to apply Christ's blood to receive forgiveness of sins, but we do not necessarily understand how to bring every block, sin or fleshly (self-powered) structure in our lives to the Cross to be crucified. We will either believe that we will go through the Christian life asking for forgiveness of sin after sin, or we will learn how to live the crucified life, bringing fleshly structures (sinful actions or reactions) to the Cross once and for all.

The world's viewpoint is usually in direct opposition to the Word of God. Some psychologists tell us we can simply re-decide and make better choices with positive thinking. Motivational speakers tell us we can do anything we set our minds to accomplish. Prosperity preachers tell us God will provide the funds for anything that we can say and believe. Personal life coaches would help us to overcome our weaknesses with a powerful new self-image. In the Bible, however, we find different keys to victorious living.

God's Word teaches us that we need to come under His training, to accept what He knows is best for us. As we grow in faith, He creates opportunities for us to trust Him even more, to become radical lovers who are unfettered in our passion for Him and our compassion for others. In order to walk through these open doors of opportunity, we have to choose to die to our self-centeredness and to "live in Christ." Patterns of sinful reactions and sinful behaviors have to be brought to the Cross for Jesus to bring them to death. Instead of defending our strongholds by tolerating, excusing or minimizing our sin, we must choose to allow God to circumcise our hearts and purify our motives. Jesus died to break the power of sin in our lives. (Romans 6)

We must discern the difference between eternal versus temporary motivations and spiritual versus fleshly sources. Was it "just me" or Jesus Christ through me? 1 Corinthians 3:11-13 says, "For no other foundation can anyone lay than that which is laid, which is Jesus Christ. Now if anyone builds on this foundation with gold, silver, precious stones, wood, hay, straw, each one's work will become clear; for the Day will declare it, because it will be revealed by fire; and the fire will test each one's work, of what sort it is." NKJV

The Holy Spirit will then orchestrate challenges that are designed to develop us, not to destroy us. We learn how to renounce the lies, doubts and ungodly beliefs spoken in the past, and to speak God's truth.

When we cry out for a transfer from "adverse-city," the Holy Spirit, our personal tutor, will give the revelation: the key is to repent of wanting pity for our problems and to speak His truth about our <u>powerful potential</u>.

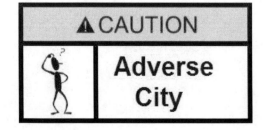

As we abide in Jesus, we learn a lifestyle of focusing on Jesus rather than on problems. We choose to partner with God, instead of focusing on disease, we focus on the opportunity to receive or minister healing. As we live by faith and walk by faith, we don't focus on lack or poverty, but we speak God's abundance and provision into existence for all that He wants done. We learn that every apparent problem is simply a stage set for us to agree with God, to declare and to decree His miracle-working power. We live by His supernatural power not our natural power.

For many believers, this is radical thinking. They are afraid to step out and allow God to activate them in supernatural power because they know their hearts are not pure. They are afraid to speak blessing and miracles into existence because they have used their words to harm others. James 3:10 says, "From the same mouth come both blessing and cursing. My brethren, these things ought not to be this way." NASB They recall that in the past they have spoken judgments against others, dishonored authorities and have doubted God. While they may have been able to modify their behavior, it is not enough. Their hearts still need to be purified.

If you have Christ in you, you have everything you need to fulfill your destiny in Christ, but most people may not know how to release this life-changing power. Believers in Jesus Christ as Lord have been called from the foundation of the earth and have His unlimited power within to be all He has called them to be. He has made unique deposits into each believer's life and has been preparing individuals for a unique gifting, a unique calling and a unique anointing.

It is God's pleasure that believers experience blessing and undeserved favor to fulfill their God-given destiny. If asked, He will give personal revelation about spiritual principles that will allow believers to pinpoint their destiny, to identify the blocks to that destiny and to be released to fulfill it. What excitement, to be able to lead believers into the knowledge of release, answered prayer and fulfillment of their God-given purpose in Christ!

The big question is how to lead them into the knowledge of getting rid of the blocks in their lives and being activated in the spiritual gifts and calling of God to be a demonstration of His love and power. When believers allow God to give them personal revelation of how to apply His principles to their lives and get the beam out of their own eyes, He will be happy to give them the keys to be activated in both spiritual gifts and calling.

Even though we are believers and members of God's family, we all struggle with our fleshly desires or basic selfishness that fuels our independent will. In order to make us ineffectual for Christ, Satan will do anything in his power to get believers to fall into sin or sinful habits. It seems that most churches do not have an accountability and restoration team in place to restore the fallen. When a leader falls, the church may do anything from hide the error due to embarrassment and shame to deny that there is a problem. When believers fall, those in the Christian community usually exhibit one of the following reactions, none of which is particularly helpful:

1. Cast the sinners out and turn them over to Satan, with no help to restore.
2. Ignore the sin, pretending it never happened; not judging, just love the sinner.
3. Forgive and forget without ministry to the sinners, their families or victims.

It's not enough to simply pray for the fallen while neglecting the area of restoration. Sin affects the whole person—body, soul, and spirit—and not only the sinners but also any people they may have wounded.

Restoring believers to God, to themselves and to the Christian community involves the leading of the Holy Spirit to discern the root of the sin and what is needed for true restoration. This heavenly discernment is absolutely necessary; only God can perceive the thoughts and intents of the heart. When confronted with their sin, fallen believers tend to display one or more of these common reactions:

1. Choose to deny, minimize, excuse, blame; feel remorse but do not repent.
2. Pretend to repent and receive a pseudo restoration, which is not lasting.
3. Truly repent, do restitution and thus truly restored.

For fallen believers who exhibit the third reaction and honestly want to rout the devil from their lives and follow the true route to blessing, there is an answer: They must come into agreement with God about their own former sinful reactions to problems in their lives. Indulgence in or defense of these sinful reactions leads to discernable patterns of sinful behavior. This is what the Holy Spirit can help them, and you, to discern in order to bring about healing.

Let's look at some of these patterns.

What are fleshly structures or patterns? Everyone has fleshly self-centered reactions whether they are a born again believer or not. Pediatricians would say the babies are born with preferences, fears, dislikes, likes, opinions or even addictions that were formed during prenatal experiences. For instance, an unborn baby who was subjected to physical, verbal or mental abuse in the womb will form reactions to the abuser and will react if that person tries to hold them in the labor room. Anxious mothers-to-be may give birth to colicky fearful babies. Early childhood wounds cause children to have fleshly reactions and fleshly behaviors before they understand the difference between spiritual responses and fleshly reactions.

Romans 7 describes the struggle that every believer experiences, as our self-centered fleshly lusts war for dominance over our spirit-led desires. Even though we can be assured that our old nature is dead once for all, as Christ died once for all (Romans 6), our flesh still remembers the self-life well and wants to be in control.

Romans 7:1-6 says the secret is to die to our "old husband" of keeping the law in our strength and to be married to another, our new Bride Groom in the Spirit, Jesus Christ. Out of this union, life is conceived and lasting fruit is born. We have died to living by the letter of the law and live out of our new personal spirit, which actually can be one with Holy Spirit. (1 Corinthians 6:17)

Ungodly Beliefs

Many believers go through their entire lives like hungry passengers on a cruise ship, unaware that fabulous meals are included in the fare. They continually beg God to give what He has already given. They may know that God's Son has already paid the price for the fare, but they are blocked from further knowledge of the contents of the dining room—or even how to find it. They may read words in the first chapter of Ephesians like "holy and without blame" but they don't really believe all these blessings, benefits, and privileges belong to them. If you try to share that they already have been given everything they need for life and godliness, they may stare at you like a cow looking at a new gate: "If I go through this new gate, where will it lead?"

There are many reasons why Christians don't seem to live the victory Christ has promised. The main reason is that God's enemy (and ours) is constantly seeking to undermine the abundant life God offers so that Christians will not enter into God's fullness. First, we must choose to believe that walking in the fullness of the Holy Spirit in victory, is a "mission possible" because Jesus died that we might be free from the law of sin and death.

Satan is out to destroy believers and their hope that Jesus Christ would want to live His life through them in love and power. God's plan is to empower us to love Him, ourselves and others. Satan's master plan is to separate us from God, ourselves and others. Satan sets up circumstances so that believers feel separated and isolated, alone in their struggles and sure that no one understands them. Yes, Christians can certainly feel brokenhearted, despondent, and inconsolable, but to remain in that state is a trick of the devil, who may have worked for decades to plant the seeds of condemnation, expectations of failure or word curses handed down from previous generations.

Satan is out to strangle faith and he will go to any extent to intimidate, sidetrack, mislead and render believers powerless. He will use events of hurt and trauma to sow ungodly and untrue beliefs about God, others or themselves in the minds of believers and build fleshly, reactive behaviors on the foundation of these false beliefs. As Christians come to wrong conclusions about themselves, others and God, Satan hopes to use these wrong conclusions to keep believers weak and ineffectual for a lifetime.

God is delighted that you are willing to partner with His Holy Spirit to help people identify and destroy Satan's strategy. For some reason, He usually limits Himself to working through human beings.

The Bible says that we determine our future by the "fruit of our own lips" or you might say, "We get what we speak." We also get what we believe for; faith works, whether negative or positive faith. There are spiritual laws that are just as sure as natural laws like gravity. We don't break the law of gravity, it breaks us. A spiritual law that has everything to do with healing, freedom and restoration, is the law of sowing and reaping.

Sowing and Reaping

Another reason for lack of vibrant Christianity is the resulting pattern of sowing and reaping. Many people today do not understand cause and effect; they think that even long-term patterns in their lives just come out of the blue. If there is a long-term negative pattern or curse in their lives, they need to run to ask God for the root cause because Proverbs 26:2 says it is not there without a cause. Patterns don't develop out of the blue. They are constructed bit by bit over time.

Anytime someone comes complaining of reaping more than their share of trouble, as an ongoing pattern, one has to ask God how they sowed the bad seeds they are now reaping and how to break the power of the cause. **The rule of cause and effect** (or sowing and reaping) applies to everyone, including believers. A sinful reaction to godly authority, for example, sows a grudging attitude that will reap a harvest of discontent and disrespect, especially if that person becomes an authority themselves.

Sowing and reaping, like gravity, is an impartial law. Whatever seeds we sow, whether good or bad, we will reap what we sow, later than we sow and more than we sow. No amount of counseling can make this reaping pattern go away and no amount of counseling can cause the receiver to be immune to God's natural and spiritual laws, like sowing and reaping. As Galatians 6:7 ESV says, "Do not be deceived: God is not mocked, for whatever one sows, that will he also reap." If a man sows one kernel of corn, he will reap about 300 kernels, no matter what his beliefs.

Ungodly Soul Ties

Ungodly soul ties develop when we enter into an ungodly covenant with another person, group or institution. It is important to formally break the ungodly part of our ties and to keep the godly ties. The fruit of the transference of spirits, ungodly beliefs, bitter expectations, inner vows, word curses spoken by them or us, will affect our lives until we renounce and break the power of our ungodly agreements with them. God is a covenant keeping God and honors the covenants we have made until we break them. We must identify and cut the ungodly soul tie by praying a prayer of agreement with someone with spiritual authority.

Soul ties can be made in many more relationships than with just sexual ones. People will come for prayer ministry to rid themselves of the residue of personal relationships, ties with denominations, error taught in books, wounds from business contracts, employers, church leadership, teachers, coaches, blood packs, vows with secret organizations, domineering or abusive relationships or even from the control of people who have already passed away. Soul ties must be broken with the power of agreement of someone with spiritual power and authority. I had been teaching about soul ties for years before I realized the power of them in my own life.

Thirty-three years after I was separated from my high school sweetheart (because my family moved to another state) he appeared in my doorway. My heart was leaping for joy, believing that I would finally have the true love I had always wanted. This powerful tie had been lying dormant for thirty-three years. I was single and available! But ... after three weeks of calls and emails, I had to admit that I was now Spirit-filled with spiritual gifts and he was not. My poor heart had to give him up AGAIN! After five weeks of tears, a pastor prayed with me to break the power of the soul tie and I was finally free to take my heart back. Good thing too ... because I met my husband, Louis, the next week!

Bitter Root Judgments

Hebrews 12:15 says to look "carefully lest anyone fall short of the grace of God; lest any root of bitterness springing up cause trouble, and by this many become defiled; ... ." NKJV   A bitter root judgment of an offense or wound in the past is one of the most common spiritual roots of current negative patterns. The more we meditate on scriptures, the more these bitter roots are brought to light, so that the sowing and reaping cycles can be broken.

If there is bad fruit on your tree, the bad root is on your tree. Believers need to take a good, long look at their lives and their sinful reactions to hurts and wounds. Are they exhibiting the good fruit of the Holy Spirit or some other kind of fruit? Where there is lots of bad fruit, there is a bad root—often a root of bitterness caused by judgmental attitude, resentment, or repressed anger, grief or guilt not completely dealt with, or even a hardened attitude of unforgiveness.

Bad fruit on MY tree is from MY own sinful reactions and hidden roots on MY tree ... not their tree!

Bitter judgments are like negative faith and faith works whether it is positive or negative. We have all been hurt by bitterroots, when someone refused to forgive us and expected us to continue to fail. When believers judge with condemnation, they are helping Satan put prison bars around the other and their sin, making it harder for them to experience the very freedom from sin that is needed. This bitter root will grow and fester within hearts and lives, so that Christians begin to believe in a twisted sense of God's truth, inhibiting their own spiritual maturity and tainting the lives of everyone around them.

The good news is that the Holy Spirit is able to show us how to pray, whether we are tracing the pattern from bad fruit to bad root or from a bad root to bad fruit. Even if the fruit has not fully blossomed yet, we can renounce our bad roots and avoid reaping crop after crop of bad fruit in the future. Luke 6:46-49 exhorts us to dig deep and to see if our foundation is built upon the "rock" which cannot be shaken.

Fleshly Strongholds

Strongholds are areas of fleshly resistance in our lives that we know are against the will of God but seem impossible for us to change. The Holy Spirit will try to convict us of sinful thoughts and behaviors but if we resist, we are in danger of developing strongholds in our lives.

Often they begin when we have reacted sinfully to hurts and have begun to tolerate sinful thoughts, followed by excusing sinful behaviors and the development of new sinful beliefs, behaviors and expectations. When we defend all these sinful reactions instead of repenting of them, we are then defending our fleshly stronghold.

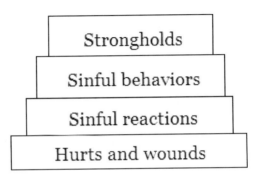

When strongholds are operating in our lives, we tend to judge others and ignore our own blind spots. Strongholds give us a false identity and we begin to agree with it saying, "I am angry" or "I am fearful" or "I am rejected" or "I am jealous." Even though we know that this is not God's higher truth about us, we feel that it is hopeless to change.

Over time, strongholds are slowly built in our lives until we resist any kind of ministry and claim our rights to react sinfully. For instance, we don't decide to have a stronghold of bitterness; we decide that because of what "they" did to us, we then have a right:

- to refuse to forgive the offender until "tomorrow"
- to resent them for today and review our record of wrongs
- to judge them with condemnation, attack or avoid them
- to imagine how we could even the score or retaliate
- to allow ourselves to rage or express our wrath to others
- to choose to hate them, not just their action
- to imagine how to eliminate them from our world
- to entertain murdering them through words or violence

When I began to pray scripture against each stronghold in my life, I was healed of twenty-four illnesses. They were documented illnesses, but physicians could only treat the symptoms. It was humbling to realize that praying scripture defeated my own personal strongholds and I was healed.

Praying the Word of God in agreement with other Christians, will break the stronghold's power to hold us and will show us how to come into agreement with God's truth about who we are in Christ. Satan's plan is to cause separation between us and God, others and even inside ourselves. God's plan is to enable us to love Him, others and ourselves.

Accepting our True Identity in Christ

The Bible has much to say about us that may sound hypocritical when we try to declare these truths over ourselves. I would say a hypocrite is someone who pretends he is someone that he is not. But I am commanded to believe that I am holy, blameless, righteous, totally forgiven and unconditionally loved and accepted, completely apart from my performance. If God says this is who I am, because Jesus died and took my sins upon Himself, am I a hypocrite to say this is who I am or a hypocrite to pretend I am not who God says I am?

Westerners are particularly prone to base their identity on their performance or lack of it. It is difficult for us to understand that our new identity is based on the true reality of who Jesus says we are: since we have exchanged our old nature for our new one. Choosing to walk as a new creature in Christ, old things having passed away and all things made new, is the first step to accepting our new identity in the true reality, God's reality.

The Bible is clear that our old man has died and we have been raised to newness of life. Romans 6:6-11 says, "Knowing this, that our old man was crucified with Him that the body of sin might be done away with that we should no longer be slaves of sin. For he who has died has been freed from sin. Now if we died with Christ, we believe that we shall also live with Him, knowing that Christ, having been raised from the dead, dies no more. Death no longer has dominion over Him. For the death that He died, He died to sin once for all; but the life that He lives, He lives to God. Likewise you also, reckon yourselves to be dead indeed to sin, but alive to God in Christ Jesus our Lord." NKJV

Fleshly Inner Vows

Fleshly, inner vows are promises or vows to ourselves in the power of our own strength: "I will never. . ." or "I will always …" These vows are powered by the power of the flesh, are not Spirit-led and should be renounced utilizing the power of agreement with someone who knows their spiritual power and authority. In the Bible, we are commanded to simply let our "yes" be "yes" and our "no" be "no" without swearing. In order to break the power of a fleshly inner vow, we must ask someone with spiritual authority to pray in agreement with us, in the Name of Jesus Christ. The most common fleshly inner vow that I know of is "I will not talk, tell, share, feel, be real or ask for what I want." This vow can seriously limit your future.

Studies show what fleshly inner vows such as "I will never grow up" or "I will never marry" or "I will never have children" have actually prevented the person from developing physically, or having a successful marriage or delivering a live child. Once renounced in agreement with someone who knows their spiritual power and authority, people were suddenly able to mature physically, enjoy a successful marriage or deliver a live child.

Bitter Expectations

Bitter expectations are almost as powerful as bitterroot judgments. When we expect others to fail, we are agreeing with the enemy and defiling others. While it is easy to expect others to continue to act like they have in the past (or the present), it is godly love and obedience to believe the best and to agree with God for their healing and deliverance from sin. (When we continue to expect others to fail us, and they do, we may also develop bitter root judgments.)

Although it's easier to feel like the innocent victim and blame others, people who truly want deliverance for themselves need to be held accountable for their ungodly reactions to the failings of others. Dishonoring or judging others for their failures or their sins may seem like a normal reaction or an easy out, but playing the "blame game" allows people to avoid responsibility for their own actions, reactions, or overreactions. Until they face the reality of their own possible contribution to the problem, whether conscious or unconscious, healing from the pain and consequences of past mistakes will not be complete.

I learned this the hard way. I had judged my father for being distant even though he had to travel for a living. Then I began to judge my tenant and spiritual leaders for being distant too. But when I repented of judging my father for being distant, I noticed an immediate change in my father, spiritual leaders and tenant, who suddenly wanted to spend time with me. I realized I was reaping the judgments that I had sowed.

Self-Directed, Christ-Directed or Christ Controlled?

You can see that Satan has lots of tricks up his slippery sleeve and he has used these same traps with generations of believers who keep on falling into them. However, the good news is that when people do admit they are part of the cause, they also have power to be part of the solution. In agreeing with God that their attitudes and actions are sinful, believers can be led into the healing presence and power of Holy Spirit to be set free to live for God with vitality and purpose.

Romans 12 says that we need to present ourselves as living and holy sacrifices, allowing our minds to be renewed. In Luke 9:23 Jesus said, "If anyone wishes to come after Me, let him deny himself, take up his cross daily, and follow Me." In Galatians, Paul teaches that those who belong to Christ are to crucify fleshly passions and lusts. Jesus died to bring flesh to death, to resurrect His life in its place and to redeem all the rewards and blessings that we missed because of our sinful reactions and behaviors.

This must be made perfectly clear: seeking deliverance without also bringing fleshly structures to the Cross for Jesus to put to death is a formula for failure. Actually, we are commanded to deal with our flesh more often than we are told to seek deliverance. Our flesh comes between us and God, excusing and encouraging us to continue in these sinful fleshly patterns, to the point that we often refuse the liberty offered by Holy Spirit. Without truly hating our fleshly patterns, we will not hate the agreements that we have with Satan's deceptions. These agreements with Satan's lies must be renounced before we can receive God's Truth and speak the Word of faith effectively. Without dying to our flesh, we cannot be Christ controlled.

Some "pre-believers" whose lives and priorities are out of control, will request ministry. They are still on the throne of their life and have not invited Christ into their life as their Savior.

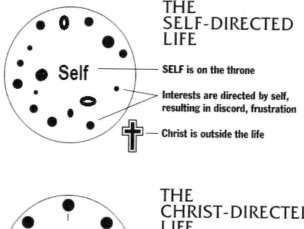

THE SELF-DIRECTED LIFE

SELF is on the throne

Interests are directed by self, resulting in discord, frustration

Christ is outside the life

Many believers try to live a Christ directed or assisted life. They may see Christ as inside of them, on the throne of their life, or they may picture Christ outside of them and assisting them to control "their life."

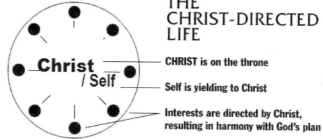

THE CHRIST-DIRECTED LIFE

CHRIST is on the throne

Self is yielding to Christ

Interests are directed by Christ, resulting in harmony with God's plan

What Apostle Paul is talking about in Galatians 2:20 is actually Christ living in and through believers, in a union with us that bears much fruit according to Romans 7:4.

Here is Galatians 2:20 paraphrased in my own words:
"My old fleshly, self-centered, unredeemed nature has been crucified with Christ; but nevertheless the real me, partaker of the divine nature, is still living; yet not I alone but Christ is living His life in me and through me. The life I live now is not even by my own faith but with the faith OF the Son of God, who loves me and gives Himself daily for me."

CHRIST IN YOU THROUGH YOU

One with Christ

One with His mind, will, way and timing

His fruit is born

Restoration ministers must ask Holy Spirit to lead them to ask the right questions to help the prayer receiver to recognize if they have invited in Christ to be their Savior and Lord.

What Happens When We Are Born Again?

Many times, although we have true compassion for our prayer receivers who desperately want peace with God, we don't know what to say to them. Maybe they prayed a prayer but aren't sure they are born again in Christ. We may not know how to tell them what born again is. We are sure that God loves them, has a wonderful plan for their life and that He came in the form of Jesus Christ to tell them so. We know that Christianity is not just a religion but being born again into the family of God. We want them to know that they will be supernaturally transformed and set free when they choose to invite Jesus Christ to come to live inside their hearts. (Revelation 3:20)

What do you believe really happens when someone is born again? Are they the same person with the same nature but they are now going to Heaven? Do they now have the old nature and a new nature? Is the old nature now dead and they have a new divine nature? What becomes new? Their soul or spirit? If the old man dies, exactly what passes away? If you are born again, are you actually able to live the Christian life?

If they are not sure they are born again, I encourage you to ask questions versus trying to persuade them that they have eternal salvation already. If someone wants to invite Jesus to be their Lord and Savior but asks you what happened to you when you prayed the prayer of acceptance, what would you say?

Here is a short list of what happened when you were born again. Read and study these blessings and privileges God bestows freely on His children.

- I will not perish but have eternal life = a new past and a new future (John 3:16).
- I am saved by grace totally apart from my good works (Ephesians 2:8-9)
- I can be absolutely sure that I am going to heaven (1 John 5:11-13).
- I have increasing faith as I know the Word of God. (Romans 10:17).
- I am adopted by God who is my *Abba*— "Father" (Romans 8:15).
- I automatically receive righteousness as a gift (Romans 5:18, 21).
- I am totally forgiven and cleansed of all unrighteousness (1 John 1:9).
- Jesus makes me holy and without blame before Him (Ephesians 1:4).

- I am partaker of the divine nature by the Spirit of God (2 Peter 1:4).
- I am born again in Spirit = primarily a spiritual creature (John 3:5).
- I know I have eternal life; I have the Son of God inside (1 John 5:12).
- My old nature dies, is buried; I am raised to newness of life (Romans 6).
- I am a new creation in Christ; all things are made new (2 Corinthians 5:17).
- I am sealed with the Holy Spirit of God (Ephesians 1:13).
- I am hopeful and not ashamed because God loves me (Romans 5:5).
- I have no fear of condemnation because I am in Christ (Romans 8:1).
- The Holy Spirit assures me that I am a child of God (Romans 8:16).
- God gives me wisdom and healing (James 1:5; 5:16).
- I have life and life abundantly because Jesus is the Life (John 10:10).
- He is my Shepherd; I am His sheep: I hear His voice (John 10:16).
- I have the fruit of the Holy Spirit who is inside me (Galatians 5:22).
- I ask, believing God's Word, and my prayer is answered (Mark 11:24).
- If I abide in Christ and His Word, I will be fruitful (John 15:5).
- I have peace with God, beyond understanding (Philippians 4:7; Romans 8:6).
- I am transformed by the renewing of my mind (Romans 12:2).
- I can do all things through Christ who strengthens me (Philippians 4:13).
- I am loved and accepted unconditionally in God's family (Ephesians 1:6).
- I am finally complete in Christ, lacking nothing (Colossians 2:10).
- I will be given everything I need for life and godliness (2 Peter 1:3).
- I have God's perfect love that casts out all my fears (1 John 4:18).
- I have love, power and a sound mind instead of intimidation (2 Timothy 1:7).
- God's truth makes me truly free from bondage (John 8:32; Romans 8:14-15).
- I can be sure that I will be resurrected and go to heaven (Romans 6:5).
- Jesus Christ in me will live the Christian life through me (Galatians 2:20).
- I am filled with Holy Spirit and gifts (1 Corinthians. 12, 14; Ephesians 5:18).
- I am one spirit with Holy Spirit, Jesus and Father God (2 Cor. 6:17; John 17).

You Can Know God Personally! – Adapted from www.cru.org

Because of God's deep love for you, He has already made all the necessary arrangements for you to enjoy His wonderful plan for your life. We aren't born again by our own efforts to reach God. We need a whole new heart or spirit that can have fellowship with God. Through the death and resurrection of Jesus Christ, you can enjoy a personal relationship with God. Jesus made it possible to bridge the chasm which separates us from God.

John 17:3 tells us, "Now this is eternal life: that they may know you, the only true God, and Jesus Christ, whom you have sent."

How can we be born again?

1 John 5:11-13 says, "And this is the testimony: God has given us eternal life, and this life is in his Son. [12] Whoever has the Son has life; whoever does not have the Son of God does not have life."

What prevents us from knowing God personally? We are separated from God because of our sin.

Romans 8:6-8: "The mind of sinful man is death, but the mind controlled by the Spirit is life and peace; the sinful mind is hostile to God. It does not submit to God's law, nor can it do so. Those controlled by the sinful nature cannot please God."

A great gulf separates man from God. Man is continually trying to reach God and establish a personal relationship with Him through human efforts, such as living a good life, philosophy, or religious efforts. But man's efforts to bridge the gap between man and God inevitably fail.

Jesus Christ is God's Son and His ONLY provision for man's sin. Through Him alone we can know God personally and experience God's love. Jesus broke the power of sin by His death and resurrection. By giving His perfect life in exchange for our sinful ones, He made the perfect sacrifice and paid the full price to open the way to God.

Romans 5:8: "God demonstrates His own love toward us, in that while we were yet sinners, Christ died for us."

1 Corinthians 15:3-6: "Christ died for our sins... he was buried... he was raised on the third day according to the scriptures... he appeared to Peter, then to the twelve. After that he appeared to more than five hundred..."

John 14:6: "Jesus said to him, 'I am the way, the truth and the life. No one comes to the Father except through me.' "

We must individually RECEIVE Jesus Christ as Lord and Savior; then we can know God personally and experience His love.

John 1:12: "As many as received him, to them he gave the right to become children of God, even to those who believe in his name."

Ephesians 2:8-9: "For it is by grace that you have been saved, through faith. This does not depend on anything you have achieved, it is the free gift of God; and because it is not earned no one can boast about it."

Receiving Christ involves turning to God from self (a spirit of repentance) and trusting Christ to come into our lives to forgive us of our sins and make us what He wants us to be. Just to agree intellectually that Jesus Christ is the Son of God and that He died on the Cross for our sins is not enough. Nor is it enough to have an emotional experience. We receive Jesus Christ by faith as an act of our will as we choose to receive Him as our Lord and Master.

Jesus Christ is waiting for an invitation to come into your life. In fact, He says, "Behold, I stand at the door and knock; if anyone hears my voice and opens the door, I will come in" (Revelation 3:20).

Perhaps you can sense Christ knocking at the door of your heart. You can invite Him in by faith right now. God knows your heart, so it doesn't matter exactly what words you use.

Here's a suggested prayer to receive Christ as your Lord and Savior:

Lord Jesus, *I want to know You personally. Thank You for dying on the Cross for my sins. I open the door of my life to You and ask You to come in as my Savior and Lord. Take control of my life. Thank You for forgiving my sins and giving me eternal life. Make me the kind of person You want me to be. Amen*

If this prayer expresses the desire of your heart, pray it right now and Jesus Christ will come into your life, just as He has promised. Once you invite Christ into your life, He promises to never leave you.

Hebrews 13:5: "God has said, 'Never will I leave you; never will I forsake you.' "

What if your prayer receiver is not a born again believer?

Years ago, a man who had been a preacher's kid applied to receive my 18 hour whole life Restoration Prayer Ministry. He read the four articles which clearly describe our Christian ministry and prayers and he sent the 10 page application. I asked one of my dear RPM interns to assist me for the four days of ministry. He flew in and she drove 3 hours to join us and we all met in Florida.

Our prayer receiver began our first session by asking, "Does it matter that I am a Mormon?" I hear God very well and heard God saying to tell our receiver, "God is not surprised and He will restore you." (Never mind that I was shocked that he never happened to mention his Mormon faith before.) But God …

God is omniscient, knowing all things, and he had told me to ask Liz to be my assistant for this receiver. That day, Liz shared her testimony of being raised as a Mormon but later learning that Jesus Christ is the ONLY begotten Son of God Most High. Only Jesus Christ is God Himself come in the flesh yet perfect in every way. Only Jesus is the Way, the Truth the Life, because He is alone is God …

God knew that Liz was more familiar with the false beliefs of the Mormon Church and especially the false claims of who Christ is. She was loving and able to kindly invite him to receive Jesus, the Name above all names, Who alone is able to provide salvation, by paying the price for our sins. He alone has proven that He has the keys to eternal life by rising from the dead and He is alive today. All the religious leaders are dead and gone. Praise God that He is always orchestrating all things for the good of those who love Him and are called according to His purposes.

Knowing the Power of Forgiveness

People requesting prayer for healing of an emotional wound of some kind may actually be seeking vindication for their feelings of pain or anger. They may want to hear words of consolation and sympathy; the thought of forgiving their offenders is the farthest thing from their mind. But forgiveness is the key that opens the door to healing.

Withholding forgiveness will not lead to healing; it will lock up the seekers in a cell just as formidable as the ones they envision for their offenders. Forgiveness sets both the offended and the offender free to be healed. Willingness to release the offender to Jesus is the choice that gives Jesus access to the wounds that need healing.

First of all, the true meaning of forgiveness must be understood. It doesn't mean denying that anything bad happened or pretending "all is well" when it isn't. It doesn't mean sweeping things under the rug, so to speak, and looking the other way in avoidance or total denial. It doesn't mean trying in our own strength to simply "forgive and forget" without coming to God for His help and healing. It doesn't mean I have to pretend that I am totally or instantly pain free or that the offender is now innocent.

Forgiveness means acknowledging the hurt and damage done and then giving up your right to get even, pure and simple. In Ephesians 4:32, we are commanded to forgive others as God in Christ forgives us—not because we deserve it but because the price for that forgiveness has already been paid. The finished work of Christ on the Cross provides the offended one the power to give up the right to get even and then place it in God's hands to deal with in His way and in His time.

Seen this way, forgiveness doesn't mean an unrepentant offender is now off the hook. Nobody "gets away" with anything; everyone reaps what they sowed, more than they sowed and later than they sowed, unless they repent. For example, if we sow criticism, we will reap more criticism than we have sown (in ourselves or from others) and we will reap it much later than we sowed it. Just as a crop is not reaped at the time it is sown, when we do reap it, it is more than we have sown and later than we have sown.

We must remember there is no double jeopardy. Either we will insist on judging and condemning them or we release them to the Judge of all the earth. Someday the offender will stand before Almighty God to give an account. Our heavenly Father will discipline them now or later, make all things right, providing vindication and vengeance for His children. In Hebrews 10:30 we read, "Vengeance is Mine, says the Lord."

Forgiveness is also not an emotion; it is a life-changing choice. There may be an emotional reaction as the Spirit sets people free and tears of joy or pain may flow, but forgiveness is not in and of itself an emotion. We don't have to feel forgiving, but we are commanded to forgive if we want to be forgiven.

In order to receive the fullness of liberty to live the abundant life, it is not only necessary to offer full forgiveness but to receive it as well. I suggest that they ask these questions and read the scripture aloud, inviting the Holy Spirit to enlighten and cleanse their minds so they can recall details of sins or sinful reactions clearly and accurately.

Did I sow it and now I am reaping it more and later?   (Galatians. 6:7-8)
Did I dishonor my parents or authorities in this area?   (Ephesians 6:1-3)
Did I judge someone? Do I now draw that to me?   (Matthew 7:1- 2; Rom. 2:1-4)
Has a bitter root sprung up in me, affecting others?   (Hebrews 12:14-15)
Have I blamed, doubted or been disappointed in God?   (1 John 4:20-21)

During my restoration ministry training, I was not happy when I was exhorted to ask forgiveness for myself five ways and to forgive others one way. I was quick to notice that it seemed to imply that my sinful reactions were at least 80% of my problem. The good news is that I can control my choices to ask forgiveness and can get the healing I need.

Biblical forgiveness is not only forgiving others but also asking for forgiveness for our own sins five ways.

I repent, asking forgiveness five ways.
Father forgive me for my sin of:

- not asking others to forgive me
- judging and not forgiving others
- my own sin and sinful reactions
- blaming or doubting You God
- not forgiving myself

After forgiving, repenting and asking forgiveness in these five ways, believers will notice they have less of a problem in the areas they have prayed about, but further inquiry of the Holy Spirit is helpful before they may know what needs forgiving five ways.

It may take more than one session of prayer to lead wounded people into the healing grace of God even for what appears to be one issue. You can take a history of events related to this issue and take note of root issues and causes as you go. The Holy

Spirit may show them (and you) many different areas that need His touch. Give them the time they need to thoroughly comprehend and digest the truth, then guide them in prayer to walk the path of healing.

Years ago, my life began to change as I learned to pray the Cross Walk Prayer from Ellen Ferry in Atlanta, Georgia. Below is my version of this amazing prayer. Feel free to use it verbatim or let believers make up their own words as they become more proficient in praying this prayer, listening carefully to the Holy Spirit and confessing anything He brings to mind.

For example, you have had a lot of critical people in your life and this has produced in you a negative pattern of having a critical attitude. Try plugging the problem "critical attitude" into the blanks in the Cross Walk Prayer to see how this works.

Cross Walk Prayer

Dear Lord Jesus,

I have a negative pattern in my life, that is not Godly and I cannot get rid of it by myself. I know that a bad fruit has a bad root. I don't want this pattern of _____ any longer. I don't want to reap this in my own life or in the people around me. Please show me the spiritual root of it and how to deal with my part of this problem (even if I am only 10% of the problem.)

Did I sow this and now I am reaping it, more and later?	Galatians 6:7-10
Did I dishonor my parents or authorities in this area?	Ephesians 6:1-3
Did I judge someone and now I draw that thing to me?	Matthew 7:1, Romans 2:1-4
Did a bitter expectation spring up in me, defiling others?	Hebrews 12:14-15
Did I make an inner vow in not to be like them?	James 5:12, Matthew 5:37

1. **I RECOGNIZE** that the reason this problem of _____ is now a pattern in my own life, is because of my sinful reaction of (dishonor, judgment, sowing the sin myself, inner vows or bitter root expectation.) The fruit is that I am reaping similar problems in others and myself according to the LAW of sowing and reaping. I am reaping this crop because of my sinful reactions to their sin. I am reaping from the sinful seed that I have sown - not from what they have sown.

2. **I REPENT** and ask forgiveness five ways. Please forgive me:

   1. for not asking others to forgive me
   2. for judging others and not forgiving others
   3. for sowing my own sin / sinful reactions
   4. for blaming or doubting you God
   5. and for not forgiving myself

for blaming or doubting You God

not asking others to forgive me

for judging and not forgiving others

for not forgiving myself

my own sinful reactions

3. **I RENOUNCE** my sin of dishonor, judgment, sowing the sin myself, bitter root expectations or fleshly inner vows. I choose to forgive them, releasing them to you, the Judge of all the earth.

4. RELEASE me from reaping this crop that is mine to reap because of my sinful reactions to others.

5. I RECKON dead on the cross all flesh that identifies with this reaction and all automatic reactions that I have developed with it. I ask you Jesus, to bring it to death, because I cannot. Create in me a pure heart that agrees with your responses.

6. RESURRECT your likeness into every area that you have brought to death.

7. RESTORE all the years that the locusts have eaten while I was disobedient.

8. I RECLAIM all the spiritual blessings that my family and I have missed.

9. REWARD us for generations to come, as we sow true discernment, grace and mercy. Thank you Lord for the forgiveness you have provided for us on the cross and all the blessings that we are free to walk in now. We believe you for them! Amen

If you want to learn the easy way and MUCH _FASTER_ ... Simply make a list of all your parent's faults (without mercy.) Assume that as a child, you probably judged and dishonored them as some point. You can include other authorities too if you really want to get freedom fast!!

This prayer is an excellent maintenance prayer as the Holy Spirit brings to mind each new ungodly belief or fleshly pattern on the road to complete liberty. Being healed, delivered and baptized in the Holy Spirit is only the beginning and God's enemy is not going to be deterred from his plan to destroy believers.

We have to learn to pray, to meditate on the Word, to declare scripture daily and to stay in agreement with God in order to maintain our freedom and appropriate all God has promised us.

Want a shortcut to healing and freedom? Stop now and make a list of all the judgments you may have made against others in the past, especially family and authorities. Then pray the Cross Walk Prayer and break the sowing and reaping cycle.

The Cross Walk Prayer will be referred to as an Exhibit after this.

Your lists of judgments, dishonor, doubting God, your own sins, etc. go here.

Discerning Repentance versus Remorse

Did you ever feel like a hurtful conflict was still unresolved even though you had sincerely forgiven those involved? Did you sense that they had no grasp of how badly they had hurt you? Did you think that trying to reconcile was almost hopeless, because they had made little or no effort to rebuild the trust they had crushed?

Your perceptions may be right! There is a huge difference between true repentance and simply showing remorse for what happened. The repentant one is honestly sorry for any hurtful words or actions and is willing to make restitution. The one who merely shows remorse may only be sorry they got caught and have no intention of owning responsibility for their own sinful responses or accountability for damages.

True godly repentance comes from a godly grief about sinning against God first of all, and secondly understanding how badly our words or actions have hurt others. It is a broken heartedness about what was done without making excuses, blaming others or presenting half-truths. A repentant attitude shows genuine concern by asking forgiveness for the hurt done.

Remorse rationalizes and expects God to condone sin or compromise. It avoids consequences, asking for forgiveness or making restitution because it cannot face its own sinfulness. Those who are only remorseful are sorry about the pain they caused themselves. They seek to cover their selfish motivations with little thought of how their actions affected the lives of others. 2 Corinthians 7:9-10 teaches that the sorrow that is according to the will of God produces true repentance without regret, but the sorrow of the world, shallow remorse, produces spiritual death in the unrepentant heart.

A biblical example of the difference between true repentance and surface remorse is found in the books of Samuel. In 1 Samuel 13-15, King Saul disobeyed God's instructions, then tried to pin the blame on his people and the prophet himself. When confronted with his sin, Saul insisted that he had indeed done the will of God and it wasn't his fault. All he seemed to care about was that the prophet would still go with him, saving face in front of the people. The prophet Samuel rebuked Saul with "to obey is better than sacrifice" (1 Samuel 15:22). Because of Saul's blatant disobedience and remorseful but stubborn heart, his kingship was taken away from him.

In 2 Samuel 12:1-23, when King David was confronted, he demonstrated true repentance when he admitted his sin without focusing on himself or condoning his actions. He accepted the truth and centered his attention on the damage he had caused, with genuine compassion. He did not rationalize what he had done but was ready to face the consequences of his sin. He was willing to change his mind and heart and work for restoration. He did a 180 degree turnaround and remained obedient and faithful to God.

Remorse alone is a feeling of sorrow but is not true repentance. As we have seen, Saulish remorse is more like embarrassment and a desire to save face, but Davidic repentance comes with a broken heart for hurting God and others. Discerning between true repentance and the feeling of remorse will help others come to full surrender, repentance to the Holy Spirit and make restoration of some relationships possible.

The able restoration minister will listen for signs of true repentance and will NOT:
1. mistake buckets of tears for true repentance
2. release the unrepentant receiver from accountability
3. minister comfort before Holy Spirit has brought them to conviction
4. require others to pretend that the offender has repented
5. endorse them to minister with an unrepentant heart
6. give them false assurance of being forgiven
7. condone attempts to appear right with God

Your notes on areas of remorse versus true repentance.

Repentance with Restitution

The Bible is full of examples of required restitution (i.e. Exodus 22:1-17; Leviticus 6:1-5; Luke 19:1-10). God understands that true repentance will result in a desire to restore what has been broken or stolen. Restitution helps to heal the wound and rebuild the love and trust. It makes complete forgiveness possible, versus presuming others will just eventually forget the hurt. By their efforts to rebuild, the truly repentant bless the hurt ones with godly comfort.

In some cases, spiritual leadership will require the offender who has "fallen" to receive ongoing restoration prayer ministry from a team of people who will hold him/her accountable. The process of restitution helps the offenders feel the depth of their offense and die to the selfish motivations that caused the offense in the first place. When offenders are required to prove their repentance by serving in a humbling way, with a brokenness and contriteness, they begin to appreciate the cost of sin. They learn to value the need to earn trust and respect by a life of integrity (Psalm 51:17).

A person who is humble before God will value the privilege of being accountable to good leadership and will voluntarily "report in" to a compassionate spiritual advisor. None of us is so mature that we do not need to be accountable for our choices and motivations. We all need to know our areas of potential vulnerability—the enemy certainly knows them! This is why Paul told Timothy to be a spiritual guide for others: "In meekness instructing those that oppose themselves; if God peradventure will give them repentance to the acknowledging of the truth" (2 Timothy 2:25).

In the meantime, no matter how deep the hurt was, we should check our own motivations to see if we desire to see the offender repent for their own sake as well as ours. Will we rejoice when they are restored, reconciled and allowed to resume their place in the body of Christ? Can we bless them with every spiritual blessing? Do we look forward to being able to fellowship with them again? We must consider ourselves lest we fall in the same way. "Brethren, if a man be overtaken in a fault, ye which are spiritual, restore such an one in the spirit of meekness; considering thyself, lest thou also be tempted" (Galatians 6:1).

Godly forgiveness involves humility of heart; it accepts any offered retribution but does not demand it as proof of the offender's true repentance. The innermost being is seen only by God and it isn't up to us to judge another believer. We are to pray and be prepared for reconciliation and restoration, even though it may not happen. The Holy Spirit may have much more work to do in many hearts. Remember the example of Jesus, who while suffering abuse and agony on the Cross, prayed for the forgiveness of His tormenters: "Father, forgive them, for they do not know what they do" (Luke 23:34).

For some people, their personal confession of repentance in private is not enough. They need to hear from a spiritual authority that they are indeed forgiven and that any lost opportunities for good will be restored. If you are a trained counselor or an ordained minister, it might be helpful to people with such tender spirits, if you would pray over them, using words such as:

As a minister of the gospel and according to God's Word, because you have forgiven those who sinned against you, I declare that the Lord has forgiven you. With the authority invested in me as a minister, I say that the power of each judgment or sin confessed here today has been broken off your life and off those you have judged. Jesus has brought every sinful seed to death on the Cross and is right now raising up His likeness in its place.

He is replacing all the years the locust have eaten (Joel 2:25) with reward and blessing as you sow new godly seeds. He is transforming your mind so that you will be a demonstration of His gracious, merciful and loving responses. As you continue to give the Holy Spirit complete control of your redeemed human nature, He will be faithful to continue cleansing by bringing any fleshly attitudes to the Cross. I will stand with you as Jesus completes what He has begun in you.

What if they never repent?

Years ago, someone attempted to kill me at least six times, followed me when I moved out of state, broke into my home and stalked me. Father God had told me not to prosecute because the offender was still homicidal and my life was still in danger. God asked me to forgive anyway and allow Him to handle the entire matter. He would not allow me to expose him to spiritual leaders or defend against false accusations. Father said that my safety depended on my obedience and that I would be alive as long as He wanted me to be. It seemed a little co-dependent to me but I obeyed.

However, Father God's requirements of me became more and more strict. On the way to a conference, I was aware that I might run in to the offender. But God … had arranged for me to hear a message on forgiveness on the radio as I drove. The preacher taught how Joseph modeled true forgiveness for us when he met his brothers again.

1. He had already forgiven them for even thinking of killing him.
2. He was not expecting any restitution for the years they had stolen from him.
3. He made no effort to expose them and hold them accountable.
4. He said that what they had meant for evil, God had used for his good.
5. He told them not to even hold their sins against themselves!
6. He didn't even require them to feel bad for what they had done.
7. He blessed them, their whole family and the nation.

In an effort to apply these insights, I sat in the back of the church so the offender would not have to face me or feel uncomfortable. I refused to fantasize about retribution or restitution. I gave up any supposed right to tell my story or to expose him.

But wouldn't you know the offender accidentally sat right in front of me in church and suddenly appeared right in front of me in the book store line. Why God, why? Again and again, God has used an offender to mature me so I can practice what I preach.

Defining Godly Discernment

Most people give others a piece of their mind instead of a word from the Spirit. To discern rightly, we have to take our urge to criticize and judge to the Cross to be crucified. We have to be willing to renounce all our ungodly reactions—past, present and future—so that we can be the pure in heart who will see God. We have to be willing to demonstrate His great grace at all times but much that is called spiritual discernment is not ministered with grace.

John 17:18 tells us that Jesus said He was sending out His disciples as Father God had sent Him. What an amazing thought! We have the same mission that Jesus had. We are called to have covenant relationships where we love others with the unconditional love and acceptance of Jesus Christ when they need it the most.

Apostle Barbara Yoder says that many people often confuse their critical or judgmental spirit with the gift of discernment. They may sense an urgency to point out the weakness of another and think that it is spiritual discernment. Have you ever been given a word that was technically correct but it defiled you because it was not given with the redemptive grace of God?

True discernment is marked by our ability to love others with God's redemptive sacrificial love. One who has invited Jesus Christ to be Lord of their life should have humility, peace and a desire to minister the unconditional love of God. True spiritual discernment sees the weakness of the other as an opportunity to lift them up in prayer and will die to its own convenience so that the other can live. We can choose to let Him manifest His love and peace through us.

True discernment will not gossip but may report a matter to spiritual leadership. It will only report the facts without adding fleshly interpretations, suspicions, innuendos or conclusions. It is motivated by Christ's heart of love to restore that person to life and godliness.

False discernment is slow to hear, quick to speak and quick to anger. False discernment is based in criticism, mistrust, suspicion and fear. It may judge by surface symptoms and surface causes, without discerning the heart intent or root causes of outward behaviors. These people are not motivated by love and peace. They may be totally unaware of the anger inside of them that comes out of their own dysfunctional past or injustices suffered. For instance, they might judge a Christian who is dependent on prescription drugs, when they should actually focus on ministering healing to the pain and rage that is smoldering inside.

Those operating out of a critical spirit will have a desire to expose the other's weakness, will attempt to elevate themselves and will forget their own deep need for the grace of God every day. Apostle Rick Joyner says that when we sow criticism, we reap blindness to our own faults, which in turn causes us to reap more criticism of ourselves. Our ability to discern ourselves, others and the Holy Spirit, depends on our ability to perceive correctly. If our past experiences have not been healed and redeemed they color our perceptions.

The veil that keeps us from perceiving correctly is the veil over our own hearts. Until we can perceive ourselves correctly and deal with the impurity in our own hearts, we will not clearly see what is in the heart of another. This is why Jesus gave us that unforgettable picture of trying to remove a speck of dust from someone else's eye when an entire log is obscuring the vision in our own eye. Or as my husband Louis says, "Take the lumber yard out of your own eye, before you focus on the splinter in the eye of another."

Hurting people may also judge themselves by surface symptoms and surface causes, never delving into the deeper root causes. They need guidance to understand, acknowledge, and take to the Cross all the root causes of their behavior.

Scripture is replete with verses that show us the spiritual roots that apply to issues today. Read and study this list, so you can start putting these truths to work for yourself and others who come to you for ministry.

Whatever we judge with condemnation in others, we will reap again ourselves. Luke 6:37: "Judge not, and ye shall not be judged: condemn not, and ye shall not be condemned: forgive, and ye shall be forgiven."

Unforgiveness, resentment and bitterness in our lives defile both ourselves and others. Hebrews 12:15: "Looking diligently lest any man fail of the grace of God; lest any root of bitterness springing up trouble you, and thereby many be defiled."

Spiritual discernment is based on God's truth and not our own opinion. Hebrews 5:14: "But strong meat belongeth to them that are of full age, even those who by reason of use have their senses exercised to discern both good and evil."

Critical attitudes cause us to be blind to our sins and we reap criticism. Luke 6:41: "And why beholdest thou the mote that is in thy brother's eye, but perceivest not the beam that is in thine own eye?"

Sin, or bad fruit, in our lives is because of bad roots on our tree. Luke 6:43: "For a good tree bringeth not forth corrupt fruit; neither doth a corrupt tree bring forth good fruit."

Whatever we sow, we will reap, reap more than we sowed and later. Galatians 6:7: "Be not deceived; God is not mocked: for whatsoever a man soweth, that shall he also reap."

We desire a pure heart and that our spirit be aligned with the Holy Spirit. Psalm 51:10: "Create in me a pure heart, O God, and renew a steadfast spirit within me."

As we chose to hold our hearts open to God, He will show us our hearts. Proverbs 20:27: "The lamp of the Lord searches the spirit of a man; it searches out his inmost being."

God is ready to comfort us when we are ready to give Him our hurts and wounds. Proverbs 20:27: "For the Lord comforts His people and will have compassion on His afflicted ones."

We can pour our hearts out to Jesus because He has experienced every hurt. Isaiah 53: 4-5: "Surely He took up our infirmities and carried our sorrows ...He was pierced for our transgressions, He was crushed for our iniquities; the punishment that brought us peace was upon Him, and by His wounds we are healed."

When we choose God's wisdom, our soul, spirit and body are in good health. Proverbs 3:7-8: "Do not be wise in your own eyes; fear the Lord and shun evil. This will bring health to your body and nourishment to your bones."

God's wisdom is embedded in our spirits as we meditate on God's Word. Proverbs 4:20-22: "My son, pay attention to what I say; listen closely to my words... for they are life to those who find them and health to a man's whole body."

As we humbly receive ministry, God is able to give us a new heart and spirit. Ezekiel 11:19: "I will give them an undivided heart and put a new spirit in them; I will remove from them their heart of stone and give them a heart of flesh."

When we submit our sinful reactions and fleshly patterns to God, He transforms our minds. Romans 12:2: "Do not be conformed any longer to this world, but be transformed by the renewing of your mind."

Anxiety or worry is usually about assuming responsibility that is not ours to assume. 1 Peter 5:7: "Cast all your anxiety on Him for He cares for you."

Praise and worship brings healing to our wounded hearts and heals our souls Malachi 4:2a: "But for you who revere My Name, the sun of righteousness will rise with healing in its wings."

When we ask others to forgive us, God is free to forgive our sins and to heal us. James 5:16: "Therefore confess your sins to each other and pray for each other so that you may be healed. The prayer of the righteous man is powerful and effective."

The way to please God is to ask in faith, believing that He is loving and faithful. James 1:6a: "But let him ask in faith, nothing wavering."

God has asked us to partner with Him in delivering the captives and healing. Luke 9:1-2: "When Jesus called the twelve together, He gave them power and authority to drive out all demons and to cure diseases, and He sent them out to preach the kingdom of God and to heal the sick."

Whatever God tells us to ask, He will surely do for our sakes and for His glory. John 14:12-15: "I tell you the truth, anyone who has faith in me will do what I have been doing. He will do even greater things than these, because I am going to the Father. And I will do whatever you ask in My Name, so that the Son may bring Glory to the Father. You may ask for anything in My Name, and I will do it. If you love Me, you will obey what I command."

Christ in us wants to minister through us just as He ministered two thousand years ago. Hebrews 13:8: "Jesus Christ is the same yesterday and today and forever."

Signs (deliverance, tongues, protection, power and healing) follow believers. Mark 16:17-18: "And these signs will follow those who believe: In My name they will cast out demons; they will speak with new tongues, they will take up serpents; and if they drink anything deadly, it will by no means hurt them; they will lay hands on the sick, and they will recover."

We choose to invite the Holy Spirit to operate in all of His gifts through us. 1 Corinthians 12:4-11: "There are diversities of gifts, but the same Spirit. There are differences of ministries, but the same Lord. And there are diversities of activities, but it is the same God who works all in all. But the manifestation of the Spirit is given to each one for the profit of all: for to one is given the word of wisdom through the Spirit, to another the word of knowledge through the same Spirit, to another faith by the same Spirit, to another gifts of healings by the same Spirit, to another the working of miracles, to another prophecy, to another discerning of spirits, to another different kinds of tongues, to another the interpretation of tongues. But one and the same Spirit works all these things, distributing to each one individually as He wills."

We choose to be spiritual first, serving and restoring others in meekness. 2 Timothy 2:24-26: "And a servant of the Lord must not quarrel but be gentle to all, able to teach, patient, in humility correcting those who are in opposition, if God perhaps will grant them repentance, so that they may know the truth, and that they may come to their senses and escape the snare of the devil, having been taken captive by him to do his will." (NKJV).

Before God can give us a spirit of discernment, love and forgiveness must mature in us. We cannot be used to free others from captivity until we can be trusted not to react sinfully to their carnality or immaturity. We cannot react to what they think, say or do. To walk in offense, criticism or judgment is to walk in self-deception ourselves. We cannot prevent feelings from coming but we can choose not to add sinful reactions which in turn produce sinful emotions.

When we are in self-deception about our own hurts, sins and strongholds, our thoughts about the behavior of others are not trustworthy. Often we will project our own woundedness or sinful motivations onto others. It's not that a minister never feels a hurt but that they chose a lifestyle of forgiveness so that they never take offense in the first place.

Prophetic people if they are operating in pride, can be the first to mistake suspicious thinking for prophetic perception. (A wise counselor hears both sides of a story before drawing conclusions.) A prophetic gift is no substitute for a humble heart that repents readily and keeps short accounts with God. A tendency to "slice and dice" others is not prophetic gifting, but judgment with condemnation. Romans 2:1 states, "Therefore you are inexcusable, O man, whoever you are who judge, for in whatever you judge another you condemn yourself; for you who judge practice the same things."

The gifts of the Holy Spirit have to pass through the condition of our own hearts as they are ministered. God's law says that we will reap what we sow, more than we sow and later than we sow. If we have sown seeds of judgment and dishonor to others, we will reap that seed in ourselves, our own ministry or in people around us.

I grieve for those who are bitter because their "call to ministry" has not been recognized by others. They feel self-righteous when they judge and criticize those who will not support their "mission." A spirit of accusation has caused them to think they are discerning others rightly, when they are actually projecting what is in their own hearts. Their friends and spiritual leadership know that they will not see clearly to minister restoration until the instinct to judge, blame or accuse has been crucified.

When we receive the grace of God to see the log in our own eye, we will not rush to accuse another of having a speck in their eye. When others find us trustworthy to minister without judgment or condemnation, they will ask for our discernment and value our wisdom and insights.

To receive true spiritual discernment, we must still ourselves inside before the Lord as a lifestyle. We must choose to aggressively become calm and be willing to hear His heart and mind in each situation. As we receive His love, peace and grace, we will be able to overflow it to others. God's desire is to bring an outpouring of great grace that will enable believers to be healed and to have enlarged hearts that discern by *agape* love and will not judge by outward behavior or performance.

Can God trust us to take that one by the hand who was the perpetrator, not the victim? To guide them to the throne of grace, where they are won by the kindness and mercy of God?   To be safe harbors for ships that are in serious danger of shipwreck? To be happy when He not only restores but promotes them?

If so, God will trust us with the secrets of men's hearts and enable us to discern the roots of the matter.   Probably, they have lost the ability to trust a perfect God, much less fallible ministers. They don't care how much we know; they want to know how much we care.   They need trustworthy people to help them learn to trust again. When we remember how much grace it takes for God to love us, the "unlovable" will come to us for His unconditional love and true discernment

People who come to you for help, spiritual insights and prayer need someone who can lead them into healing with an unfettered understanding of God's unlimited grace. Before you start administering restoration to anyone else, be sure your own life is in order. If you sense yourself to be anything less than a clean vessel, purified by the blood of Christ and anointed for His service, you may find it helpful to talk things over with God, using the following prayer as a guideline.

This prayer can also be utilized for people who are afraid to delve into their past or who are genuinely confused about their spiritual condition and have no idea how to proceed.

Prayer for discernment

Lord, I thank You for Your Word that gives me direction and understanding to discern and face the truth about myself. I ask for Your anointing to be able to recognize self-destructive habits or life patterns that produce bad fruit because of a harmful or sinful root. Bring healing and comfort for present hurts and wounds; then look with me, through the clear eyes of Your love, into my past. Show me how, where, and when this hurt began and give me the courage to confront whatever You reveal. Together, in Your power, we can overcome anything.

Forgive me for judging those I held responsible for aiding me in planting my sinful roots. Open my mind and my memories to discern the harmful roots in my past that have developed destructive habits or life patterns over the years, resulting in damaged or worthless fruit. Hew Your axe of grace into my harmful or sinful roots and free me to produce good fruit worthy of a child of God.

I freely forgive anyone who nurtured or encouraged the growth of fruit that was detrimental. Father, You alone can guide me through the tangled forest of my past. You have seen my life from its very beginning. Nothing surprises or shocks You, for You already know all about me and still You continue to amaze me with Your constant love.

I forgive myself for allowing my mind and body to be led into destructive habits and life patterns. Help me see my sinful reactions with clarity so that the power of forgiveness can bring down the walls of resentment, anger, and pain I have built.

Lord, as I partner with You to minister to others, I lay everything I think I know on the altar: all my training, all my experience and every method that has worked in the past. Open my spiritual ears to hear on 3 levels: mind, heart and spirit. Open my eyes to see past their sin to their painful wounded roots and how You want to heal them. Give me keen discernment to know how to partner with Your Holy Spirit to bring them to repentance for their sinful reactions. Be that skillful detective in me that would notice what is conspicuously absent in their story.

Most of all, may I be a demonstration of Your gentleness, only offering ministry where I am clearly invited. May I be in perfect concert with Your will, Your way and Your timing. May I have the true heart of a minister who comes only to restore in humility, knowing that except for your grace, there go I. Amen.

Your notes on discernment versus a critical or judgmental attitude go here.

What is 18 Hour Restoration Prayer Ministry (RPM)?

I'd like to explain a little about our 18 hour ministry of restoration through prayer. Of course, I believe the best and quickest way for you to learn how the Holy Spirit ministers to restore lives is to receive our 18 hour Restoration Prayer Ministry (RPM) yourself. I suggest that you read four articles describing RPM and the 10 page application before you call. You can make the minimum of six appointments for individual prayer ministry by contacting me, Carlotta Waldman, through our original main web site, Cross Walk Life, at www.CrossWalkLife.com or our new simple site at www.RestorationPrayerMinistry.com.

This book is designed to be a guide to Issue-Focused Prayer Ministry, whether for one or more sessions. This section is designed to briefly describe the whole life 18 hour Restoration Prayer Ministry that I offer. RPM is not just teaching, or analyzing or talking bad habits to death. It is not presuming that we can use the steps that worked yesterday. It is not telling Jesus how to heal a person or telling the person what to imagine through visualization. It is not just praying that they will forget the pain, leave the past behind or even that they will not hurt anymore. It is not deliverance or healing alone. It is an integrated ministry addressing all the issues that Holy Spirit reveals when I interview you about issues in your entire life.

As we address spiritual root causes versus counseling only surface symptoms, RPM is the most thorough method I have found to remove blockages in a person's life and to empower them to fulfill their God-given potential with joy. We are actually enabled by God to see past the surface problem to the hidden roots and we invite Him to touch every problem area.

We offer a minimum of six sessions designed to address the most common problem areas. Usually, the first six sessions are as follows:

1. We take your history to uncover generational patterns, ungodly beliefs, bitterroot judgments, bitter expectations, dishonor, word curses, hurts, suppressed memories, bondages, etc. If necessary, the history may be taken over two sessions.
2. We renounce over two hundred long-standing generational sins and destructive patterns.
3. We identify false identity areas and replace these deceptions with your true identity. We pray to release blocked areas, emotions and break the power of ungodly soul ties.
4. We pray and replace ungodly belief systems, bitter root expectations, self-powered inner vows, judgments, word curses, etc. with Godly beliefs and responses.
5. We invite Jesus to show us or tell us how He will personally touch partially healed hurts, take our pain and render us healed people who are safe to partner with Him in healing other people.
6. We come against every demonic bondage, habit or mind-set that is holding us back and retake the promises and blessing that rightfully belong to us.

In the fifth session of healing hurts, our prayer receivers simply ask Jesus to come and reveal the root areas that need healing. We wait quietly as He shows us what wounds need to be healed and what walls need to come down. He knows where the original pain is hidden and the lies that were embedded. If Jesus is allowed to take the walls down, He will become the protector Himself. He takes the power out of the lies and the pain out of the memories.

In the extended Restoration Prayer Ministry, we pray thoroughly over every root that is revealed, whether it was inherited from ancestors, ungodly beliefs, unhealed hurts or oppression and bondage. Prayer receivers consistently tell us that where their pain may have been 7-10 on a scale of 1-10, it is a ZERO now! Jesus offers them His truth instead of lies and supernaturally clears their minds of false beliefs and false identity as they declare their godly beliefs and true identity each day.

Please note: Healing with vision is not imagining that Jesus is there, but experiencing a live interaction with our living Lord. It is not re-decision therapy or cognitive work, where one might mentally choose to make new choices or draw new conclusions out of their own resources. It is not visualization, where the counselor suggests a certain vision or outcome; neither do we "coach Jesus" telling Him what He should do.

Healing with vision is a prayer to invite Jesus to appear with His own methods of healing without any coaching. During healing prayer sessions I say very little, never suggesting what our prayer receivers should see. My role is reduced to being a scribe: I take notes as our clients see the open vision and dictate it to me and I usually take at least eight or nine pages of detailed notes. Sometimes I see Jesus too and I am healed as well. There is always more grace than we need when we are in His presence.

In RPM, we provide an opportunity for a person to invite Jesus Christ to tell them or show them their wounds, roots or walls (without analysis). Jesus is then invited to touch each one supernaturally, just as He did many times in the New Testament. He does—and our prayer receivers marvel that their lifetime of painful memories and the power of the enemy's lies is gone instantly. His actions or words may be very simple or brief. He may only tell them truth that you or I could have told them. The difference is that His anointing, power and presence breaks every yoke and heals wounds effectively and immediately.

The main reason people need RPM is that none of us can see our own blind spots. Therefore, having a counselor or minister to help us see our open doors and blocks is key to knowing what to pray about, to renounce, to confess and what to break the power of.

Restoration Prayer Ministry is cooperating with Holy Spirit as He transforms your spirit-man in the spiritual realm. You can't heal your heart with your head. By the power of God's Holy Spirit, we address all possible spiritual and psychological causes. RPM has proven to be a very thorough and effective ministry for helping people find freedom. For instance, we often pray all eight RPM prayers asking forgiveness five ways over every spiritual block.

Sometimes Restoration Prayer ministers use methods that not everyone understands, like speaking healing "from conception on," loosing and binding, bringing their fleshly structure of selfishness to the Cross to be crucified, confessing one to another, repentance with restitution, words of knowledge and wisdom, prophetic visions and dreams, or even healing through worship and dance.

Restoration Prayer ministers impart a balance of the Word of God and faith in motion. I think of a restoration prayer minister as a liberator with true grit, who gets involved, who will love the unlikely to life and who will take risks to help a lost lonely heart find safety in the love of God. It is about demonstrating faith to bring someone into the very presence of God, right here and now, so they can be healed, forgiven, set free, restored and transformed in whatever way God wants to do it.

RPM is a passion to know the heart of God and His purposes for a person, knowing that the secret of healing is to do whatever our loving Father says to do. It is a compassion for people that constrains us to say "yes" when Jesus decides to set the captive free, even if He does it in ways that we have never heard of before. It is destroying the works of the devil so that people can be filled with the Holy Spirit in every area of their life (1 John 3:8b; Ephesians 5:18).

It is not behavior modification or just learning to "act more like Jesus." It is coming against religious counterfeit spirits that have replaced believers' "first love and true worship in spirit and truth" with "performance for the approval of God by works." It is receiving the righteousness that Jesus gave us as a gift (Romans 5) and believing Him when He says that we are made holy, blameless and righteous by His work on the Cross (Ephesians 1). It is demonstrating how to allow Jesus to live a holy life in our bodies (Galatians 2:20).

Restoration Prayer ministers are often the former "walking wounded" who are now transformed by the amazing power of the resurrected Christ within them. Like the prophets of the Old Testament, they are willing to do anything their heavenly Commander says, even if it means going against the established "religious traditions and rules."

It may mean finding that one lost sheep on skid row, in a bar, a casino, a cult or across the tracks. It can mean following God's call despite the fact that they have not been to seminary. It can mean meeting rejection or ridicule because the ministers are women ministers, former addicts, murderers or thieves. This may look like breaking the "rules" but it is not rebellion against God. It is a holy war against "religious legalism:" defiance against a spirit of control that says only perfect performers can be transformed into prayer ministers.

For me, it included making the commitment to be trained up in the Elijah House School of Prayer Counseling Ministry so that I would have more of a diagnostic knowledge to balance my intuitive and prophetic insights. It meant studying to show myself approved for months and becoming a healed person who could partner with God in healing people. I appreciated the Elijah House School so much that I recorded my own version of the first year school and put it online so people all over the world could attend for free. See www.NowFaith.TV

I like to introduce myself as the former woman at the well because, like her, I am smacking "religious legalism" in the face. She was a woman who was rejected by Jews on account of her race, rejected by religious leaders because of sexism, rejected by neighbors on account of her serial marriages and for being a failure at love. But the woman at the well became the first evangelist appointed by Jesus himself and she reached her entire town the same day!

The most powerful thing Restoration Prayer ministers do is to let someone know that God believes in them, right now, with unconditional love, before anyone else has any hope for them. Restoration Prayer ministers have to see people as God sees them and love their slumbering spirits to life. Maybe they are captives who act like alcoholics, crack heads, adulterers or murderers today, but they may be called to be raised up as missionaries tomorrow. We have to be able to say to them what no one else will say, in truth and in love.

A Restoration Prayer Minister sees according to their potential, not their past. Restoration Prayer ministers have to lay down every talent and knowledge they think they have on the altar daily, in deference to depending on the Anointing to break every yoke. God may want to heal as they kneel, sing, dance like David danced, use mud and spit or absolute silence. Jesus is coming in unconventional ways. We have to know Him and His voice.

The main agenda of Restoration Prayer ministers is to bring every selfish fleshly structure to death on the Cross. We ourselves might not have come to Jesus if we had known that God wanted to kill our pride, wreck our schedules, take away every crutch, destroy our self-centered ways and give us His broken heart for others instead. We have to learn to rest in His opinion of us, in His ability to live His life through us and to be satisfied with Jesus as our Source.

The prayer ministers of tomorrow may not be the ones with the great business cards, expensive videos or impressive church growth. They may be the ones with tattoos and crazy hair who are not afraid of sinners for they know their language and they will do whatever it takes to destroy the works of darkness. They are willing to admit their own need for ministry. They know demons are real and deliverance is for today. They may pray a little differently, without all the flowery phrases, but demons are afraid of them because they speak with spiritual authority in the name of Jesus. They know their true identity in Christ. **Nothing will be impossible to those that believe!**

Part 2:
Issue-Focused Prayer Ministry
in One Session

Take the helmet of Salvation and the Sword of the Spirit, which is the Word of God. And pray in the Spirit ...
Ephesians 6:17-18

Introduction to Part Two

Having been raised by strong Christian parents, I was blessed with a solid biblical foundation. I had also worked 25 years (off and on) as a Registered Nurse in inpatient Mental Health. In both environments, Christian churches and in secular mental health, people were counseled or admitted for the same issues year after year. In spite of all my access to good teaching and training I had also suffered with self-destructive patterns, sins and downward spirals of my own.

It was not until I first attended an Issue-Focused Ministry Seminar, led by Chester and Betsy Kylstra, Founders of Restoring the Foundations International that I had real hope. They had begun a solid biblical restoration ministry that would actually heal, set free and empower believers to walk in the fullness of the Spirit-filled life (versus despairing of ever finding out how the Christian life works.) The seminar didn't fit into my mental health grid and they spoke a Christian-eze that was unfamiliar to me, but the Spirit of God assured me that this ministry offered a way for lay ministers, priests, pastors and other believers, who had the compassion of Christ, to approach a one-time prayer ministry appointment with confidence.

Like many of you, I had already spent much time and money receiving "Christian counseling" that was supportive, a safe place to emote and somewhat enlightening, but they had not even defined my surface causes correctly much less my root causes. One dear pastor had faithfully taught me who I was in Christ for ten years but had not taught me what co-dependence was and that I was exhibit A. Therefore, sincere as we both were, I continued to be known for attracting the 'bad apples' and failed relationships with deceptive people.

In my experience, my Christian counselors were loving and kind hearted but did not know how to address my issues from all sides at once. Therefore the enemy got away, if you will. They approached me according to their gifting, whether healing, deliverance, merciful listening, discerning spirits of deception, preaching scriptures or by using the latest fad in Christian counseling. I and my friends began to feel disillusioned, wondering if Christianity worked.

 In all fairness to them, I could also sense that many pastors actually dreaded requests for pastoral counseling because their seminary education had not prepared them to deal with the ever expanding variety of maladies afflicting the body of Christ today. In an effort to recognize their limitations and to be responsible, they either just listened, tried to talk my issue to death, analyzed me or referred me to someone else. I thought to myself, there ought to be a book, seminar or training that would prepare pastors, prayer ministers and priests to at least minister to their hurting sheep for one session, with more understanding, insights and an appropriate prayer.

But God ... Who had planted His desires in my heart, also had a plan to train me and others, how to minister to one issue effectively. The Kylstra's taught me how Holy Spirit usually leads them to minister to the most common problem areas. This chapter is my version and adaptation of their "Issued-Focused Ministry." (Chester and Betsy Kylstra, Founders of Restoring the Foundations International, Hendersonville, NC. www.RestoringtheFoundations.org)

Biblical Basis for Restoration Prayer Ministry
The Bible is replete with BIBLE VERSES regarding ISSUES and spiritual roots.

BAD FRUIT: If we have bad fruit on our "tree" it is because of bad roots on our tree.
Luke 6:43 For a good tree bringeth not forth corrupt fruit; neither doth a corrupt tree bring forth good fruit

ROOT CAUSES: We reap more than we sowed, and reap later than we sowed.
Galatians 6:7 Be not deceived; God is not mocked: for **whatsoever a man soweth,** that shall he also reap.

SPIRITUAL DISCERNMENT: We must learn to discern based on God's truth.
Hebrews 5:14 But strong meat belongeth to them that are of full age, even those who by reason of use have their senses exercised to discern both good and evil.

DISCERN OURSELVES: Critical attitudes cause blindness to our own ungodly beliefs.
Luke 6:41 And why beholdest thou the mote that is in thy brother's eye, but perceivest not the beam that is in thine own eye?

HEALING: Lord, I was only partially healed! Heal me - spirit, soul and body - 100%!
Jeremiah 6:14 They have also healed the hurt of My people **slightly, [partially]** saying, 'Peace, peace!' When *there is* no peace.

JUDGMENTS: Whatever we judged / condemn in others, we will reap again ourselves.
Luke 6:37 **Judge not,** and ye shall not be judged: condemn not, and ye shall not be condemned: forgive, and ye shall be forgiven:

UNFORGIVENESS: Unforgiveness, resentment and bitterness in our lives defiles others.
Hebrews 12:15 Looking diligently lest any man fail of the grace of God; lest any root of **bitterness springing up** trouble you, and thereby **many be defiled;**

DISHONOR: Whatever we do not honor in our parents, we reap in ourselves or others.
Exodus 20:12 Honor thy father and thy mother: that thy days may be long upon the land which the LORD thy God giveth thee. .

INNER VOWS: Are made in our own strength are not spiritual and should be renounced.
James 5:12 … **swear not,** neither by heaven, neither by the earth, neither by any other oath: but let your yea be yea; and your nay, nay; lest ye fall into condemnation.

CURSES: Spoken over us and by us over ourselves can be broken.
Galatians 3:13 Christ has redeemed us from the curse of the law, having become a curse for us (for it is written, "Cursed is everyone who hangs on a tree")

SOUL / SPIRIT HURTS: Usually the open door for our ungodly beliefs and reactions.
Psalm 34:18 The Lord is close to **the brokenhearted** and saves those who are crushed in spirit.

HOLY COMFORTER: Is ready to comfort us when we are ready to give Him our hurts.
Proverbs 20:27 For the Lord comforts His people and will have compassion on His afflicted ones.

DISAPPOINTMENT WITH GOD: Every rift with others is also a rift with God.
Psalm 41:4 ... "O Lord have mercy on me; heal me, for I have **sinned against You."**

RESTORATION: Restoring others in meekness.
2 Timothy 2:24-25 KJV And the servant of the Lord must not strive; but be gentle unto all men, apt to teach, patient, 25 In **meekness instructing those that oppose themselves**; if God peradventure will give them repentance to the acknowledging of the truth; …

OUR FLESHLY PATTERNS: We confess our sinful patterns to God, He transforms us.
Romans 12:2 Do not conform any longer to the pattern of _____, but be **transformed by the renewing of your mind**.

ANXIETY AND FEAR: Usually about assuming responsibility that is not ours to assume.
1 Peter 5:7 Cast all **your anxiety** on Him for He cares for you.

CONFESSION OF SINS: When we confess to others, God is free to forgive our sins.
James 5:16 Therefore **confess your sins** to each other and **pray for each other** so that you may be healed. The prayer of the righteous man is powerful and effective!

DELIVERANCE: God asked us to partner with Him in delivering in setting captives free.
Luke 9:1-2 When Jesus called the twelve together, He gave them **power and authority** to drive out all demons and to cure diseases, and He sent them out to preach the kingdom of God and to heal the sick.

EQUIPPING: Five-fold ministers and believers are called to equip His church.
Ephesians 4:11-12 And He gave some to be apostles, some prophets, some evangelists, and some pastors and teachers, for the **equipping of the saints** for the work of ministry, for the edifying of the body of Christ,

STRONG FOUNDATIONS: Wise men dig deep and lay a strong foundation upon a rock.
Luke 6:47-48 I will show you what he is like who comes to me and **hears my words** and puts them into **practice.** He is like a man building a house, who **dug down deep** and laid the foundation on rock.

KEYS TO THE KINGDOM: We choose to be good stewards, using them often.
Matthew 16:19 And I will give unto thee the keys of the kingdom of heaven: and **whatsoever thou shalt bind** on earth shall be bound in heaven: and **whatsoever thou shalt loose** on earth shall be loosed in heaven.

SPIRITUAL GIFTS: We are commanded to kindle afresh the gifts that are within us.
2 Timothy 1:6 For this reason I remind you to **fan into flame the gift of God,** which is in you through the laying on of my hands.

PRAY IN TEAMS: Prayer under pastoral authority is wise. Pray in teams and avoid being a needless casualty of war. Ask a team of intercessors to pray for you, your team and your prayer receivers.
Proverbs 11:14 NKJV Where there is no counsel, the people fall; **But in the multitude of counselors there is safety**.

KNOW WHY WE DO ISSUE-FOCUSED PRAYER MINISTRY

JESUS SAID He had several PURPOSES in coming.

1. I have come that they may have life, and that they may have it <u>more abundantly</u>. John 10:10
2. The Spirit of the Lord is upon me, because he hath anointed me to preach the gospel to the poor; he hath sent me to <u>heal the brokenhearted, to preach deliverance to the captives, and recovering of sight to the blind, to set at liberty them that are bruised</u> ... Luke 4:18
3. Christ <u>redeemed us from the curse</u> of the law by becoming a <u>curse</u> for us, for it is written: "Cursed is everyone who is hung on a tree." Galatians 3:13
4. <u>Blotting out the handwriting of ordinances that was against us</u>, which was contrary to us, and took it out of the way, nailing it to his cross; and having spoiled principalities and powers, he made a shew of them openly, triumphing over them in it. Colossians 2:14-15
5. … that He might <u>destroy the works of the devil</u>. 1 John 3:8

SATAN'S MASTER PLAN to kill, steal and destroy usually begins early in life as he tries to cause you to be broken-hearted and to feel <u>separated</u> from others, yourself and God.

- Sows seeds of <u>sin</u> into our <u>ancestors</u>
- He tempts ancestors to <u>hurt or wound</u> us
- He tempts us with <u>ungodly beliefs</u>
- He tempts us with <u>sinful behaviors</u>
- We <u>defend</u> ungodly beliefs and behaviors
- He has <u>built a stronghold in us!!!</u>
- He uses <u>open doors of unconfessed sins</u> as legal permission to harass and oppress us.

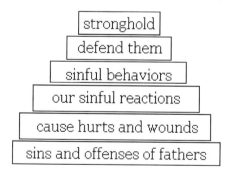

The Bible says we don't need to fear of any curse touching us, unless there is unconfessed sin. A curse causeless, shall not come. Proverbs 26:2

GOD HAS PROVIDED SIMPLE SOLUTIONS for these sinful reactions and with the help of the Holy Spirit in Issue-Focused Prayer Ministry, the open doors will be revealed and closed!! <u>Having a head knowledge of what Jesus has provided is not enough. Issue-Focused Prayer ministry helps us APPLY scripture appropriately to individual strongholds and situations.</u>

WHAT IS ISSUE-FOCUSED PRAYER MINISTRY?

Issue-Focused Prayer Ministry is a commitment to receive ministry for 1 session (or more) in order to receive God's healing, truth and freedom regarding one issue.

We fill out a **questionnaire regarding one issue.** Most of the blocks to our progress today are from ongoing unresolved issues which began in the past. We want to forget the past and leave the issues behind but couldn't because they are also current.

ISSUES

SURFACE ISSUE - losing jobs

SURFACE CAUSE - conflicts

ROOT ISSUE - authority issues

ROOT CAUSE - can't trust God

1. **Close open doors from generational sins**
   We confess the sins of our ancestors (4 generations) and obey scripture: renouncing their sins and our own. We repent of our sinful reactions and judgments of them. We repent of participating in their sin or blaming or doubting God. Then we forgive our ancestors and ourselves. (Jesus took the curse on the cross for us, releasing us from reaping what has been sowed. Galatians 3:13) (Exodus 20:5 .... for I the LORD thy God am a jealous God, visiting the iniquity of the fathers upon the children unto the third and fourth generation ...) (If they shall confess their iniquity, and the iniquity of their fathers ... Leviticus 26:40)

2. **Close open doors of ungodly beliefs of all kinds**
   We write out our ungodly beliefs about ourselves, others and God and we replace them with truths that agree with God's higher truth. We repent of judgments, dishonoring parents, bitter expectations, inner vows, false identity, etc. (Casting down imaginations, and every high thing that exalteth itself against the knowledge of God, and bringing into captivity every thought to the obedience of Christ. 2 Corinthians 10:5) (... a root of bitterness springing up trouble you, and thereby many be defiled. Hebrews 12:15b)

3. **Close open doors of word curses**
   Word curses are negative words spoken over us and/or by us about ourselves. They don't agree with God's Truth about us and they undermine our true identity in Christ. Usually, they contain a deception or a lie even if they appear to be a fact. As they lodge deeply in our hearts, we either believe them or tend to wonder if they are truth. It takes the Cross of Christ and the power of a prayer of agreement to break word curses. (Be transformed by the renewing of your mind Romans 12:1-2) (Curses taken on the tree. Galatians 3:13)

4. **Close open doors of ungodly soul ties**
   There are godly soul ties and ungodly soul ties. We pray to break ungodly soul ties which were born out of ungodly agreements and/or ungodly relationships. Our relationship may have been teacher/student, male/female, parent/child, pastor/member, coach/player, etc. We keep the godly soul ties if the relationship basis or covenant was godly. (Isaiah. 58:8-9)

5. **Close open doors of disappointment with God**
   Many times, we were tempted to blame God for the works of the devil. Either we didn't trust God or His will and ways or His timing. Disappointment, dejection, discouragement, doubt, depression and disillusionment are fertile ground for ungodly beliefs about Father God, prayer, His Word, His plans for us, His provision, His faithfulness, etc.(1 John 4:20)

6. **Close open doors of partially healed hurts and wounds**
   We invite Jesus to touch the hurt and He really does meet us in person to touch and heal. The lie that the enemy sowed into you with the hurt, is replaced with truth that Jesus brings. The door to mental or demonic strongholds based upon hurt is now closed too! (Surely He took up our infirmities and carried our sorrows. Isaiah 53:4)

7. **Close other open doors of hidden spiritual roots and suppressed memories**
   From childhood on, many were able to block or suppress painful memories. Many times, the most painful memories are not recalled until we are in our 30s or 40s. We may have had dreams, flashbacks or body memories of the pain. If we ask the Holy Spirit, He may bring a memory into our recall (but never use pressure or hypnoses to rush the process.) The seasoned prayer minister always waits on Holy Spirit to lead and does not push.

8. **Close open doors to oppression, addictions or bondages**
   We tear down strongholds in prayer in the name of Jesus! Bondages were built on our unbelief and wounds but after this thorough ministry to the other areas, the enemy has no more legal permission to oppress. (Luke 11:21-22 When a strong man armed keepeth his palace, his goods are in peace, but when a stronger than he shall come upon him, and overcome him, he taketh from him all his armour wherein he trusted …)

9. **Cross Walk Prayer**
   We gain more freedom and prayer in new areas, as we continue to pray these prayers and learn to ask for forgiveness 5 ways, for our own sinful reactions.

10. **Pray to be filled with the Holy Spirit**
    Receive the power, fruit and gifts of the Holy Spirit. (… but be filled with the Spirit. Ephesians 5:18b)

Know Your Limitations and Calling

If you have ever been to a person who called themselves a counselor and a few hundred dollars later you found out they had no license, no degree, no oversight and no insight, you know why we must include this page. Let's be real about what God has called us to do and what we are not called to do. The most powerful way you can succeed is to stay within the scope of ministry that Holy Spirit will empower you to do. Let's look at the various roles of a ministry team.

God the Father, Son and Holy Spirit
1. Heal broken hearts and set the captives free
2. Convict people of sin and true repentance
3. Restore the rewards, blessings and years the locusts have eaten
4. Fill people with Holy Spirit resurrection power
5. Orchestrate all things concerning ministry times
6. Choose what memories to surface for ministry
7. Are all powerful, all knowing and present everywhere

Professional psychiatrists, psychologists and licensed counselors
1. Have earned advanced degrees under supervised practice
2. Prescribe, diagnose, treat, practice therapy and counseling
3. Take referrals to do counseling
4. Do interventions and admit to ER for evaluation
5. Manage treatment of patients with a diagnoses

Restoration Prayer Ministers know the scope of their ministry
1. Do prayer ministry not psychological counseling
2. Do active listening to receivers to hear their issue
3. Do active listening to Holy Spirit to hear His prayer strategy
4. Release Jesus Christ within to minister in His power and love
5. Minister within the limits of their experience and skill
6. Minister according to their spiritual gifts and faith
7. Minister with the power and authority given by God
8. Minister according to their ordination as a licensed minister (or not)
9. Do not fix people; they point them to Jesus the healer

Qualities in a good prayer minister
1. Humble, approachable, teachable, correctable
2. Anointed and available
3. Assertive not aggressive
4. Open, understanding and not defensive
5. Confident in Christ, not in experience and training
6. Responsible, disciplined and accountable
7. Submitted to God's chain of authority
8. Loving, serving and deferring to others
9. Good team member or leader as needed
10. An intercessor and prayer warrior

Prepare to Minister

PREPARE YOUR MIND, HEART AND BODY

- Consider time involved and make a firm commitment.
- Take your personal inventory of any unconfessed sin.
- Be prayed up and praised up! NO open doors!
- Learn to pray loosing and binding prayers.
- Put on the armor of God. (Ephesians 6:11-18)
- Learn to be still, listen and receive God's love.
- Demonstrate God's power, presence and anointing.
- Be a team player under authority – no lone rangers.
- Confidentiality is a must! Only share with your supervisor.

PREPARE YOUR SPIRIT TO MINISTER

- Wait for the move of the gentle courteous Holy Spirit.
- Practice using your spiritual ears and eyes to discern.
- Ask for supernatural words of wisdom and knowledge.
- Hear God tell you how to encourage, exhort and console.
- Have faith in God's promises and speak them.
- Believe for redemption in their spirit, soul and body.
- Believe Jesus died to heal broken hearts and set captives free.
- Remember the anointing breaks yokes - not talking it to death.

PREPARE YOUR TEAM TO MINISTER

- Clear your proposed ministry strategy with your leader.
- Set appointment time(s) and confirm with your team.
- Have: Bible, ministry guide, prayer card, confidentiality agreement and permission to minister and evaluation.
- Highlight critical related areas on the questionnaire.
- Begin your Issue-Focused Prayer Ministry work sheet.

PREPARE WITH PRAYER IN ADVANCE

- Praying in the Spirit unlocks mysteries.
- The Holy Spirit intercedes with groans we cannot express.
- He will give us words of knowledge and wisdom.
- We receive wisdom from our intercessors and leadership.
- Ask the receiver to fill in the IF ministry questionnaire.

Issue-Focused Prayer Ministry Questionnaire – one line answers

(Ideally, your prayer receiver will bring this completed questionnaire and the Commitment, Referral, Waiver of Liability and Confidentiality with them to the first session.)

Key to Abbreviations

Issue = Issue selected for ministry
SOF = Sins of Fathers (and mothers)
UGB = Ungodly beliefs

WC = Word curses spoken over us or by us
Hurts = Partially or unhealed hurts
DO = Demonic oppression and bondages

1. ISSUE: Identify <u>one issue</u> that we will be praying about this time. (one line answers)

    _____

2. ISSUE: How is your life or relationships affected by this problem? (one line answers)

    _____

3. SOF: How old were you when the problem began?

    _____

4. SOF: What sins of your ancestors contributed to this problem?

    _____

5. SOF: What other family members had this problem?

    _____

6. SOF: What were similar problems or situations in your childhood or teenage years?

    _____

7. UGB: What lie or ungodly belief do you have about yourself as a result?

    _____

8. UGB: What lie or doubt do you believe about God as a result?

    _____

9. UGB: What negative expectations or judgments to do you have of people as a result?

    _____

10. How have you judged or dishonored parents or authorities for having similar problems?

_____

11. UGB: What negative expectations do you have about your future now?

_____

12. WC: Has anyone spoken negative words or word curses over you related to this issue?

_____

13. WC: Have you spoken word curses about yourself that relate to the problem?

_____

14. UGB: Who do you have ungodly soul ties with as a result?

_____

15. HURTS: How have you been hurt by people related to this problem?

_____

16. HURTS: How have you been disappointed with God related to this problem?

_____

17. HURTS: Have you had dreams or nightmares related to these hurts

_____

18. HURTS: What ongoing difficulty, damage or pain does it cause?

_____

19. HURTS: On a scale of 1-10, how painful is this problem? (10 being very painful)

_____

20. DO: What religious or occult issues have contributed to forming this problem?

_____

21. DO: In what ways has the devil oppressed or harassed you related to this issue

_____

22: DO: What bondages, habits or addictions have you used to deal with this issue?

_____

23. DO: What demonic spirits may have been transferred to you?

_____

24: DO: What lies does the devil speak to you related to this issue?

As you review their answers, you can begin to clearly define the issue needing prayer.

Interview Worksheet and Ministry Plan	
Questions 1-2 **Identify one issue**	Choose one issue or current problem
Questions 3-6 **Sins of the fathers (SOF)**	**Generational patterns:** old and current Word curses
Questions 7-14 **Ungodly beliefs (UGB)**	**Ungodly beliefs** about others, God or self Ungodly soul ties
Questions 15-19 **Soul Spirit Hurts (HURTS)**	**Soul / Spirit hurts** - Hurt by others? God? Disappointment with God Hidden memories or roots
Questions 20-24 **Demonic Oppression (DO)**	**Demonic Oppression** - Open doors Bondages, addictions, downward spirals, torment

We suggest that you ask every prayer receiver and team to sign a form like the one below in order to protect your teams and prayer receivers from misunderstanding and accusation.

Commitment, Referral, Waiver of Liability and Confidentiality

___ Oversight Copy   ___ Prayer Minister's Copy   ___ Receiver's Copy

EXPECTATIONS OF YOUR COMMITMENT

It is expected that you have a sincere desire to overcome whatever problems or issues are hindering you and that you will cooperate fully with your Prayer Minister and the Holy Spirit in order to facilitate receiving God's help. Your Prayer Minister may ask you to pray, to fast and to do some outside "homework" in conjunction with your ministry. He/she also may ask you to be accountable to him/her for some specific problem areas of your life or for some specific behaviors.

The outcome of this ministry time will also be directly related to your commitment to spend daily quality time in meditation on God's Word, in prayer and to walk in obedience to the Holy Spirit. The ministry prayers require sincere decisions to confess, renounce and repent of sinful reactions and sinful behaviors. Only Jesus Christ can heal us (spirit-soul-body), restore our souls, renew our minds and deliver us from demonic oppression.

REFERRAL

If your Prayer Minister is not equipped or able to minister to your particular need or if you need longer term ministry, he/she may, in conjunction with the Pastor(s) and/or their designated representative, refer you to appropriate help.

WAIVER OF LIABILITY

I understand that I will be seeing a Prayer Minister who will be able to listen, support, encourage, pray and minister to me to help me overcome my problem(s) and to grow in my Christian life. I accept that he/she is not a licensed or professional pastor or counselor. The result of this ministry is dependent on my cooperation with the plan and power of the Holy Spirit and no guarantee of specific results are implied.

WAIVER OF CONFIDENTIALITY

I am aware that all statements that I shall make to the Prayer Minister (and to any other assistant present) are of a confidential nature, including all written information and that legally and ethically these may not disclose without my written consent. However, I waive my right to "complete" confidentiality in the following situations:

- I accept that my Prayer Minister may give a verbal summary report of the ministry to his/her oversight person.
- I accept that my Prayer Minister may consult with the Church Pastors, oversight person, Church Counselors, and/or others in a supervisory position concerning his/her ministry to me with the purpose of providing me with more effective ministry.
- I accept that the Church Pastors, and/or their designed representatives, will be informed of any ongoing, willful sin in my life with which I am not willing to receive freedom and healing.
- I acknowledge that Pastors, Counselors, Prayer Ministers, or any other persons involved in working with adults and children in a helping setting are either encouraged or required

by law to disclose to the appropriate person, agency, or civil authority any harm, or potential harm, that a person may attempt or desire to do to one's self or to others.

- I acknowledge that Pastors, Counselors, Prayer Ministers, etc., are also required to report any reasonable suspicion of physical or sexual abuse that has been done or that is being done to a minor child.
- I accept that all Pastors, Counselors and Prayer Ministers at _____ Church or Ministry reserve the right to make such reports as mandated by law whether or not they confer with me first.

By my signature below, I acknowledge that I have read and understand the "Commitment, Referral, Waiver of Liability and Confidentiality" and that I accept the expectations and stated conditions and limits of liability and confidentiality.

Signature: _____Date: _____

Printed Name: _____Date of Birth_____

Address: _____ Apt. _____

City/State//Zip: _____

Home Phone: _____ Cell or work phone: _____

Prayer Minister's Name: _____ Home Phone: _____

Prayer Minister's Name: _____ Home Phone: _____

Referred to: _____ Date Referred: _____

Witness: _____

Prayer Minister Comments:

_____

_____

NOTE: This form was NOT written by an attorney and we suggest that you have one drawn up that will be appropriate for the scope of your ministry.

Leader's Opening Prayer (Example)
Lord, we thank You for the gift of salvation including full healing and freedom from all that affects us. We thank You for the gift of eternal life. We thank You for manifesting Your love, power, presence, and anointing, to bring forth what You desire in _____'s life. Lord, we choose to **submit to You** as our Father God. We are under Your authority and receive the spiritual authority that You promised to give to all believers who submit to You. Lord, we choose **to use the authority You give us** against Satan and his plans.

In the Name of Jesus Christ, we cancel every assignment of the enemy against us, everyone and everything we care about, our pets, possessions and properties. We say that **no devil can hear or see** what is going on in this building and forbid any distraction, interference, or harassment. We **repent any way we have spoken agreement with fear, doubt, and unbelief**. Lord, we thank You for Your divine protection over each one of us, our homes, children, possessions, and over this ministry room. We say we are in **an entirely safe place** where only the Holy Spirit of God can affect us, in the Name of Jesus Christ.

Holy Spirit, we invite You to be in charge of this meeting. We depend on You to lead, guide, and direct us. We ask You to bring forth Your will, in Your Way and in your timing. We ask You to go to the **back rooms of our hearts** where even we don't go and to heal and restore. Lord, we thank You for ministering to us. We don't give the credit to a method or a person but we **give You all the honor and glory** for what happens here during this ministry session. Amen!

Member's Submission Prayer (Example)
Lord, I am here because **I need Your healing and freedom**. I ask You to heal and deliver me, and to put fresh hope in my life. I thank You for loving and accepting me just as I am, yet loving me too much to let me stay as I am. Lord, **help me take responsibility** for my sinful choices. Open my eyes to every way I have been in disagreement with You or have disobeyed You.

Lord, I **confess my sins** before You and the sins of my family and ancestors. I choose not to hold them responsible for the effects of their sins on my life. **I release them** from any way I blamed them for my sins. I depend on Jesus' death on the Cross and His shed blood for my forgiveness and restoration and declare that Jesus Christ is **my Lord and my Master**.

I invite You, Holy Spirit, to **help me see the deceptions** that I have believed. I am ready to have my **mind renewed**. Thank You for Your **undeserved favor and grace** to carry me and soften my will. Lord, I need You to **heal and redeem every painful experience**. Please **expose the deceptions** and clarify my perceptions. Bring Your healing to my hurts and **blocked emotions**. I invite You, **Holy Spirit** to lead us.

Lord, You are my Deliverer. **Set me free** from every ungodly influence and every torment. We choose to use the authority You have given us over all the power of the enemy and to **renounce every deception**. I choose to be **totally set free and to continue** to walk in Your freedom. I commit to abide in **Your Word and in prayer daily.** Holy Spirit, be the revealer of Truth and be **my Comforter.** In the Precious Name of Jesus Christ I pray. Amen!

Where are we?
First establish where we are in our spiritual walk.
John 3:3   Jesus answered and said unto him, "Verily, verily, I say unto thee, except a man be BORN AGAIN, he cannot see the kingdom of God." KJV

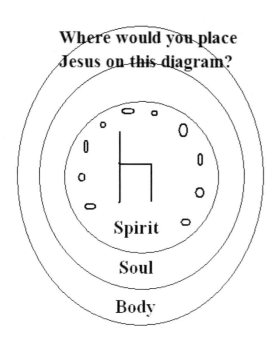

Where would you place Jesus on this diagram?

Spirit

Soul

Body

1 John 5:11-13a   And this is the testimony: that God has given us eternal life, and this life is in His Son. **He who has the Son has life; he who does not have the Son of God does not have life.** These things I have written to you who believe in the name of the Son of God, that **you may KNOW that you have eternal life** ... NKJV

Romans 7:18   For I know that **nothing good** dwells in me, that is, **in my FLESH;** ...NAS

John 10:10   The thief does not come except to steal, and to kill, and to destroy. I have come that they may have life, and that they may have it **more ABUNDANTLY.**   NKJV

2 Corinthians 5:17   Therefore if any man be **IN CHRIST,** he is a **new creature: old things are passed away;** behold, all things are become new. KJV

2 Peter 1:4   Whereby are given unto us exceeding great and precious promises: that by these ye might be **partakers of the DIVINE NATURE,** having escaped the corruption that is in the world through lust. KJV

1 Corinthians 6:17   But the one who joins himself to the Lord is **ONE SPIRIT with Him.**

Galatians 5:24 And they that are Christ's have **crucified the FLESH** with the affections and lusts. KJV

Galatians 2:20 KJV	**Carlotta's paraphrase**
I am crucified with Christ:	My **old nature is crucified** with Christ
nevertheless I live;	but **my born again divine nature lives**
yet not I,	but **not just I alone**
but Christ liveth in me:	but **Christ lives inside me**
and the life which I now live in the flesh	and the life which I am living now
I live **by the faith of the Son of God,**	**I live by His faith inside me**
Who loved me, and gave himself for me.	**because He loved me and died for me!**

Forgiveness is the First Key to Freedom and the Most Misunderstood

Forgiveness Is
A decision of the will to obey God
Giving Jesus access to heal your hurt
To let go of resentment and bitterness
To cancel plans or thoughts of revenge
To let go of demands for restitution
To release your right to be vindicated
To turn it all over to God to judge
Remembering that Jesus paid the price
Hoping for restoration to some level

Forgiveness is the first key to your
healing, restoration and freedom.
Forgiveness helps break the chain that
ties you to the hurt or other person.

Forgiveness does NOT mean
You feel like forgiving them
Forgetting or erasing your past
Never feeling the hurt again
God will never punish the offender
God will not ever require them to pay
Insisting on proof that you were innocent
Hoping they will feel guilty forever
The offender will owe you forever
No safe boundaries or discernment

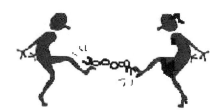

Forgiveness is Scriptural

Mark 11:25-26 And when you stand praying, if you hold anything against anyone, forgive him, so that your Father in heaven may forgive you your sins. But if you do not forgive, <u>neither will your Father who is in heaven forgive your sins.</u>

Mathew 18:34-35 In anger his master turned him over to the jailers to be tortured, until he should pay back all he owed. "This is how my heavenly Father will treat each of you <u>unless you forgive your brother from your heart.</u>"

Isaiah 43:25 I, (even) I, [am] he that blotteth out thy transgressions for mine own sake, and <u>will not remember thy sins.</u>

1 John 1:9 If we confess our sins, he is faithful and just to forgive us {our} sin, and to <u>cleanse us from all unrighteousness.</u>

Forgiveness is NOT Negotiable! We ask forgiveness for ourselves 5 Ways!

Horizontal: We ask others to forgive us for our sin, for judging them and we forgive them.
Vertical: We ask God to forgive us for doubting Him and ask forgiveness for our own sin.
Circle: We forgive ourselves for thoughts, words, deeds and for falling for deception.

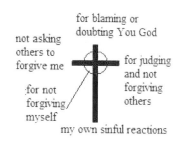

Test Yourself: Do You Need Ministry?

Many people who have already received a good measure of healing may ask for help in knowing if they would benefit from Restoration Prayer Ministry. I believe there is always "more" in life - more freedom, more life, more power, more ways to stretch in believing God.

If you would like to assess yourself today, you may take the following four tests. What percentage of the time are you believing what God's word says about you? How much are you still basing your self-worth on your ability to please others and what others say about you?

To score: 1 = often, 2 = sometimes, 3 = rarely

Fear of failure test:

1. Because of fear, I often avoid participating in certain activities.
2. When I sense that I might experience failure, I become nervous and anxious.
3. I worry or feel a floating anxiety.
4. I am a perfectionist and procrastinate if I can't do it perfectly.
5. I am compelled to justify my mistakes or make my point heard.
6. There are certain areas where I must succeed or I become depressed.
7. I become angry with people who interfere with my success or competence.
8. I am self-critical.

Fear of rejection test:

1. I get nervous and avoid certain people who might reject me.
2. I am uncomfortable around those who are different from me.
3. It bothers me when someone is unfriendly to me.
4. I am basically shy but I try to determine what people think of me.
5. Sometimes I try to impress others.
6. I am critical of others.
7. I become depressed when someone criticizes me.
8. I don't know what motivates some people and I usually don't ask.

Fear of punishment/punishing others:

1. I fear what God might do to me or that He will punish me.
2. After I fail, I worry about God's response.
3. When I see someone with difficulties, I wonder what they did to deserve them.
4. When things go wrong, I tend to think that God must be punishing me.
5. When I fail, I am very hard on myself.
6. I get angry when someone who is immoral or dishonest prospers.
7. I tend to focus on the faults of others and want them to receive correction.
8. God seems harsh to me.

<u>Shame test:</u>

1. I often think about past failures or experiences of rejection.
2. There is guilt, shame, anger, or fear in my past that is still painful to me.
3. I seem to make the same mistakes over and over again.
4. There are aspects of my character that I don't believe I can ever change.
5. I feel inferior, flawed or defective.
6. I am generally disgusted with myself.
7. I feel that certain experiences have basically ruined my life.
8. There are aspects of my appearance that I cannot accept.
9. I feel that I have lost the chance to experience a complete, wonderful life.

Now total your scores into one total score.
33 - 58: Fears and shame form a general backdrop and dominate your beliefs about yourself, God and others.

59 - 82: When you experience problems, your beliefs and decisions are still affected by fears, guilt, angers or shame from your past.

83 - 99: You usually walk in agreement with God's love and acceptance (or you have suppressed your emotions or are greatly deceived about yourself!)

This test was adapted from tests in *Search for Significance* by Robert S. McGee.

WHAT IF I AM THE INNOCENT VICTIM?

Although I easily recognized that I had attracted a long list of deceptive men, I sincerely did not know why. I saw myself as a basically innocent Christian woman who did not sleep around, "drink, dance, chew or go with those who do." I had no clue how I was "opening doors" for more and more spirits of deception to attack me. Honesty was my policy and I told my counselor that I hated deception. She pointed out that I actually hated the deceivers too and had judged them over and over. The more I sowed judgmental attitudes (condemnation) with unrighteous judgment (not true spiritual discernment) the more I reaped deceitful men. At the time, this made no sense to me and I continued to sow judgmental attitudes but finally I came back and asked for help to tear down the strongholds in my own life.

Issue-Focused Ministry Plan

Restoration Prayer Ministry is the most thorough ministry approach that I know of because we discern and minister to each issue eight ways. Our two page questionnaire, ministry plan and eight RPM prayers are coordinated to provide integrated ministry versus just one approach such as solely a healing approach or deliverance.

For illustration, we will say that the receiver's issue is that of being critical. Our ministry plan is gathered from the one line answers on the two page questionnaire and might look like this:

As you review their answers, you can begin to clearly define the issue needing prayer.

Interview Worksheet and Ministry Plan	
Questions 1-2 **Identify one issue**	**Choose one issue or current problem** I have become quite critical.
Questions 3-6 **Sins of the fathers (SOFRC)**	**Generational patterns:** old and current Critical mother and grandmother
Questions 7-14 **Ungodly beliefs (UGB)**	**Ungodly beliefs**: All women are critical. **Word curses:** I am a failure and deserve criticism. **Ungodly soul ties:** with Mother and Grandmother
Questions 15-19 **Soul Spirit Hurts (HURTS)**	**Soul / Spirit hurts** - Hurt by others? God? **Disappointment with God** – Choosing my Mom **Suppressed memories** – Scars from criticism.
Questions 20-24 **Demonic Oppression (DO)**	**Demonic Oppression** - Open doors to self-hate Bondages, addictions, downward spirals, torment

Questions 1-2:   We identify the primary issue and insert it into the ministry plan.
Questions 3-6:   We choose 1-2 generational patterns that relate to our primary issue.
Questions 7-14: We write quotes that are ungodly beliefs, word curses or ungodly soul ties.
Questions 15-19: We choose 1-3 soul or spirit hurts which can include hurts from people, disappointment with God, suppressed memories or wounds.
Questions 20-24: We ask Holy Spirit what demonic spirits are behind their oppression.

For each of the eight areas on the right side of the ministry plan there is a corresponding prayer similar to the one above. Then the prayer minister will lead the receiver to pray, forgiving others and asking forgiveness for their own sin so that they can legally renounce and break the power of each related area. In each case, the prayer minister will remind the receiver to fill in the blank with the related area, i.e. being critical.

This manual provides teachings, scriptures and a suggested prayer for each area. For example, in this first prayer for the first ministry area, the prayer minister will lead the receiver to insert "being critical" in the first two blanks. The blank in line 7 will be filled as Holy Spirit prompts them to receive specific freedoms and blessings instead of criticism.

<u>Sins of the Fathers and Resulting Curses</u> (SOFRC)

1. I *confess* the sin (iniquity) of my ancestors, my parents, and my own sin, of
_____.
2. I *forgive* and *release* them for passing these sins on to me and the resulting curses.
3. I ask You to *forgive* me, Lord, for this sin, for yielding to it, to the resulting curses and for doubting You God.
4. I *repent* of this sin and for judging them.
5. I **forgive** myself for participating in this sin.
6. I **renounce** the sin and curses of _____ and break the power of it and all resulting curses through the redemptive work of Christ on the Cross and His shed Blood.
7. I **receive** God's freedom from the sin and from the resulting generational curses. In their place I **receive** _____.

Now that you understand how to hear God for a ministry plan and how to pray for each related area, let's look at the associated teaching that we suggest. It provides enough teaching and scripture to clarify God's Word but not enough to cause confusion.

Each Ministry Session

Now to put it all together, we will begin each ministry session with these ingredients.
1. Welcome them, do introductions, thank them for coming and express your joy!
2. Pray the leader's opening prayer and lead them in the receiver's prayer.
3. Review the limited waiver of liability and confidentiality very briefly.
4. Locate the rest room, tissues and explain that we will take short breaks.
5. Discuss their questionnaire answers briefly, giving them time to clarify.
6. 1-5 should take less than ½ hour, leaving more time for prayer than talking.
We will lead in ministry to each related area, one at a time, for about 15 minutes each.
1. Share the teaching and scriptures for one area i.e. SOFRC.
2. Answer pertinent questions for biblical understanding.
3. Pray the related prayer over the related issues in the ministry plan.
Then we repeat this process until we have prayed over all eight areas in about three hours.

Freedom from Sins of the Fathers and Resulting Curses (SOFRC)

The most common generational issues involve committing the same sins that our ancestors did. Often people will call to say that they are acting like their father or mother.

Deuteronomy 28 and other passages are clear that when we idolize or do not worship God and God alone, we bring curses into our lives. They become part of the inheritance that we leave our descendents. Jesus Christ died to take these curses upon Himself. **We can pray and receive His provision** to break the power of the sinful patterns and the resulting generational curses.

COMMON CURSES from generational sins

- **Abandonment**
- **Barrenness/Miscarriage**
- **Disease/Illness**
- **Failure**
- **Fears (of all kinds)**
- **Poverty**
- **Sexual Impurity**

Exodus 20:5 is clear that the sins of the fathers do go down 3 and 4 generations. Just as we prayed a prayer of salvation, we must pray to appropriate Jesus' death and forgiveness for these sins as well, in order to be totally free of generational patterns.

When the Bible says to CONFESS the sins of our fathers as sins, we are not **REPENTING** of them (or responsible for their choices.) We are agreeing with God that their sins were sins.

Sins of the Fathers Scriptures

Exodus 20:5-6
You shall not bow down to them or worship them; for I, the LORD your God, am a jealous God, punishing the children **for the sin of the fathers to the third and fourth generation** of those who hate me, NIV

Leviticus 26:40a, 42
"'But if they will **confess their sins and the sins of their fathers**… I will remember my covenant with Jacob and my covenant with Isaac and my covenant with Abraham, and I will remember the land. NIV

Galatians 3:13
Christ redeemed us from the curse of the law by becoming a curse for us, for it is written: "Cursed is everyone who is hung on a tree." NIV

Jesus Christ died on the Cross and shed His blood so that we could be forgiven and we could be free of the curses brought into the family by the unconfessed sins of our ancestors.

EXAMPLES OF GENERATIONAL ISSUES YOU MAY HEAR:

I hate it but I am doing the same gross sins, just like my father and grandfather did.
I am told that my sharp tongue sounds like my mother and grandmother.
My grandparents and parents were poor and now we are poor too.
I have the same illnesses that the men in my family had. Will I die prematurely too?
I can't believe I am treating my children the same way my parents treated me.
My children have the same issues that my parents and grandparents had.
No matter how hard I try, the people I date turn out to be just like my parents.

Sins of the Fathers and Resulting Curses

1.   I *confess* the sin (iniquity) of my ancestors, my parents, and my own sin, of
_____.

2. I *forgive* and *release* them for passing these sins on to me and the resulting curses. (Can add a new specific.)

3. I ask You to *forgive* me, Lord, for this sin, for yielding to it, to the resulting curses and for doubting You God.

4. I *repent* of this sin and for judging them.

5. I **forgive** myself for participating in this sin.

6. I **renounce** the sin and resulting curses of _____, and break the power of it and all resulting curses through the redemptive work of Christ on the Cross and His shed Blood.

7. I **receive** God's freedom from the sin and from the resulting curses.   In their place I **receive**
_____.

Notes

Testimonies of Freedom
from Sins of the Fathers and Resulting Curses (SOFRC)

Stubbornness and rebellion

I was staying with my mother a short time after my father had died. During that time I had both a disturbing dream and a demonic presence manifest itself in my mother's home. When I asked the Lord to show me what it was, He responded by showing me that stubbornness and rebellion were in my family line. This was very noticeable in both my father and grandfather and had been passed down to me through the ancestral line. I could sense that this curse was trying to have a hold over my own life now that my father was no longer alive.

The Holy Spirit then reminded me of 1 Samuel 15:23, which says, "Rebellion is as the sin of witchcraft and stubbornness as the sin of idolatry." I had good reason to believe this was because my father and his father were heavenly involved in Freemasonry. As soon as I got home, I prayed the restoration prayer for Sins of the Fathers and Resulting Curses. After praying this prayer, I have stayed with my mother many times and have not been worried by any evil encounters. The Blood of Jesus broke the power of this ancestral sin and curse over me and has set me free from its consequences.

Generational Sins Revealed Through Dreams

I had been living a fasted life for about 3 and half years working on my relationship with God so that I would not miss the destiny He had for me life. Then God gave me a dream where he told me that I need prayer for inner healing and deliverance to break the power of generational curses.....which at one point in my Christian life I did not believe in.

I actually knew a few people whom I had done some inner healing and deliverance prayer work prior to this, however, I knew I was not to use them. It took time and prayer to find Carlotta, then it took time to get an appointment but I knew I was with the person whom God had wanted me to get restoration prayer with.

What I liked about working with Carlotta, was she made me feel comfortable and was just herself with me, very professional but at the same time so knowledgeable. I was nervous in the beginning before the first session but I was determined to find freedom from the generational curses that had haunted me my whole life.

So when we were praying the protection prayer in the beginning my stomach was hurting about half way through for the first three days ... but after we prayed and broke all the generational curse that can pass down through your ancestors forgiving them and after asking forgiveness 5 different ways I was experiencing freedom at a new level for the first time in my life.

I had actually thought it was not possible for me, that it was for other people. Prior to the prayer, I went on a 40 day vegetable and water fast. I was determined to give myself the best chance for deliverance as I could.

When we finished the third day of praying and breaking off of the generational curses, I had a dream that night. In the dream I was in my bedroom and as I woke up the walls were glowing with a soft white light. As a matter of fact everything in my room was glowing with a soft white light, my room where I lived had been completely cleaned out. I walked around wondering where all of old stuff had gone and even looked in the closet of the house and it was completely clean as well. I thought in the dream that the someone had come in and cleaned my house and I was upset because I thought how will I find anything now......

When I woke up later and realized that God had shown me that all of ancestral or generational curses that I had lived with my whole life were gone I was so relived. I felt very good both physically, spiritually and emotionally after each session with Carlotta.

She breaks it down into 6 three hours sessions. By the fourth session, most of the hindrances have left after working through the ungodly beliefs and all of them by the deliverance session. I have been doing very very well since the last session and it has been almost one month since the sessions ended. The freedom from the constant pressure of the generational curses has finally stopped in my life.

Carlotta has so many years of experience and has been given an anointing for this. Her methods are very thorough and I was impressed with depth of her knowledge of the spiritual realm and times we are living in. The first thing they teach you about inner healing prayer or restoration prayer is that you always need tune ups, everyone needs them like a physical, so I am constantly asking God to show me blind spots in my life as my walk with Lord continues.

It is hard to describe freedom when you have felt this pressure on you your whole life. I had read so many books on the subjects and even received a degree in counseling but it didn't bring any relief to my life. I was looking for this freedom since I was 12 years old when it first started, I am now 54 years old and very thankful for Carlotta's persistence and determination to get herself free and then to show others the path to freedom.

Blessings to all looking for freedom as I was. In His grip

Another prayer receiver shared this testimony verbally:

She had lived in serious financial distress for years, had no car and was paid poorly. Part of this poverty had been due to her own involvement in occult practices and immorality and some of it was due to generational sins and the resulting curses. When she had repented of her sins and testified at church, rather than affirming her, the membership shunned her and she lost her Christian friends too.

It was not easy for her to do Restoration Prayer Ministry because it is one thing to get out of the occult but yet another thing to get all of the occult out of you. Sometimes, demons would rise up and fight back but she persisted, renounced them, cast them out and overcame.

In the third session, we prayed prayers of agreement and she confessed all of the sins of her ancestors and repented of her own sins. The power of the generational curses was clearly broken and she was free of reaping what they had sown into her inheritance. Now she was free to sow good seed and to reap financial blessings.

Father God graciously gave her a confirmation that very day. When the mail came, there was a card from a lady that she did not know. She had written an apology because she had not obeyed God months before, when He first asked her to write. She enclosed a nice check and a note of blessing. Incredible as it might seem, Father God knew what day the generational curses and curse of poverty would be broken. He arranged a check and blessing to arrive that very day! Our gracious Heavenly Father had planned it so the blessing would arrive the very day that she confessed their sin and repented of her own!

Ungodly Beliefs (UGB)
How to Identify and Replace

Ungodly beliefs usually begin when we are hurt or offended. We are tempted to have sinful reactions and behaviors and to draw ungodly conclusions, develop ungodly expectations and to think ungodly beliefs.

Ungodly beliefs may sound like facts but they are not in agreement with God's Word and are not God's best for us to live by. After we pray, confessing them as sin, renouncing them, repenting of living by them and asking forgiveness 5 ways, their power is broken. After we pray asking forgiveness, it is much easier to hear God as He tells us His higher Truth.

WHAT ARE UNGODLY BELIEFS?
(UGBs)
Ungodly Beliefs are anything you believe, judge, dishonor, vow or expect which does not agree with God's Word, His nature or His character.

WHAT ARE THE RESULTS OF BELIEVING UGBs?
You speak doubt or unbelief.
You fall for more deceptions.
You judge and condemn others.
You overreact to current situations.
You damage or defile your relationships.
You are in agreement with devils vs. God.
Separate you from others, God and yourself.
You begin to defend your fleshly strongholds.

WHY FORMALLY RENOUNCE UGBs?
What you believe matters to God!
They result in more defilement and hurt.
UGBs are agreement with the Deceiver.
They include ungodly negative expectations.
What you believe determines your reactions in a time of crisis and determines your future!

YOUR GODLY BELIEFS WILL BE A BLESSING!

Meditate on 2 Timothy 2:24-25 KJV

UNGODLY BELIEF SCRIPTURES

Romans 12:2 And be not conformed to this world: but be ye transformed by the **renewing of your mind,** that ye may prove what {is} that good, and acceptable, and perfect, will of God.

Proverbs 23:7 For as he **thinketh** in his heart, so {is} He ...

Exodus 20:12 **Honor** thy father and thy mother: that thy days may be long upon the land which the LORD thy God giveth thee.

James 5:12 But above all things, my brethren, **swear not**, neither by heaven, neither by the earth, neither by any other oath: but let your yea be yea; and your nay, nay; lest ye fall into condemnation.

Luke 6:41 And why beholdest thou the splinter that is in thy brother's eye, but perceivest not **the beam** that is in thine own eye?

Galatians 6:7 Be not deceived; God is not mocked: for whatsoever a man soweth, that **shall he also reap.**

Identify Related Ungodly Beliefs

Check each ungodly belief that directly relates to the issue you chose for prayer ministry today. Then fine tune them or write the exact ungodly belief you said or thought in the past. Even old inactive ungodly beliefs must be renounced and replaced with Godly beliefs.

Feeling Inadequate or Inferior?

If I try to step out, I will fail again.
My family/friends will discourage me.
My contributions will be rejected.
I never have the money to succeed.
I have to meet people's expectations.
The struggle will be too hard for me.
I will disappoint or hurt people.
I am not trained and equipped.
If I fail, I will lose people's approval.
I don't have the gifts that I will need.

Feeling controlled or dominated?

I have to do what other people say.
If I obey God it makes people angry.
I am easily controlled by criticism.
It is not safe to share my feelings.
I have to make everyone happy.
Isolate and avoid unwanted advice.
People will not agree with my vision.
If we disagree, I must be wrong.
I don't have options or choices.
If it needs to be done, I have to do it.

Feeling depressed or discouraged?

I dwell on what might go wrong.
I can't speak to people or groups.
My interests and motivation are low.
I am not able to concentrate anymore.
I can't forgive offenses of the past.
If others know me they will reject me.
No one will ever love and accept me.
I failed; I deserve to be punished.
It is not OK for me to express anger.
This is the way I am; there's no hope.

Feeling abused or intimidated?

I am shameful and defective.
Submission means tolerating abuse.
Exposing abuse only makes it worse.
I resent people who take advantage.
I am to blame for the abuse I get.
Don't share, tell, feel, ask or be real.
I shouldn't get angry at manipulation.
Their reaction will ruin my future.
Everything I do and say is wrong.
I never have normal relationships.

Feeling trapped by a sense of duty?

I have to fix everyone's problems.
I have to meet the standards of others.
I am unworthy and the most unlikely.
I am only able to do menial tasks.
I will always be taken advantage of.
I rescue people from consequences.
I'd rather do it myself than confront.
My preferences are never important.
I will be criticized and unappreciated.
I deny my own needs until I burn-out.

Feeling far away from God?

My prayers are seldom answered.
God seems distant and uninvolved.
God could never totally forgive me.
God short-changed me; I can't succeed.
If I fail, God will never accept me.
I am not sure of my eternal salvation.
God should have intervened for me.
Why hasn't God released me to minister?
God doesn't love me like He does others.
God requires too much and is not fair.

Identify ungodly beliefs regarding Satan and God.

I renounce Satan's Lies	I receive God's Truth that says
Whatever God says is not true.	God is truth. I invite Him to show me truth. I choose to know Father God personally.
God is unfaithful and doesn't answer me.	I choose to be willing to seek Father God's face and to know His faithfulness.
What if I belong to Satan? to darkness?	I choose to live in the light and Truth and struggle there vs. in the darkness.
Jesus Christ won't heal me.	I choose to open my eyes and ears to the love and healing power of Jesus Christ.
I don't believe that God loves me.	Father God loves me perfectly. I do not earn His love; it is His gift to me.
God is distant and at fault for everything.	I choose to believe God is a personal God and He has my best interest at heart.
There are many holy books; they are not true.	I receive the Holy Bible as Truth: the only inerrant, infallible, inspired Word of God.
Satan tortures me; God doesn't care.	Father God offers me unlimited grace and favor when I choose Him as my Lord.
Jesus Christ offers me hope then disappoints me.	Jesus Christ sustains me with new vision, hope and will never let me go or reject me.
God is not creator. I don't owe Him anything.	I am accountable to my loving Creator. His love constrains me to obey Him.
God sets me up to fail, then punishes me.	God loves me and He makes a way of escape from temptation.
I can't feel God's love; He wants to kill me.	I embrace His love; I die to my selfishness, self-proclaimed purpose, destiny and goals.
There are many God's.	There is one True Holy God, who alone is omniscient, omnipotent and omnipresent.
We can all evolve into a God.	I live in a one power universe. I am God's created being. I am under His protection.
I will be like God - controlling my own life.	I am accountable to Father God, who alone is in control. I bow to Him in humility.
I take care of myself; God is not dependable.	I am grateful to Father God for all His benefits and I safely depend on Him.
I have to earn God's approval but I can't.	I am loved and accepted unconditionally totally apart from my performance.
I must be my own Savior.	Jesus Christ alone is perfect and able to take my sins and punishment upon Himself.
I served Satan; God will send me to Hell.	I am free to choose life, Father God, love, salvation, Heaven or to choose Hell.
If I make Jesus Lord, He will force me to _____.	Love is not love if it is forced; Jesus Christ is a gentleman who loves me to Himself.
I cannot handle love; it will destroy me.	Father God will not destroy my identity but will cast out my fears with perfect love.

God will crush my personality.	Father God is life and resurrects a new spirit in me that can love and be loved.
God will set me up to hope and then destroy me.	Love only destroys that which is not love and not pure.
I could never live the Christian life.	Jesus Christ offers to live His life from inside me, in His power, as I abide in Him.
Satan may be able to block my salvation.	I have invited Jesus in as my Lord and have eternal salvation. I am his child forever.
God is out to criticize and condemn me.	God lets me share the glory when I succeed and takes my punishment when I fail.
God is an evil parent who is capricious.	Father God embraces me and can only act in love to me. I am His love to others.
God holds my mistakes and sins over my head.	When I confess my sin, Father God totally forgives me and restores me.
God will take away my freedom.	Jesus sets me free to be what I was created to be, in my full inheritance as His child.
God will let me be persecuted even if I do obey.	I embrace the cup of Christ's suffering and persecution for righteousness sake.
God withholds from me and shames me.	God will fill me with His Holy Spirit, His gifts, His fruit, His power and His glory.
God does not answer all my prayers.	I choose to believe that God knows what is best; I accept His way, will and timing.
I tried tithing to God and was not blessed.	I give out of gratitude to God to build His Kingdom, with no strings attached.
God will use me and abuse me.	I am a bondservant, giving my all to the Kingdom of God, asking nothing in return.
I am evil and am bound to sin intentionally.	Father chose to love and forgive me when I was His enemy, not caring about Him.
Jesus did not stop my evil torturers.	Teach me your ways oh God and I will embrace your love, leaving justice to you.
How can a loving God allow evil?	Father God created us all with free choice because love is not love if it has no choice.
God is small and we do not need Him.	Father God is my source and I trust Him for miraculous intervention in my life.
God doesn't answer my questions.	In all eternity, I may not understand who God is because He is God and I am not.
Recovery will take years or is impossible.	When I make Jesus Christ my Lord, His anointing breaks every yoke and bondage.
I can masterfully save myself.	Jesus Christ is God Himself, come to earth, to offer me His life in exchange for mine.
We are all sons of God as much as Jesus is.	In the beginning Jesus Christ created me in His image: body, soul and spirit.
I am garbage and without identity.	I am His beloved, cherished, the apple of His eye, precious in His site, chosen and authorized to express His heart.

Before the Prayer on Ungodly Beliefs

I always explain four things before we actually pray:

1. An ungodly belief may sound like fact but contains a lie that the enemy of our soul wants us to believe forever. For instance, I don't doubt that they were rejected but I know that God does not want them to believe that they will always be rejected.
2. A godly belief usually has at least two sides to it. There is the general scriptural truth that has always been true i.e. God loves and accepts me unconditionally. There is also their own choice to believe or receive truth i.e. I choose to believe and receive God's unconditional love and acceptance, completely apart from my performance.
3. We never begin a godly belief with "I will" or "I will never" as in a vow.
4. I tell them I will coach and teach with each related area and each prayer.

Ungodly Beliefs (UGB)

1. I *confess* my sin (and if appropriate, my ancestor's sin) of believing the ungodly belief(s) that _____ and for any way I have **blamed you** God.
2. I *forgive* those who contributed to my forming this UGB, including myself and _____.
3. I ask You, Lord, to **forgive me** for living my life by it and for anyway I have judged others, based on this UGB.
4. I *forgive* myself for believing this ungodly belief.
5. I *renounce* and **break** my agreement with this UGB, and the agreement that I have had with deception, the power of darkness and with demons.
6. I *choose* to **believe** the godly belief that _____.

Explain that word curses are negative words that cause damage to a person's hopes or identity like, "You will never amount to anything" or "Your will never get it."

Word Curses (WC)

1. **I forgive** those who cursed me with the spoken word (and if appropriate) including myself, by saying _____.
2. I **repent** for receiving this curse and judging myself.
3. I ask You to **forgive me**, Lord, for giving it place in my life. I receive Your forgiveness.
4. I **renounce** and break the legal rights/power of this curse in my life based on the shed Blood of Jesus and His finished work on the Cross.
5. I **release** all related fleshly structures to You and ask You to bring them to death on the Cross.
6. I **cancel** all judgments and all work of all demons associated with this curse by the power of the Blood and the Cross of Christ.
7. I **receive** God's Truth that says I am _____.

Ungodly Soul Ties
Another source of negative energy or power in our being

This page is written so that the receiver can read the entire page and prayer out loud and list their ungodly soul ties. They answer every question by writing a list of initials or names.

Ungodly soul ties develop when we enter into an ungodly covenant with another person, group or institution. It is important to formally break the ungodly part of our ties and to keep the godly ties. The fruit of the transference of spirits, ungodly beliefs, bitter expectations, inner vows, word curses spoken by them or us, will affect our lives until we renounce our ungodly agreements with them. God is a covenant keeping God and honors the covenants we have made until we break them. We must identify and cut the ungodly soul tie by praying a prayer of agreement with someone with some spiritual authority.

TEST YOURSELF: (Ungodly soul ties can be made with relationships of all kinds.)

Whom have I been previously knit to and ungodly residue of these relationships still affect me?
Have I had ungodly relationships with denominations that taught error or religious pride?
Have I come into agreement with error taught in books or media that bore ungodly fruit?
Have I made an ungodly contract in business, as a partner, an employee or an employer?
Have I had ungodly soul ties with religious groups, cults, churches, leaders or members?
Have I had an ungodly soul tie in a mentoring, teacher, coach or student relationship?
Have I had ungodly packs, blood packs, dedications, baptisms or vows with secret organizations?
Have I had a ungodly tie in a relationship that included dominance, control, demands or manipulation?
Have I been programmed to have ungodly soul ties and not be consciously aware of them?
Have I had covenant relationships which included intimidation, fear, coercion or abuse?
Am I still haunted by the words, pressure or control of people who have passed away?

You can pray to break your ungodly soul ties in groupings like: parents, siblings, employers, co-workers, church leaders, dating/marriage relationships, cults or secret organizations… etc.

SUGGESTED PRAYER TO BREAK UNGODLY SOUL TIES:

In the Name of Jesus Christ, Son of the Most High God, I submit myself completely to you and ask forgiveness five ways. I confess all my sins of attitude, action and sexual sins, as well as the ungodly soul ties. I ask You, Lord, to forgive me for my sins that resulted in an ungodly soul tie. I ask forgiveness for the ways that I have judged others. I ask forgiveness for any way I blamed you, Lord, or were angry and resentful against You for the harmful effects of this relationship. Lord, I receive your forgiveness. Thank You for forgiving me and for cleansing me.

Lord, I choose to forgive myself for letting this soul tie affect my life and relationships.

I choose to forgive each person that I have been involved with in any ungodly way. I cut and break my ungodly soul ties with _____. I pray that You would cause him/her to be all You want him/her to be and that You would cause me to be all that you want me to be.

Lord, please cleanse my mind from all memories of ungodly unions so that I am totally free to give myself to You (and to my mate if applicable.) Restore and return the broken torn portions of my soul and destroy anything that has come into me through an ungodly soul tie. I renounce and cancel assignments of evil spirits attempting to maintain these ungodly soul ties.

Lord, I thank You for restoring my soul to wholeness. Let me walk in holiness by Your grace. In the Name of Jesus Christ, Son of the Most High God, I pray. Amen.

I suggest that our receiver write the down initials of all the ungodly soul ties that came to mind as a record of which ones were covered in this session.

Healing Soul and Spirit Hurts (SSH)

God's master plan is to enable you to love Him with all your heart and to love others as yourself but **Satan's master plan is to SEPARATE** you from others, from God and yourself but Satan wants to isolate you and convince you to defend your rights to harbor sinful reactions and behaviors. If you refuse to forgive, Jesus will not be able to heal you.

In Luke 4:18, Jesus said, "The Spirit of the Lord is upon me, because he hath anointed me to preach the gospel to the poor; he hath sent me to heal the broken-hearted, to preach deliverance to the captives, and recovering of sight to the blind, to set at liberty them that are bruised, ..."

 Satan tempts us to have ungodly reactions so he can build fleshly strongholds in our lives. For instance, he tempts us to harbor rage, unforgiveness, resentment, bitterness, wrath, retaliation, violence (and ultimately suicidal or homicidal thoughts or actions.)

YOU ARE NOT YOUR PAST!

Don't let your past define your future! But God does want you to invite Him to heal you. He wants you to have lasting healing in your life. Then you will be free to fulfill your destiny in His power.

Denial for Survival!

Will you be real with God? In the past, you may have denied the hurt or "stuffed" the pain just to survive. Ask the Lord to help you to be real with yourself. You don't have to relive the memories but you can ask Jesus to reveal the memories that are the root of your issue today.

To receive a healing, it is important to share your real feelings with God. He will not be surprised or shocked. He already knows how you feel. He is not waiting to punish you. Will you risk being real?

How do we receive healing that lasts?
by being diligent about forgiving.
by being real honest with God.
by giving the pain or offense to God.
by letting God speak/show us His truth

Big steps to receiving healing:

1. Forgive others
2. Renounce lies
3. Release the hurt
4. Ask Jesus to heal

King David was a man after God's own heart. He is a model showing us how to be real with God. In Psalm 142, David "pours out his complaint" to the Lord honestly and then receives God's truth.

Soul/Spirit Hurts Scriptures
Isaiah 53;4
Surely he hath borne our griefs, and carried our sorrows ...
Psalm147:3
He healeth the broken in heart, and blindeth up their wounds.
Psalm 23:2-3
He maketh me to lie down in green pastures: he leadeth me beside the sill waters. He restoreth my soul: he leadeth me in the paths of righteousness for his name's sake.

About the Soul/Spirit Hurts Prayers

In 2003, Jesus began to appear in spiritual visions to heal most of our receivers in person through open visions. I have learned to lead them to say the first line of this prayer and then fix their eyes on Jesus for five minutes or so until HE TELLS them or shows them what He will heal that day. If He appears to them or begins to tell them how He is healing them, I will be quiet the entire time except to direct their conversation or prayer back to Jesus instead of to me.

If He does not appear to them and they do not hear Him, then I lead them to pray over the hurts we have already identified. More often than not, He will take over this session if allowed.

Soul/Spirit Hurts (SSH)
1. I *Ask* You Holy Spirit to reveal the hurt You want to heal today (**Listen/watch** patiently as He tells or shows it to you. Wait 1-5 minutes and begin to talk directly with Jesus.)
2. (Be honest with God about how you feel.) Lord, I pour out my heart about the hurt, pain, fear, anger, frustration …
3. I *forgive* _____ (parents, siblings, peers, others) for inflicting this hurt and causing me pain.
4. I ask you to **forgive me,** Lord, for hurting others out of my hurt. I *repent* of this sinful reaction, sinful behavior and my attitude.
5. I *forgive* myself for letting this hurt control me and open doors to strongholds in my life.
6. I **release** this hurt to You, Lord, and I **receive** Your healing touch. Please show me or tell me how you are healing me today. **Listen/watch** as He does. (Listen several minutes for Jesus to tell you or show you how He is healing you today.)
7. **Thank you** for redeeming every hurt and taking the pain.

Many times, Holy Spirit will immediately take them to memories of hurts and disappointments with God. We follow His leading and continue in prayer to ask forgiveness for doubting God.

Disappointment with God
Dear God, I **confess** that I have misjudged You and blamed You for things that You did not do. I choose to repent and stop today.
1. I ask You to **forgive me** for my sins against You.
2. I **affirm** that You are good and want only the best for me.
3. I choose to **receive You** as Lord of my life and to **believe** You cause all things to work together for good, to mature me so I will be able to rule and reign with You in eternity.
4. I **put the "blame"** where it really belongs, on Satan's kingdom. I choose to stop blaming You, God, and will take responsibility for my own choices under the guidance and control of the Holy Spirit.
5. **Thank You** for new freedom, new ability to trust and a renewed relationship with You. I receive it in the Name of Jesus.

True Stories About Healing Hurts

My favorite thing about doing Restoration Prayer Ministry is that it is not a new gimmick or method, with an agenda of steps or lists. It is a simple meeting with Jesus, the Truth, a touch, a vision or healing encounter. It is increasing trust and learning to relate to God's power on an ongoing basis. It is not a new dependence on a Christian counselor, but learning to relate to God in supernatural ways, as a lifestyle. Usually, our receiver has an open vision of Jesus healing.

In our healing hurts sessions I am quiet. (First miracle!) I ask them to invite Jesus to show them or tell them what He wants to heal today and direct all their conversation to Jesus. They may pour their heart out to Him but then they look and listen to see what Jesus does to heal them Himself. This is not visualization because I don't suggest anything. Jesus does it all and they tell me.

Dancing with Jesus again: She reported: God took me back to years ago, when my daughter was missing for 6 weeks. My husband, an abusive alcoholic, was worse than no support at all. When I found out that she had been brutally murdered, it damaged my ability to trust God. My passion had always been for worshipping God, in song and in dance. I felt that Jesus wanted to heal me and He actually asked me to dance with Him. As I doodled, I drew a stick figure of myself dancing, but my heart was too broken; I couldn't draw Jesus in. I couldn't dance with Him.

Now years later, Jesus was asking me to dance with Him again. I looked in my wallet to find the scrap of paper of that simple drawing, from years ago. I gasped when I saw it. Today, Jesus had drawn Himself in - dancing with me. I promise you: I did not draw it. Jesus drew it. He wants to dance with me and complete my healing. We've been dancing ever since.

Covered with green slime: I really wasn't trying to make a vision from Jesus happen, but it did. Jesus took me to a dark igloo like place that was deep down in my heart. A younger me was at the door and definitely did not think it was a good idea to let Jesus in there. I persuaded him and opened the door. Inside the walls were completely lined with shelves that were loaded with green slime, like in the Ghost Busters movie. I knew that Jesus wanted to clean the room up and that represented cleaning my heart. I gave him permission and he began. He not only removed the slime, he removed the shelves and then he removed all the walls. Suddenly, I could see the whole world outside. I knew that Jesus had set me free.

My identity and trust restored: I have to give honor and thanks to God for changing my life. Through Restoration Prayer Ministry, at Cross Walk Life, he revealed things to me that I have had suppressed for years. I discovered that I have had a 14 year old side of me that has dominated my life for 18 years. At 14, I became the provider for my family of five. For the next 12 years, I felt like I had to do everything and regardless of what I did, it was not good enough. I always felt the need to prove myself as a strong young man and to earn respect. I grew up fast with many responsibilities and had no one to depend on or to instruct me. I missed my childhood and learned to depend on myself instead of God. I was always wanting to be in control of everything. Jesus showed me that my true identity is not based on how others perceived me, but in God's Truth about me. As I allowed Truth to touch the 14 year old inside, God healed me and restored my ability to trust.

Open visions of healing during worship: (Carlotta: I silently prayed for this young man without telling him a word about visions and God did it all. In fact, he continues to have frequent spontaneous visions since then.) He reported: While I was worshipping at our home group, God suddenly gave me an open vision, taking me down a deep dark tunnel, to a room inside myself that I didn't even know existed. It was where a "little version of me" lived, who had been hurt and was hiding in shame for many years. I knew that it was up to me to choose to open the door and allow Jesus to come into that room. Jesus cleaned the room, touched me and set me free to become all that I am destined to become. Praise God! This is a day of suddenlies!!

Freedom from defensiveness with my children: Although I had already had other types of counseling for these same things, Restoration Prayer Ministry at Cross Walk Life set me free in three stages of my life.

At age 7, I was angry because my parents were alcoholics and were mentally abusive. At age 12, I was molested by my cousin and was overcome by shame, guilt and fear. I created little ones inside me put up walls of defense that still separated me from God, as an adult. Even now, I have been afraid to totally trust him. Jesus used Restoration Prayer Ministry to help me to let go of a pride that I wasn't aware of, trying to control everything and the need to be defensive. I was able to recognize and deal with defensive walls (of indifference and stubbornness) that I would put up when things didn't go my way. Actually, I was surprised to find out that these were the same areas that I have been dealing with in my children! Thank you for the freedom that truth brings!

A new boldness and ability to love replaced my timidity, need to protect myself and defensive buttons: In May, I had the awesome opportunity to attend a Restoration Prayer Ministry seminar and learn the techniques used to bring total healing and restoration into the lives of those that would receive. Shortly after, I scheduled my own sessions and now I've noticed many of my buttons that others could push are broken, as in gone. I don't get hooked into feeling defensive and needing to protect myself. My speech patterns are much bolder and people respond favorably, even if I'm telling them something that could be perceived negatively. Instead of feeling timid in unfamiliar settings, I'm connecting with perfect strangers and feeling love and compassion for them like I never thought possible. Most interesting of all, I've got a new desire for my husband which I believe is the result of a complete healing of the wounds from my abused   past.

In the last two and a half weeks, I've continued to see daily the effects of my Restoration Prayer Ministry. Additionally, I've stepped out and prayed with my first prayer receiver and the results were amazing! More to come on that, later. I look forward to helping bring about real change in the lives of any and all who would choose it. I now see myself as a facilitator in the Kingdom of God, and I'm excited!

Jesus is Healing though Open Visions

As I prepared to teach a men's class, I knew that Jesus wanted me to demonstrate His desire to heal in miraculous ways, through open visions. I simply impart faith to believe that Jesus will appear to the receiver and heal him -- through his spiritual eyes, spiritual ears, spiritual senses and/or through spiritual touch. (See Acts 2:17 and Joel 2:28 And it shall come to pass afterward, that I will pour out my spirit upon all flesh; and your sons and your daughters shall prophesy, your old men shall dream dreams, your young men shall see visions.)

We pray binding every other spirit that might try to interfere and then we invite Jesus to come and to heal any area that still needs more healing. **Jesus comes in an open vision,** takes them to the wound, melts their walls, heals the hurt and imparts new life to them. (When Jesus heals, they are healed!) All I do is ask a couple questions and take notes, as they dictate the vision to me! I am not allowed to add anything new because Jesus is God and He is able! All I do is take notes and direct their attention back to what Jesus wants to do.

Demonstration of healing through an open vision: I asked for a volunteer receiver and explained the above. I prayed a protection prayer and then asked the receiver to command his mind to rest, to operate out of his spirit and to fix his eyes on Jesus. I explained that Restoration Prayer Ministry is not just about praying to Jesus but also about receiving from Jesus in prayer believing He is true to His Word.

Carlotta: Why don't you just fix your eyes on Jesus and invite Him to come and to heal any area that still needs healing. Don't try to think or to figure anything out. Just wait and He will come.
Receiver: (Prayed to invite Jesus to any area of his life and waited about one minute.) Jesus is taking me back to when I was a boy... I am there. I am talking to my mother about my Dad.... I am hurting because my brothers and sisters know who their Dads are but I don't know who mine is. I am so angry because all she ever tells me is his name and no more. I am angry again because she won't talk about him.
Carlotta: Jesus has taken you to this anger, so go there.
Receiver: I am so angry that she won't tell me where he is. I am angry because I feel like I am nobody. All my brothers and sisters know who their Dad is. She never married my Dad. I don't know who I am....
Carlotta: Where is Jesus?
Receiver: He is standing there listening ....Now he is showing me that I have bitterness against my Dad. Sometimes, I hate him. Why hasn't he come around since the day I was born? Why can't I even meet him? Why doesn't he want to know his son? Sometimes, I feel like I hate him but I have never met him. Sometimes, I am angry at God too....
Carlotta: You are doing well. Just pour out your heart to Jesus.
Receiver: (He tells Jesus about all the difficulties he had trying to become a young man without a father -- for about 10 minutes. He sits there staring silently, looking very sad and abandoned.)
Carlotta: What is Jesus doing now?
Receiver: Jesus is showing me that I am angry because I have tried to meet my Dad for 30 years. Even since I have been in prison, I have written letters trying to locate him. My sisters have helped me and they did finally find him, not 45 minutes from here. They got his address and I wrote him a letter introducing myself.... I sent him pictures of me and my family.... I told

him how much I have always wanted to meet him.... I told him how I have invited Jesus into my life and I am a changed man now.... I invited him to come to see me here at the prison....

Jesus is showing me my hatred for my Dad because he never even opened my letter. He just wrote "Return to Sender." I don't want to hate him but sometimes I do. Why doesn't he come here to see me? I don't want to have hatred and bitterness in my life!

Carlotta: Would you like to ask Jesus to take the anger, hatred and bitterness?

Receiver: Yes. (He prays and asks Jesus to take it all.)

I can see Jesus holding my heart in His hands. I don't see all of Jesus now, only His hands. My heart is in His hands, just my heart -- no veins or anything. He is just holding my heart and healing it. Now, I feel an unbelievable peace coming over me. An indescribable peace. Everything is OK now. He is flooding me with peace.

Carlotta: What about the anger, hatred and bitterness now?

Receiver: It is all gone, all gone.

Carlotta: You don't have to say that for my sake. Really now. On a scale of 0-10, how is the anger now?

Receiver: I am serious. It is 100% gone. Jesus has taken it all! It's OK now. I don't have to be angry and bitter anymore.

Carlotta: When Jesus comes with His healing touch, He completely heals doesn't He? When Jesus heals, He usually does something very simple, like holding your heart and says very little. He doesn't say much but what He does is 100% effective. You can invite Him back into your heart anytime, any day. He is always willing to meet with you and to touch areas of your life.

Actually, He may even be able to pray for your father more effectively through you now. He may give you words of knowledge about his weaknesses and needs. You will be able to intercede for him more effectively now that your prayers will be more about him and less about you.

Satan's plan was to gain access to our lives "while we were down" by attacking us with deep hurts and offense. While we were in pain, he infected us with lies about the offender, ourselves and even about God. His goal was to isolate us from others, from God and even to separate us from our true selves. Jesus came to heal us, body - soul - and spirit, to heal the broken hearted. Included in our salvation, we have forgiveness of sins and healing. If we ask Jesus for a fish, He will not give us a snake. If we ask Him to come to us and to heal us, He will. He is coming to heal in open visions more often than in any other way. He does all things well.

Restoration Prayer Ministry is not about short commanding prayers or long analytic ones. It is not visualization where the receiver is told what to visualize. It is not like Theophostic where you identify the original hurt and lie etc., and not like topical Christian analytic counseling with a prayer at the end. Restoration Prayer Ministry is transformation ministry that includes healing hurts simply inviting Jesus to come in an "open vision" and to do whatever He wants to do! Jesus is given complete freedom to heal, melt walls, deliver, impart truth, dance or whatever He knows is best.

All I have to do is impart faith to believe that Jesus wants to visit us with His healing power.

Suppressed Memories and Spiritual Roots

Please note that often our receiver does not know to share suppressed memories on the initial interview. These suppressed, often painful, memories may contain the deeper root causes that need prayer. Our receiver will usually share little more than the surface symptoms and causes on the questionnaire because they genuinely do not remember or do not know the root symptoms and root causes.

Do not take offense as if they had planned to deceive you. Keep on asking gentle questions until Holy Spirit is ready to bring these memories to their recall. Remember that people are testing us to see if we are safe people to confide in and if we can personally handle their truth. It is a hard word, but I call it "emotional rape" if you insist on blurting out "what you think God has shown you" instead of waiting on green lights from Holy Spirit. We wait on Holy Spirit to see if He is showing our receiver the root symptoms and causes before we pray. If we pray each line of this prayer slowly, waiting for revelation after each line, Holy Spirit may continue to reveal more.

Survivors of serial abuse will also initially present surface symptoms and surface causes because they have developed brilliant survival skills to block painful memories. As little children, they may have dissociated from unspeakable pain by compartmentalizing painful memories and unresolvable conflicts. The most brilliant children develop the ability to actually dissociate their consciousness into different "parts," who are assigned different tasks, i.e. suffering daily incest.

Each new "part" will master the ability to "detach" themselves from their current surroundings in order to minimize how much pain the core person feels and remembers. The core person may not remember these painful memories at all for decades, until these amnesia walls begin to break down. We must be gentle and patient. I will write much more on this in manual two and three.

Spiritual Roots and Suppressed Memories
1. Lord please **tell me or show me** any hidden memory that contains the starting point of my issue/problem. Reveal how this memory and the spiritual root or deception has affected my life. (**Share** what the Lord reveals: _____.)
2. Lord, show me the areas of my life that this hurt has damaged:
_____.)
3. **Show me or tell me** the lies or deceptions buried in this memory.
(**Share** the lies or deceptions _____.)
4. **I turn my eyes** on You Jesus and invite You to show me or tell me how you are healing my hurts. (Share _____.)
5. Lord Jesus, I **ask you** to take all the hurts and lies and replace them with your Truth about myself, about others and about You.
6. I choose to **believe and receive** Your Truth _____.)
7. (**Measure** the pain now: 0 = gone and10 = very painful.)
8. (**Give thanks** if the pain is gone. If not, ask Jesus to show what healing is still needed and pray this prayer again.)

Freedom from Demonic Oppression (DO)
Jesus Said He Came To Destroy the Works of the Devil!

Who can cast out devils?

Jesus said, "Believers shall cast out demons." You don't have to be "Super Christian" to cast out demons. Just be a believer! Mark 16:17

Jesus commanded you to -- in spiritual power and authority -- in His name.

The "Don'ts" of casting out demons:

- Don't be shy or beg them
- Don't get scared of evil
- Don't expect to throw up
- Don't yell at the demons
- Don't be weird or spooky
- Don't close your eyes

It is not necessary to yell or to be dramatic when you do deliverance. Every demon knows he has to bow when we command them in the Name of Jesus owning our spiritual power and authority and the resurrection power we have in Christ.

The "Do's" of casting out demons:

- Do have a partner or team
- Do have intercessors praying
- Do ask forgiveness 5 ways first
- Do get into agreement with God
- Do confess sins of the Fathers
- Do break the resulting curses
- Do set your will to choose freedom
- Do remember all demons are liars
- Do command each demon leave
- Do keep insisting until they leave
- Do command them never to return
- Do replace them with good
- Do discern their open eyes
- Do address pains or tightness
- Do use scriptures and praises

Demonic Oppression not Possession

1 John 3:8 …**For this PURPOSE** the Son of God was manifested, that he might destroy the works of the devil.

Acts10:38 How God anointed Jesus of Nazareth with the Holy Ghost and with power: who went about doing good, and **healing all that were OPPRESSED** of the devil; for God was with him

Mark 16:17 And these signs shall follow them that believe; **In my name they shall cast out DEVILS;** …

God's plan: "Little by Little"

In Exodus 23: 29-30, God gives a "picture" of the process of taking back all God has promised you. He says that the **giants would be driven out** "little by little" rather than all at once. As we gain spiritual strength we overcome and take back our "land."

Even Jesus prayed more than once when the blind man did not see clearly after one prayer. Study Luke 1-9 to map how often Jesus prayed for healing and deliverance together.

So whether your vision is to win the world to Christ or to get rid of your own baggage, BELIEVING Biblical Truth will make you FREE!

Demonic Oppression and Bondage (DO)

1. I **confess** my sin of agreeing with the demons of _____ and forgive all who may have influenced me to sin.

2. I **repent** for giving place to the demons of _____.

3. **I forgive** myself for the pain and limitations I have allowed the demons to inflict upon me.

4. In the Name of Jesus, I **renounce** and break all agreement with the demons (stronghold) of _____, including all associated demons of _____, _____, _____, etc.

5. I **take authority** over the demons (stronghold) of _____ and command you demons of _____ to leave me now based on the finished work of Christ and my spiritual authority as a believer.

6. In the Name of Jesus Christ of Nazareth, the Anointed One, Who has given me spiritual authority, I **command** the demons of _____ to go to the dry uninhabited places and never come back.

7. In its place I choose to **receive** _____.

Lastly: Lord Jesus, I receive You as my Lord. I ask you to take control of my life in every way. Fill me with Your Holy Spirit and His power, anointing and fruit. I choose to receive the gifts of the Spirit and yield my life to You for Your glory and purposes. Amen

Why I prefer integrated ministry

We use this integrated ministry of praying over issues in eight different ways in order to effectively close all the open doors to demonic oppressions. For example, we do this by recognizing, repenting, renouncing and replacing the ungodly beliefs with God's Truth. We ask our receivers to say these godly beliefs for forty days like Jesus did in the wilderness, in order to give Holy Spirit ample time to transform them and to renew their minds.

Luke 11:24-26 [24] When the unclean spirit is gone out of a man, he walketh through dry places, seeking rest; and finding none, he saith, I will return unto my house whence I came out. [25] And when he cometh, he findeth it swept and garnished. [26] Then goeth he, and taketh to him seven other spirits more wicked than himself; and they enter in, and dwell there: and the last state of that man is worse than the first.

TEST: What Does the Bible Say About Deliverance?

☐ The Bible says Christians can have demons or be demonized.

☐ Father God gave both Adam and Eve dominion over the earth.

☐ Demon possession is never mentioned in the Greek New Testament.

☐ We don't need to ask demons for their name or to ask them questions.

☐ Jesus never turned anyone away who asked for healing and deliverance.

☐ Demons can cause Christians to have emotional turmoil or mental torment.

☐ Listening to palm readers, horoscopes or psychics opens doors to demons.

☐ Demons cannot oppress us unless we have unconfessed sin in our life.

☐ Jesus usually cast out demons of infirmity and commanded healing.

☐ Deaf and dumb spirits can also cause illness like epilepsy.

☐ Demons like Leviathan break up covenant relationships and marriages.

☐ It is abominable to consult the occult, the dead, mediums or familiar spirits.

☐ Prophetic people may get into divination in their lust to give powerful "words."

☐ Spiritists and occult leaders may heal people using demonic power.

☐ Satan uses believers to accuse the brethren before the throne day and night.

☐ Spirits of intimidation want to prevent us from operating in spiritual gifts.

☐ Our own sinful reactions and fears open doors to demonic oppression.

☐ This is a one power universe and Satan only has delegated power.

☐ We speak our own future with negative thoughts, doubts, worries or fears.

☐ We welcome a spirit of death when we say, "This is killing me."

☐ All believers have inherited spiritual power and authority over demonic spirits.

☐ When we refuse to repent, we oppose God and open ourselves up to captivity.

☐ Our choices determine whether we are afflicted by demons or not.

☐ Sin - over time - draws demonic powers to Christians and non-Christians.

☐ Demonic spirits can transfer from another person to us if we are fleshly.

☐ Demonic spirits will most often question, "Has God really said ....?"

☐ Spirit guides and "spirits of ancestors" are usually demonic spirits.

☐ Demonic spirits cannot read my mind and are not all-powerful.

☐ Deliverance is usually not lasting when inner healing is not done first.

☐ Many incurable illnesses (cause unknown) are caused by demonic spirits.

☐ All believers have power to and are commanded to cast out demons.

☐ Every demon has to bow at the Name of Jesus Christ, the Anointed One.

☐ Demons like to talk through believers to accuse others and Father God.

☐ Demons love it when believers don't believe in demons.

Testimonies about Deliverance

For me my journey to healing and freedom has seemed long. *I had tried for many years, both in the flesh and in the Spirit to get right with God. There has always been a part of me that wanted God more than anything else, but at different times of my life it seemed that my desire for God was overcast by the reality that life is unfair.*

Having been through many deliverance sessions, where the strongholds of my life were successfully defeated by the name and blood of Jesus, I had become tired of going around the same mountain over and over again. Struggling to be who God wanted me to be - the perfect little girl who didn't disobey, didn't speak out of turn, didn't laugh, and didn't cry; I would cry out to God. "What is wrong with me?" "Why did you create me if I was to be so messed up?" "What use am I if I cannot get this right?" "Why am I here?" "If to choose you is to choose pain then I want nothing of it!"

*Through Restoration Prayer Ministry (RPM), I found out that what I **believed** God wanted me to be and the **truth** of who God wants me to be are two very different things. God has been so faithful for so long to work within the realms of who I believed I was in Him - my reality. But there came a time when, He had done all that my reality would allow Him to do, and if I was to fulfill my purpose in God, He could no longer be restricted by my reality. God has used Restoration Prayer Ministry (RPM) to destroy my reality, so that I could live in His!*

*God has caused me to realize that though deliverance is very effective and necessary, there are times when it is not enough. The most common scriptures that capture the essence of deliverance are Mark 3:27 and Luke 11:21-22. Both scriptures talk about binding the strong man (the enemy) and taking the house back. However if we have an ungodly belief system that has not been exposed and replaced by God's truth, these ungodly beliefs can cause us to reopen the door to the enemy (consciously or not), and we actually invite him back, we return to him the power that was taken away during deliverance. **So even though deliverance is successful in getting rid of him, we can sabotage it by our ungodly beliefs.***

*Typically, a person who has been through deliverance is expected to also go through inner healing in order to maintain their deliverance. However, having been through Restoration Prayer Ministry, I recognize that there are times when we can experience a level of inner healing and still have ungodly beliefs. So we walk around partially healed, and by our own self-will and determination we are 'making' it work. We spend a large amount of time trying to keep the door(s) to the enemy closed in our **own** strength rather than allowing the **Holy Spirit** to do it. So when the stresses and the pressures of life come, we do not have the strength to keep them closed, and they are swung open again, and the thing that you thought you had once conquered overwhelms you once more. Restoration Prayer Ministry provides you with effective tools that enable you to let the **Holy Spirit** keep the door(s) closed.*

My Pastor once had a vision of my heart and she said that it was covered with vines and that God was going to cut the vines down, but that it would take time before He could uproot them. I believe that there are times when we are not ready or able to receive complete healing or deliverance and all God can do is kick the strong man out in order to slow down the process of destruction in our lives. However, at the right time He is able to completely restore us. **Restoration Prayer Ministry is a tool that God has used in my life to achieve complete wholeness – and it is beyond inner healing.**

By revealing my ungodly beliefs, and replacing them with God's truths about me, I have begun the process of realigning my spirit with the Word of God, and so allowing my spirit to rule my whole being. I have experienced complete healing, and as a result, I **am free to be who God has predestined me to be.**

During Restoration Prayer Ministry

I received Restoration Prayer Ministry over the phone.

Being over the phone I was concerned about how relating to the minister would be. However within 2 hours they made me feel comfortable enough to open up. They related to me extremely well, to the point that sometimes I forgot I only met them recently.

What I found amazing was the way that they allowed the Holy Spirit to take something that could be considered a 'formula' and transform it to my specific to my needs, so I walked away with tools that were effective and individual to me and me alone.

Every area of my life has been affected by RPM. From the way I look at myself, to the way I look at God and consequently the way I look at others. Restoration Prayer Ministry has impacted me in every area of my psyche – apart from being very therapeutic to just be able to say your deepest darkest thoughts or beliefs and not get judged, the Holy Spirit has used Restoration Prayer Ministry to reveal to me the depth of love that God has for me.

The scripture that talks about the "old wine skins", at the end of Luke 5, became a reality to me. God replaced my old wines skins, my false comforts, the things that were so familiar to me, that I did not consciously realize that they did not align with the Word of God.

My heart has been changed to be able to receive and give love. My mind has been freed to hand over control to my spirit and not fear making a mistake. Through Restoration Prayer Ministry, I have been able to release control – control of my emotions, my relationships, my friendships, my reputation, and my environment on every level. My self-worth, my self-esteem has been impacted by the love of God. My ability to receive intimacy from God and from others has been restored.

I have walked away **free to be who I am in Christ, who Christ created me to be** *– and it is a wonderful sense of freedom. My whole view or landscape of the way I see my life and the lives of others has been changed to be seen through the eyes of Christ!*

Jesus died on the cross so that we can live life, and live it more abundantly! I pray that everyone who reads this will have a transforming encounter with the intense love of God.

In His love,

The Life Changing Cross Walk Prayer

Years, ago my life began to change, as I learned to pray the Cross Walk Prayer from Ellen Ferry, an Elijah House counselor in Atlanta, GA. I had been stuck in the wilderness for about 18 years, making the same big mistakes over and over.

I (Carlotta) always wanted to be free and to see others set free to reach their potential: to see the "stuck" places in their lives removed. So much time and money had already been wasted in going to counselors and ministers who were not trained adequately. As a mental health nurse (off and on for 25 years) I wondered, "When will all this counseling take effect?" It was time to admit that these methods were not working. I was "walking down the same street and stepping in the same holes again and again.

I was a slow learner. I kept trying to make Ellen understand that most of my issues were because someone else had made bad choices. I believed that I was usually only about 10% of the problem and therefore almost innocent. It took me about two years to really grasp the fact that only my sins and sinful reactions could create a fleshly stronghold in my life. Actually, this is very good news. <u>All I had to do was to come into agreement with God about my own sinful reactions and behaviors in order to tear down the strongholds.</u>

People don't get "cause and effect." They may think that even long term patterns in their life just come out of the blue. If there is a long term negative pattern in your life, the Bible says to ask God because it is not there without a cause. Prov. 26:2 Where there is lots of bad fruit, there is a bad root. My counselor told me if the bad fruit is on my tree, the bad root is on my tree. Finally, I began to identify my sinful reactions and behaviors and took responsibility that my sin was sin too!! I was reaping the sins that I had sown, not the sins that the other party had sown.

Once I repented of my own sinful reactions, dishonor of others, judgmental attitudes, bitter expectations and fleshly inner vows, I could ask Jesus to bring those bad seeds to death on the Cross and set me free of the sowing and reaping pattern I had built. Jesus would not only forgive individual sins but bring the whole fleshly pattern to death!!!!

Getting deliverance without bringing fleshly structures to the cross for Jesus to put them to death, is a formula for failure. Actually, we are commanded to deal with our flesh more often than we are to get deliverance. Without truly hating our fleshly patterns, we will not hate the agreements that we have with deceptions.

I didn't like Ellen's answer at first. I wanted to be the innocent victim and to blame others for patterns in my life. However, the good news is that if you are part of the cause, you also have power to be part of a solution. I could repent of my own sins and ask Jesus to bring my fleshly structures to death on the Cross, even if the other people never repented. Whoohoo!

The Cross Walk Prayer - An excellent maintenance prayer

Dear Lord Jesus,

I see that I have another negative pattern in my life, that is not Godly and I cannot get rid of it by myself. I know that a bad fruit has a bad root. I don't want this pattern of _____ any longer. I don't want to reap this in my own life or in the people around me. Please show me the spiritual root of it and how to deal with my part of this problem (even if I am only 10% of the problem.)

Did I sow this and now I am reaping it, more and later?   Galatians 6:7-10
Did I dishonor my parents or authorities in this area?   Ephesians 6:1-3
Did I judge someone and now I draw that thing to me?   Matthew 7:1, Romans 2:1-4
Did a bitter expectation spring up in me, defiling others?   Hebrews 12:14-15
Did I make an inner vow in not to be like them?   James 5:12, Matthew 5:37

1. **I RECOGNIZE** that the reason this problem of _____ is now a pattern in my own life, is because of my sinful reaction of (dishonor, judgment, sowing the sin myself, inner vows or bitter root expectation.) The fruit is that I am reaping similar problems in others and myself according to the LAW of sowing and reaping. I am reaping this crop because of my sinful reactions to their sin. I am reaping from the sinful seed that I have sown - not from what they have sown.

2. **I REPENT** and ask forgiveness 5 ways. Please forgive me:

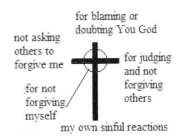

    for not asking others to forgive me
    for judging others and not forgiving others
    for sowing my own sin / sinful reactions
    for blaming or doubting you God
    and for not forgiving myself

3. I RENOUNCE my sin of dishonor, judgment, sowing the sin myself, bitter root expectations or fleshly inner vows. I choose to forgive them, releasing them to you, the Judge of all the earth.

4. RELEASE me from reaping this crop that is now mine to reap because of my sinful reactions to others.

5. I RECKON dead on the cross all flesh that identifies with this reaction and all automatic reactions that I have developed with it. I ask you Jesus, to bring it to death, because I cannot. Create in me a pure heart that agrees with your responses.

6. RESURRECT your likeness into every area that you have brought to death.

7. **RESTORE** all the years that the locusts have eaten while I was disobedient.

8. **I RECLAIM** all the spiritual blessings that my family and I have missed.

9. **REWARD** us for generations to come, as we sow true discernment, grace and mercy. Thank you Lord for the forgiveness you have provided for us on the cross and all the blessings that we are free to walk in now. We believe you for them! Amen

If you want to learn the easy way and _MUCH FASTER_ ... Simply make a list of all your parent's faults (without mercy.) Assume that as a child, you probably judged and dishonored them as some point. You can include other authorities too if you really want to get freedom fast!!

Part 3:
Deeper Life Ministry Issues

Appreciation and Credits

I want to express my appreciation for all the revelation knowledge that I have received from the following ministers on the subject of freedom in Christ and tearing down personal strongholds.

I am especially grateful to these authors for permission to use lists and explanations:

A More Excellent Way by Pastor Henry Wright
Shattering Your Strongholds by Liberty Savard
Epic Battles of the Last Days by Rick Joyner
Restoring the Foundations by Chester and Betsy Kylstra

I want to thank these authors for the clarity I gained from their diagrams and materials:

The Exchanged Life by Charles Solomon
The Anger Ladder teaching by Dr. Ross Campbell
Mentoring and Fathering by Schultz and Gaborit
Breaking the Power of Intimidation by John Bevere
Religious Spirits sermon by Jack Deere
Leviathan and Behemoth by John Eckhardt
Who I am in Christ teachings by Dan Stone and Jim Moon
Transformation of the Inner Man and Restoring the Christian Family
by John and Paula Sandford
and Who I Am in Christ (anonymous)

I owe a debt of gratitude to my precious volunteers who volunteered their time
to compile, convert from audio, edit, post and proof these insights:
Liz James, Eleanor Parks, Rita Owens Michelle Hathaway, Dan Baker,
Dottie Smith and Tara Wentworth.

Big, big hugs to my husband, Louis, for loving me, accepting me unconditionally,
and supporting me in my true identity in Christ.

Carlotta P. Waldmann, M.A.
A former "Woman at the Well"

My Testimony

I was diagnosed with twenty-six illnesses and had documentation to prove it. I had made many big mistakes and the same ones, over and over. I had prayed for my healing and freedom with only occasional relief, until I began to hear about spiritual roots to illness. If there was a spiritual solution, I wanted to align my thinking with God's thinking and get into a position to receive the healing that Jesus died to provide for me. Healing was provided with my salvation, for my body, soul and spirit. He forgives all my sins and heals all my diseases. Psalm 103:3

I had already received ministry from Restoring the Foundations International but there were deeper life issues and strongholds that needed more work. When I began to study how to tear down personal strongholds by praying in agreement with scripture, I began to make some real progress. I collected sixty pages of Bible verses so that I could pray, "It is written …" like Jesus did in Matthew 4. I prayed against one of these strongholds: anger, unforgiveness, dishonor, separated thinking, rejection cycles, accusation, pride, etc. every day.

Within three months, I was healed of twenty-four out of twenty-six illnesses! I have to give God the glory for supernaturally healing me. I realized that the keys were simple: I had to receive deeper life truths, renounce the lies in my mindsets and swing the Sword of the Spirit to do warfare against my own strongholds. I chose relevant scriptures and began to pray like Jesus did in Matthew 4: "It is written ..." I was healed by agreeing with and declaring the truth of God's Word. Whether I was sick from side effects of medications, natural exposure to illness or ungodly reactions and attitudes or side-effects, God healed it all!

Next, I compiled my notes and reviews to write an accredited college course, "Tearing Down Personal Strongholds." This course is available on CD or as a download in our resources store at www.cwlinc.com. Now I am making the high points available to you in this manual. The Bible has not lost its power and God's Word never comes back void!

Psalm 103:2-4 2 Praise the LORD, O my soul, and forget not all his benefits--
3 who forgives all your sins and heals all your diseases,
4 who redeems your life from the pit and crowns you with love and compassion,
Lord, we receive your salvation, forgiveness, healing and ask you to redeem ….

3 John 2 Dear friend, I pray that you may enjoy good health and that all may go well with you, (prosper) even as your soul is getting along well.
Lord, I choose to prosper as my soul lines up with your truth.

1 Thessalonians 5:23-24 23 May God himself, the God of peace, sanctify you through and through. May your whole spirit, soul and body be kept blameless at the coming of our Lord Jesus Christ. 24 The one who calls you is faithful and he will do it.

Isaiah 5:13 Therefore my people will go into exile for lack of understanding;
their men of rank will die of hunger and their masses will be parched with thirst.
Lord, we press into your Spirit of understanding and knowledge.

Sin or Temptation or Stronghold

Our first challenge as an author and reader is to come into agreement with some biblical definitions. I like to minister God's Truth by putting my finger on a verse. Below are common questions asked by prayer receivers who are being harassed in their minds. However, various new translations of the Bible have actually brought more confusion to these difficult questions.

TEMPTATION OR SIN?
James 1:12-15
12 Blessed is the man who perseveres under trial, because when he has stood the test, he will receive the crown of life that God has promised to those who love him. 13 When tempted, no one should say, "God is tempting me." For God cannot be tempted by evil, nor does he tempt anyone; 14 but each one **is tempted** when, by his **own evil desire**, he is **dragged away** and **enticed**. 15 Then, after desire has **conceived**, it gives **birth to sin**; and sin, when it is full-grown, gives birth to **death**.
Lord, we receive discernment and power to resist the six steps of temptation (in the verses above in bold.) We agree that a temptation is not yet a sin but we must learn to discern when sin is "birthed."

A WAY OUT OF SINFUL PATTERNS?
1 Corinthians 10:12-13
12 So, if you think you are standing firm, be careful that you don't fall! 13 No temptation has seized you except what is common to man. And God is faithful; he will not let you be tempted beyond what you can bear. But when you are tempted, he will also provide a way out so that you can stand up under it.
We choose to receive Your way out of temptation and freedom from strongholds.

REBELLION, DIVINATION, PRIDE OR WITCHCRAFT?
1 Samuel 15:23
23 For rebellion is like the sin of divination, and arrogance like the evil of idolatry. Because you have rejected the word of the LORD, he has rejected you as king."
We loose ourselves from rebellion (witchcraft) and arrogance (stubbornness or idolatry) and bind ourselves to the truth of the word of God.

IS SIN FROM MY FLESH, OLD NATURE OR ME?
Romans 7:18 NASU
18 I know that nothing good dwells in me, that is, in flesh. For the willing is present in me, but the doing of the good is not.
Lord, we ask You to bring all of our fleshly structures to death on the Cross because we cannot overcome them by ourselves.

My intent is to provide scriptures for meditation to help us all understand the scriptural context and intent. Deeper life truths have come to me when I have studied these key scriptures. Many of these scriptures, associated with each issue, would also be helpful to our prayer receivers. Feel free to print them out and recommend that they meditate on them during the week.

Flesh, Self or Old Nature?

THE WORD OF GOD EXPLAINS ITSELF.
Hebrews 4:12-13
12 For the word of God is living and active. Sharper than any double-edged sword, it penetrates even to dividing soul and spirit, joints and marrow; it judges the thoughts and attitudes of the heart. 13 Nothing in all creation is hidden from God's sight. Everything is uncovered and laid bare before the eyes of him to whom we must give account.
Lord, we give You permission to reveal every fleshly structure and every "creature."
I choose to discern and overcome strongholds by praying, "It is written …"

FORMER TRANSLATIONS IN THE NIV CONFUSED OLD NATURE AND FLESH.
Romans 7:18-19
18 I know that nothing good lives in me, that is, in my **sinful nature**. [?] For I have the desire to do what is good, but I cannot carry it out. 19- For what I do is not the good I want to do; no, the evil I do not want to do-this I keep on doing.
Lord, we choose for our spirits to be in agreement with Your Spirit.
The former NIV said our issue was a risen old nature (Zombie theology!) The new NIV agrees with other translations that our issue is with flesh. Not the old man who died in Romans 6.

THE LATEST NIV HAS CLARIFIED THAT OUR ISSUE IS WITH OUR FLESH.
Romans 7:18
18 For I know that **nothing good dwells in me, that is, in my flesh**; for the willing is present in me, but the doing of the good is not.

WE OVERCOME WHEN OUR MIND AND SPIRIT AGREE WITH GOD'S WORD.
Romans 7:22-23
22 For in my inner being I delight in God's law; 23 but I see another law at work in the members of my body, waging war against the **law of my mind** and making me a prisoner of the law of sin at work within my members.
Lord, I choose for my mind to agree with my spirit and Your Spirit, not my flesh.

OUR OLD MAN IS DEAD; OUR FLESH OPPOSES OUR NEW SPIRIT!
Romans 7:24-25
24 What a wretched man I am! Who will rescue me from this body of death? 25 Thanks be to God-through Jesus Christ our Lord!
I am a spiritual creature; my true self agrees with the truth of God's Word.

Galatians 5:16-17
16 But I say, walk by the Spirit, and you will not carry out the desire of the flesh.
17 For the flesh sets its desire against the Spirit, and the Spirit against the flesh; for these are in opposition to one another, so that you may **not do the things that you please**.

Partakers of the Divine Nature

Some of the most liberating and empowering studies that I have done were on our new nature in Christ now that we are new creatures who are partakers of a divine nature. I suggest that you share these scripture meditation lists with receivers who have deeper life questions.

OUR OLD MAN WAS CRUCIFIED WITH CHRIST. WE ARE NO LONGER SLAVES.
Romans 6:5 For if we have become united with Him in the likeness of His death, certainly we shall be also in the likeness of His resurrection, 6 knowing this, that our old self was crucified with Him, that our body of sin might be done away with, that we should no longer be slaves to sin; 7 for he who has died is freed from sin. 8 Now if we have died with Christ, we believe that we shall also live with Him, NAS

NOTHING GOOD DWELLS IN MY FLESH BUT FLESH IS NOT THE NEW ME.
Romans 7:18a For I know that nothing good dwells in me, that is, in my flesh …

WE HAVE RECEIVED A GIFT OF RIGHTEOUSNESS THROUGH JESUS CHRIST.
Romans 5:17 For if by the transgression of the one, death reigned through the one, much more those who receive the abundance of grace and of the gift of righteousness will reign in life through the One, Jesus Christ. NAS

THE OLD MAN HAS PASSED AWAY AND WE ARE NEW CREATURES.
2 Corinthians 5:17 Therefore if any man be in Christ, he is a new creature: old things are passed away; behold, all things are become new. KJV

WE ARE PARTKERS OF THE DIVINE NATURE OF JESUS CHRIST INSIDE US.
2 Peter 1:4 Whereby are given unto us exceeding great and precious promises: that by these ye might be partakers of the divine nature, having escaped the corruption that is in the world through lust. KJV

WE ARE NO LONGER SEPARATE BUT JOINED TO THE LORD IN ONE SPIRIT!
1 Corinthians 6:17 But the one who joins himself to the Lord is one spirit with Him. NAS

WE CRUCIFY THE FLESH WITH ITS PASSIONS AND LUST.
Galatians 5:24 And they that are Christ's have crucified the flesh with the affections and lusts. KJV

Galatians 2:20	**Carlotta's paraphrase**
I am crucified with Christ:	My old nature is crucified with Christ
nevertheless I live;	but my born again divine nature lives
yet not I,	but not just I alone
but Christ liveth in me:	but Christ lives inside me
and the life which I now live in the flesh	and the life which I am living now
I live by the faith of the Son of God,	I live by His faith inside me
who loved me, and gave himself for me.	because He loved me and died for me

Are you primarily your spirit, soul or body? Primarily a natural or spiritual creature?

Body, Soul and Spirit diagrams adapted from "Exchanged Life" by Charles Solomon

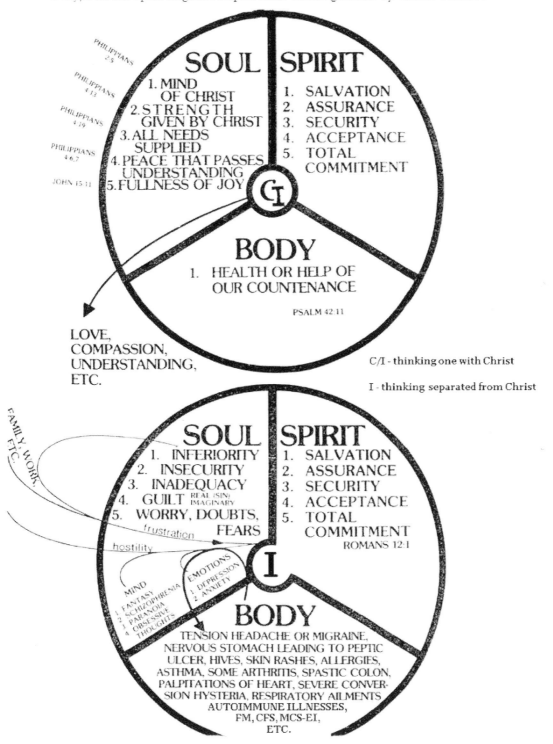

SEPARATED THINKING	ONE SPIRIT WITH HIS SPIRIT
Old Testament thinking – temporary anointing	New Testament thinking – indwelt by God's Spirit
Please come be with us today; I am on my own	Christ in me and I in Him, I am never alone
Unregenerate nature separated from Christ	Partaker of Divine Nature, one spirit with Him
Old man still alive, slave to sin	New creature, old passed away and buried
Treadmill of the law, striving, do's and don'ts	Christ fulfills the law in me as I rest in Him
Two power universe, don't trust authority	All power is delegated by God, submission
Christianity is a code of ethics to live up to	Intimate relationship as a Bride, trust, loved
Head knowledge about God	Truth of the Logos Word, Rhema revelation
External guidance and opinions	Spirit-led, Spirit bears witness, accountability
Theology, doctrine, dispensations, traditions	Experiencing God daily in line with the Word
Self-effort, holiness by works	Anointed, righteous as a gift by grace
Conscious, cognitive reasoning, rationalism	Dreams, visions, words of wisdom, intuition
Accused, guilty, condemned, punished	Totally forgiven, blameless, holy by the Blood
Pleading with God for help, inadequate	Comforter, teacher, power, fruit, gifts inside me
Used by God, poverty, door mat, unfulfilled	Edified, trained, equipped, partnering with Him
Unworthy, performing to earn acceptance	Worthy, unconditionally acceptable by the Cross
Identity based on opinions of others or my own	Identity based on God's Truth about me
Figure out God's will with cognitive thinking	Spiritual eyes, ears, senses, mind, discernment
Insecurity, based on circumstances	All needs supplied, peace past all understanding
Soul in charge, double-minded, doubtful	Spirit-led, single-minded, all works for good
Visible, material, temporal, world values	Unseen, spiritual, eternal realities are my base
Hopeless, victimized, powerless to change	Overcomer, victorious, delegated authority
Workaholic, scarcity mentality, hoarding	Serving, abundance, sowing into the Kingdom

Strongholds or Set Free?

THE UNSEEN ETERNAL IS THE TRUE REALITY, NOT THE SEEN TEMPORAL.
2 Corinthians 4:18
18 while we look not at the things, which are seen, but at the things, which are not seen; for the things, which are seen, are temporal, but the things, which are not seen, are **eternal**.
In the Name of Jesus, we loose ourselves from the temporal and bind to the eternal.

GOD HAS PROMISED TO CRUSH SATAN UNDER WHO'S FEET? OUR FEET.
Romans 16:20
20 The God of peace will soon crush Satan under your feet. The grace of our Lord Jesus be with you.
Lord, we receive your peace, not Satan's and ask you to crush Satan under our feet and to destroy his works.

JESUS CHRIST IS THE STRONGER MAN WHO SPOILS THE STRONG MAN.
Luke 11:21-22
21 When a **strong man**, fully armed, guards his own house, his possessions are safe. 22 But when **someone stronger** attacks and overpowers him, he takes away the **armor** in which the man trusted and divides up the spoils.
When the strongman has my house, he is at peace, has the goods, and I am tied up in the basement. When Jesus has the house, I am at peace and my possessions are safe.

JESUS CAME TO GIVE US ABUNDANT LIFE AND DESTORY THE DEVIL'S WORK.
1 John 3:8b
The reason the Son of God appeared was to destroy the devil's work.

WE ARE ANOINTED TO PREACH, HEAL, PROCLAIM LIBERTY AND SET FREE.
Isaiah 61:1
The Spirit of the Sovereign LORD is on me, because the LORD has anointed me
to preach good news to the poor. He has **sent me to bind up the brokenhearted,**
to proclaim freedom for the captives and release from darkness for the prisoners,
Jesus was sent to bind the brokenhearted (easy prey for strongholds).

A stronghold is something that we know is against God's will and way but we feel helpless to change it or get free from it.

Satan's master plan is to cause you to be brokenhearted and to become fleshly.

Satan's master plan is all about	**God's master plan to restore us to be**
Separating you from God	One with God
Separating you from yourself	One with ourselves
Separating you from others	One with others

LORD, we choose to be one with You, ourselves and others by Your power.

TRUE FREEDOM BRINGS THE ABILITY TO LOVE
Luke 10:27
27 He answered: "'Love the Lord your God with all your heart and with all your soul and with all your strength and with all your mind'; and, 'Love your neighbor as yourself.'"
God's plan is for us to love God, others and ourselves, reconciling us to oneness.

WE CHOOSE TO BE ONE AS JESUS CHRIST AND FATHER ARE ONE.
John 17:10-12
11 I will remain in the world no longer, but they are still in the world, and I am coming to you. Holy Father, protect them by the power of your name-the name you gave me-so that **they may be one as we are one.**

Strongholds are erected by our wounded souls to protect us from further pain and rejection. Demonic spirits gain access to us when we are vulnerable and might agree with them.

- Trauma and hurts cause broken-heartedness.
- We indulge in sinful patterns of thinking.
- We allow sinful behaviors.
- We defend our right to think and behave sinfully.

WE DEMOLISH STRONGHOLDS WITH SPIRITUAL WEAPONS AND DIVINE POWER.
2 Corinthians 10:3-6
3 For though we live in the world, we do not wage war as the world does. 4 The weapons we fight with are not the weapons of the world. On the contrary, they have divine power to **demolish strongholds**. 5 We demolish **arguments** and every **pretension** that sets itself up against the knowledge of God, and we take captive every **thought** to make it obedient to Christ.

Years ago, we all delegated power to our minds and our minds are intent on remaining in control. A stronghold is what our minds use to defend a sinful belief against outside opposition. Satan knows what activates our strongholds and triggers us to fortify them and to erect new strongholds to protect our deceptions.

We choose to loose our minds from strongholds that lodge in our imaginations, pretensions, arguments and intellect, renouncing the belief that we are helpless to come into agreement with God's will and way again. **We bind our minds in joyful obedience to the truth** that makes us free from captivity.

WE CHOOSE TO USE THE KEYS OF THE KINGDOM TO LOOSE AND BIND.
Matthew 16:19-20
19 " I will give you the keys of the kingdom of heaven; whatever you bind on earth will be bound in heaven, and whatever you loose on earth will be loosed in heaven."

According to Strong's Concordance: In these verses, this kind of <u>binding</u> is to tie, gird, join together for the effectual working of every part, knit together. This kind of <u>loosing</u> is smashing, crushing, destroying or lacerating. Flesh cannot be cast out, but must be brought to Jesus and taken to the cross to be crucified. Now we can practice what we learned in Part One.

Common Issues, Resources and Prayers

Abuse, Conflicts, Pain and Challenges

Every restoration minister must be familiar with the most common issues of survivors of abuse. One out of 5 people have experienced some type of abuse and need prayer. Repeated or ritual abuse produces unbearable conflicts and **pain** which will lead to false beliefs and identity, dissociation or denial that people can really be this bad. Some children have a very ingenious God-given gift to dissociate from horrendous pain so their real core personality can survive. Their identity is fractured in many pieces but at least they have divided the tasks of survival several ways and are alive and functioning. When they dissociate from the pain, they can create different parts of them to deal with different painful aspects of their life. They may come to you presenting their "super Christian" parts but also have extremely wounded parts.

Statistics say 1 out of 4 girls and 1 out of 6 boys have been abused. The percentages of people who have dissociated or have fractured identities have increased too. In any group of people at least 1 out of 100 people will have dissociated to survive intense pain. You can bring healing to them just by empathizing with their seemingly impossible tasks as a little child. In spite of impossible odds, abused children search for a way to find normal. They try to:

Build trust on some level	With untrustworthy deceitful people
Find safety or security	In unsafe homes, schools or environments
Be in control of their life	In unpredictable situations with capricious people
Have some personal power	Although they feel helpless and beat down
Bond with caretakers	Who are dangerous, evil or negligent
Learn some self-control	While he/she is used for the abuser's needs
Find some healthy comfort	In a place where there is no healthy coping
Take some initiative	Although they survive by obeying the abuser's will
Become capable of intimacy	Where intimacy is perverted and repulsive
Find or preserve his/her identity	While defined as a whore and a slave
Believe in a merciful God	While their life has no hope or meaning
Forgive evil abusers	While abusers take no responsibility for abusing
Deal with hurts and betrayal	With dissociated parts of their consciousness
Deal with daily abuse of all kinds	While they are demeaned and depersonalized
Cope with the reality of facts	By altering the facts in their mind

Nancy Cole, Psy.D. says abused children try to assimilate violently contradictory ideas and false information (love/abuse, mommy/pain, daddy/sex, childhood/torture, play time/terror) into one belief system. "The child must simultaneously know and not know. She is forced, in order to preserve her primary relationships, to take what doesn't make sense and then make it make sense. It is not a possible task-not if the child adheres to normal cognitive operations. It becomes possible only through strenuous denial, dissociation, and splitting. . . . She [then] finds she cannot solve problems because she has so perfectly mastered her capacity to deny problems."
~ 2007 Shield of Faith Conference: Focus on Conflict

When you interview survivors, you may sense that you are hearing from parts of many age levels. Each age level will need ministry appropriate to their age. These parts, fragments or sub personalities cannot be cast out. They must be healed. They may call these inner parts, little one, fractures, personalities, parts or by name. This subject will be addressed in the third book of this trilogy, our advanced manual.

SELF TALK: How Can I Help Survivors of Abuse?

The first way I can help is to admit that I won't have all the answers. What people want from me is unconditional love and acceptance, while they find their healing and their true identity. If I am able to patiently stand with others, who need healing but may sometimes test me, may sometimes seem to "not need me," then I will be able to welcome them, affirm them and to be available when they do need me.

I must learn to fight the forces of darkness in a spiritual battle, in the invisible realm through intercession, when the survivor cannot fight for themselves. God will give me the revelation I need for the fight as we go, words of wisdom and knowledge, information that we would not normally know in the natural. He will enable me to discern the debilitating lies, false accusations, false self-image and destructive words that the devil uses to fragment, destroy and enslave survivors.

I need to speak words of faith daily, believing that God loves, redeems every experience, takes the pain away and equips anew because He has a very good plan and purpose for their life. I can speak healing often, knowing that God's desire is to make all the weak places strong, transforming the darkest places of their heart into beacons of light, which eventually be strong enough to help others. I can learn how to bear another's burden without being drowned in their unspeakable pain.

I can agree with the prayer that Jesus prayed in John 17, that we would all be one as He and the Father are one. I can choose to be a safe person, worthy to hear the confidences that I am entrusted with. I choose to believe that God desires to restore each one to wholeness as we gain the courage to trust Him with areas that have sometimes been suppressed for many years.

My prayer for prayer ministers who desire to help survivors, goes like this:

Lord, you are a spring of compassion, welling up in me that will never run dry. You know all of the deep wounds and effects of abuse in this precious one's heart. You know the angers that rage and the questions that have gone unanswered. Only your goodness can undo all the unspeakable evil that has been done to this innocent child.

Help me, Lord, to no longer deny the unbelievable, to let go of my shallow agendas and to get seriously involved in helping the helpless. Help me to sort out my own questions like, "Where is God in abuse?" I choose to trust You on behalf of those who have no faith, to go back in time and to restore all the years that have been stolen, to restore all the blessings that have been lost and to replace all the dead empty places with fullness of life. I believe You, Lord, for a whole network of helpers who are committed to providing safe understanding relationships for survivors and their families as they courageously believe for wholeness again.

Lord, tell me when to write encouraging notes, when to call and listen, when to invite them out for fun, when to just be there for them, when to ask for professional help and when to take care of myself. Lord, help me to discern how to love each part of this person's fragmented personality to life with your grace and inexhaustible compassion. Love each child within, appropriately for their age, with your creative spontaneity.

Lord, as I walk through the process of healing with this one, I trust You to replace our horror and shock with understanding, our grief with your healing balm, our broken-heartedness with new hope, and our resentment, rage and bitterness with a willingness to let-go and let you be the judge and jury on our behalf. Help us to let go of futile attempts to collect this great debt and to let you repay all that was lost.

I choose to give permission to this one to be an important person, with needs, preferences, choices, safe boundaries, God-given identity and purpose and freedom to be interdependent, rather than dependent on me. I will keep speaking the truth of their God-given inheritance in Jesus Christ, to be unconditionally accepted, totally forgiven, to be loved and loveable.

I pray they will have the courage to heal and to try on that new identity - having been forgiven and made holy, righteous and blameless totally apart from their past and performance. My prayer is that I will be a demonstration of the passion of Jesus Christ, who came to earth to take every pain, grief, shame, fear and every horror upon Himself, replacing it all with His love, joy and peace past understanding. His heart alone is big enough to not only contain all the pain - but to take it all away, making us safe healed people who can partner with Him in healing people. Amen

NOTE: I have been praying like this for many years and I believe that I wrote this article and prayer. No plagiarism is intended. If you think otherwise, please send the proper credit to post.

I encourage you to be very careful to take responsibility as a prayer minister to:

1. Be honest about your limitations, credentials and calling.
2. Do not pretend that you have been equipped to minister to survivors, if you have not.
3. Do not let anyone tell their entire painful story to you if you know you should refer them.
4. Refer them as soon as possible to myself or someone who is called to survivors of abuse.
5. Continue to pray and be there for them as this prayer has described.
6. Pray for a team of intercessors for yourself and your prayer receivers.
7. Receive our 18 hour Restoration Prayer Ministry before you begin this area of ministry.
8. Pray our protection prayers before each session or contact.
9. Pray cleansing prayers over all people and locations involved after each session.
10. Remember that Holy Spirit does all the supernatural healing, miracles and deliverance.

If Holy Spirit leads you to meet with them again, please review the sample ungodly beliefs in Part 2 in order to pray with more discernment. Exercise gentleness and patience at all times.

Accusing Spirits

Test Yourself for Signs of an Accusing Spirit

Satan's name means "accuser" and "slanderer." Satan knows that he can cause a rift between you and God if he causes a rift between you and others and yourself. He will constantly try to get you to believe lies about your brothers and sisters. How can he accuse the brethren day and night? He sets you up to do his work for him.

Revelation 12:9-11
9 The great dragon was hurled down-that ancient serpent called the devil, or Satan, who leads the whole world astray. He was hurled to the earth, and his angels with him.
10 Then I heard a loud voice in heaven say: "Now have come the salvation and the power and the kingdom of our God, and the authority of his Christ. For **the accuser of our brothers, who accuses them before our God day and night, has been hurled down.**
11 They overcame him by the blood of the Lamb and by the word of their testimony; they did not love their lives so much as to shrink from death.

My intent is to offer tools to help you to discern others rightly in order to offer to pray with them to find healing and deliverance. The tests I have written are not approved by licensed counseling professionals but they are based on scriptural descriptions of spirits of accusation. I pray that you will not take this test in order to focus on the splinter in your brother's eye but will first of all deal with the lumber yard in your own eye. Beware of temptation to judge your brother but instead you will put on a garment of humility, restoring the one whose foot is caught in a snare, hoping he will be restored. These brief descriptions and self-tests are by no means sufficient to equip a lay person to be a counselor.

Galatians 6:1-3
6:1 Brothers, if someone is caught in a sin, **you who are spiritual should restore him gently.** But watch yourself, or you also may be tempted. 2 Carry each other's burdens, and in this way you will fulfill the law of Christ. 3 If anyone thinks he is something when he is nothing, he deceives himself.
We choose to intercede with the heart of God and place the Cross between them and the enemy until their eyes and ears are opened to see how they are being used by the evil one.

Romans 2:1
2:1 You, therefore, **have no excuse,** you who pass judgment on someone else, for at whatever point you judge the other, you are condemning yourself, because you who pass judgment do the same things.
LORD, loose us from taking credit for our maturity and bind us to glorifying our Savior.

We also take every criticism of ourselves to Holy Spirit first and ask Him to convict us of any truth in it, without receiving any lies embedded in it.

Ungodly belief: I had a right to judge with condemnation, to accuse or to dishonor people in word or deed as I said _____ .

Check	Warning Signs of accusing spirits
	1. Refuse to rejoice in God's restoration in another.
	2. Define another by their past behaviors or choices.
	3. Keep a record of wrongs (unpaid debts according to us).
	4. Focusing on the splinter in their eye.
	5. Bitter expectations that they will sin again.
	6. Judge others for accidental mistakes as if it were intentional.
	7. Judge God's heart when things don't work out your way.
	8. Blame others for your own choices or failures.
	9. Accuse others or yourself while talking to the mirror.
	10. Accuse others for being less mature than you.
	11. Defend yourself by accusing others right back.
	12. Refuse to reconcile with a person who has changed.
	13. Hold people to their past behaviors and attitudes.
	14. Keep a record of wrongs and demand retribution.
	15. Bigotry or intolerance for other opinions.
	16. Competition to prove you are better than another.
	17. Comparing another negatively without mercy.
	18. Setting unreasonable non-Biblical standards.
	19. Believing the worst or speaking the worst.
	20. Listening to accusations, gossip and slander.
	21. Repeating accusations, gossip and slander.
	22. Taking offense as you assume wrong motivations.
	23. Presuming to know another's unspoken intentions.
	24. Demeaning another while exalting self.
	25. Judging another for their inability.

26. Cutting another down out of envy or jealousy.

27. Resentment based on your ability to read minds.

28. Humoring misunderstandings versus going to the other.

29. Acting like judge and jury for another or yourself.

30. Judging another for your own behaviors while excusing yourself.

31. Refusing to forgive one who truly repents.

32. Scapegoat or blame game mentality.

33. Blaming others for causing the misfortune in their life.

34. Self-condemnation or condemning others.

35. Self-criticism, self-accusation and self-deprecation.

36. Playing Holy Spirit to convict another of probable sin.

37. Judgmental condescending attitudes and comments.

38. Focusing on another's weakness instead of strengths.

39. Over reacting with anger based on past issues.

40. Wishing God would judge and punish them now!

41. Self-hate, self-doubt and self-punishment.

42. Self-sabotage when good opportunities come.

43. Perfectionism and criticism of imperfect performance.

44. Suspicion of another's unspoken motivations.

45. Sexist prejudice against your own gender or others.

46. Unbiblical restrictions on ministry styles.

47. Accusations that other worship styles are not godly.

48. Refusal to honor new moves of Holy Spirit.

49. Blaming God for not being there for you.

50. Maligning the character of God, others or yourself.

Grade: Give yourself 2 points for every warning sign that you checked. The higher the score, the more likely that accusing spirits are working in your life. It is not enough to say, "Oops! I didn't mean that." In order to tear down this stronghold, you must truly repent of your sinful reactions and pray asking forgiveness five ways for your own sin. Pray with someone with spiritual authority and make this a life-style!!

Please see the ungodly beliefs prayer and deliverance from oppression prayer (See exhibits in Part 4) in order to get freedom from ungodly beliefs, lies, fleshly structures and demonic oppression.

Bitterness and Unforgiveness
Verses to meditate on for more insights

LORD, I INVITE YOU TO REVEAL ANY BITTER ROOT OF UNFORGIVENESS IN ME.
Heb 12:12-15
12 Therefore, strengthen your feeble arms and weak knees. 13 "Make level paths for your feet," so that the lame may not be disabled, but rather healed. 14 Make every effort to live in peace with all men and to be holy; without holiness no one will see the Lord. 15 See to it that no one misses the grace of God and that no **bitter root** grows up to cause trouble and defile many.
Lord, you took all my roots on the Cross, but I have let some spring back up and have defiled many.

I CHOOSE TO FORGIVE OTHES IN THE SAME WAY YOU HAVE FORGIVEN ME.
Matthew 18:35
35 "This is how my heavenly Father will treat each of you unless you forgive your brother from your heart."
Lord, I have been turned over to the tormentors because of unforgiveness.

I RELEASE YOU TO RESTORE OTHERS THROUGH MY PRAYERS AND ACTIONS.
Galatians 6:1-3
6:1 Brothers, if someone is caught in a sin, you who are spiritual should restore him gently. But watch yourself, or you also may be tempted. 2 Carry each other's burdens, and in this way you will fulfill the law of Christ. 3 If anyone thinks he is something when he is nothing, he deceives himself.
Who will be "spiritual" first?

SHOW ME MY BLINDSPOTS ABOUT GOD, OTHERS OR MYSELF.
Romans 8:1
8:1 Therefore, there is now no condemnation for those who are in Christ Jesus,
(KJV added, "who walk not after the flesh, but after the Spirit.")

TEACH ME TO RELEASE OTHERS FROM DEBT AND TO FORGIVE FROM MY HEART.
Matthew 18:18
18 "I tell you the truth, whatever you bind on earth will be bound in heaven, and whatever you loose on earth will be loosed in heaven.
In the Name of Jesus, I bind myself to the truth of God and loose myself from the lies of the enemy and self-deception.

I CHOOSE TO KEEP SHORT ACCOUNTS WITH GOD REGARDING MY OWN SINS.
Matthew 6:14-15
14 For if you forgive men when they sin against you, your heavenly Father will also forgive you.
15 But if you do not forgive men their sins, your Father will not forgive your sins.

What if God really does forgive us in the same way that we forgive others?

Are you ready to test yourself again? We can only impart what we have received.

TEST YOURSELF FOR BITTERNESS – adapted from teachings by John and Paula Sandford particularly in their original version of "Transformation of the Inner Man."

1. Does my unforgiveness, resentment or bitterness hurt anyone?

2. Do I have to forgive before they truly repent?

3. Was the open door to this stronghold the sinful way that I reacted?

4. When they sinned and I reacted did I minister death to them?

5. Did I claim my personal rights or assert myself?

6. Does my bitterness imprison them in the very behavior that I hated?

INDICATORS OF UNFORGIVENESS IN YOUR LIFE:

-   Are you unhappy to see him/her when they approach?

-   Do you avoid fellowship with them?

-   Do you still rehearse what you could have said?

-   Do you still think of things you could have done to retaliate?

-   Have you lost spiritual power?

-   Are you having trouble entering into God's presence?

-   Are your prayers falling to the ground?

-   Do you have physical problems, aches and pains that have no cure?

-   Do periods of despondency return quickly after joyful times?

-   Is your sleep disturbed? Not restful? Troubled with dreams?

-   Does wrath, strife and hatred really belong with witchcraft and walking by the flesh?

-   Does it seem like blame is just a normal reaction?

-   Does my relationship with this person interfere with my relationship with God?

-   Isn't this just human nature? Isn't it prideful to think you can be free of sinful reactions?

-   Isn't it healthy to have a fear of trusting them again?

- Am I operating as a voice for God or Satan? As a medium?

- Do I feel like I have a right to judge those who commit gross sin and never repent?

- Do I expect God to forgive me fully while I do not forgive them?

- Can thoughts of unforgiveness, resentment, wrath or retaliation cause illness?

Give yourself 4 points for each question. Score _____

Make notes here of areas where Holy Spirit asked you to repent, pray, forgive, ask for forgiveness or let go.

Signs of the Bitterness Stronghold

All of us can empathize with those who have been deeply wounded. Our calling as Restoration Prayer Ministers is to empathize with the person but not to sympathize with their sinful reactions and offenses taken. With true discernment, we will know how to love our receiver and still come against their fleshly or demonic strongholds by swinging the Sword of the Spirit in power. It is one thing to pour out our hearts to God but yet another to resist God's Truth and to hold on to sinful reactions. I have found the following very simple definitions to be helpful for receivers to identify unspoken sinful reactions in their heart as well as sinful behaviors.

Unforgiveness – refusal to let the offender off the hook (even if God has already forgiven them)

Resentment – to hold onto hard feelings or emotions toward the offender

Judgment – to usurp God's place as judge, to decide or conclude with condemnation, to sentence

Revenge – to fantasize or execute a plan of retaliation, exposure, punishment

Wrath – to be enraged, infuriated, livid and other evidences of indulging in malice

Hatred – intense ill will without guilt, refusing conviction of sin, defending hateful reactions

Self-hatred – self-targeted hatred (which often alternates with hating the offender)

Violence – to cause injury, to intimidate with force, imaginations of action to do harm

Elimination – to hope or plan to remove, get rid of by "accident" or on purpose

Murder – to plan or actually kill the offender or their reputation with words or actions

Discern when they have truly repented of believing they had a right to judge, dishonor or react in sinful ways.

Ungodly Beliefs (UGB)
1. I *confess* my sin (and if appropriate, my ancestor's sin) of believing the ungodly belief that _____ and for any way I have **blamed you** God.
2. I *forgive* those who contributed to my forming this UGB, including myself.
3. I ask You, Lord, to **forgive me** for living my life by it and for anyway I have judged others, based on this UGB.
4. I *forgive* myself for believing this ungodly belief.
5. I *renounce* and *break* my agreement with this UGB, and the agreement that I have had with deception, the power of darkness and with demons.
6. I *choose* to accept and **believe** the godly belief that _____.

Once the power of the ungodly beliefs is effectively broken, it is easier to hear God for godly beliefs. Encourage your receiver to declare for 40 days to transform their thinking.

They may need to repent of word curses they have believed or said over the offenders. See the exhibits for all of the restoration prayers.

Then our receiver is in a good position to cast out all associated demonic spirit right away.

Demonic Oppression and Bondage (DO)
I. **confess** my sin of agreeing with the demonic spirits of _____ and forgive all who have influenced me to sin.
2. I **repent** for giving place to the demons of _____.
3. **I forgive** myself for the pain and limitations I have allowed the demons to inflict upon me.
4. In the Name of Jesus, I **renounce** and break all agreement with the demons (stronghold) of _____, including all associated demons of _____ , _____ , _____ , _____ , etc.
5. I **take authority** over the demons (stronghold) of _____ and command you demons of _____ to leave me/us now based
on the finished work of Christ on the Cross and His shed Blood.
6. In the Name of Jesus Christ of Nazareth, the Anointed One, Who has given me spiritual authority, I **command** the demons of _____ to go to the dry uninhabited places and never come back.
7. In its place I choose to **receive** _____.

1 John 1:7-9
 7 But if we walk in the light, as he is in the light, we have fellowship with one another, and the blood of Jesus, his Son, purifies us from all sin. 8 If we claim to be without sin, we deceive ourselves and the truth is not in us. 9 If we confess our sins, he is faithful and just and will forgive us our sins and purify us from all unrighteousness.
Dear Jesus, show me if I can turn 360 degrees and want fellowship with everyone.

1 John 4:18
18 There is no fear in love. But perfect love drives out fear, because fear has to do with punishment. The one who fears is not made perfect in love.
Make me a conduit of Your perfect love to others and overcome my fear.

Matthew 5:7
Blessed are the merciful, for they will be shown **mercy.**
I release You, Jesus, to be Your mercy through me to those who need it the most.

James 4:11
11 Brothers, do not **slander** one another. Anyone who speaks against his brother or judges him speaks against the law and judges it. When you judge the law, you are not keeping it, but sitting in judgment on it.
Lord, I choose to obey Your law and to respect You as the judge of the earth.

Ephesians 6:11-13
11 Put on the full armor of God so that you can take your stand against the devil's schemes. 12 For our struggle is not against flesh and blood, but against the rulers, against the authorities, against the powers of this dark world and against the spiritual forces of evil in the heavenly realms. 13 Therefore put on the full armor of God, so that when the day of evil comes, you may be able to stand your ground, and after you have done everything, to stand.
I choose to swing the sword of the Spirit, truth of God's word, in faith, receiving the riches of the gospel of peace and His gifts of righteousness with my salvation. I pray always under the leadership of Holy Spirit and declare and decree His Word!

Romans 2:1
1 You, therefore, have no excuse, you who pass judgment on someone else, for at whatever point you judge the other, you are condemning yourself, because you who pass judgment do the same things.
Lord Jesus, I repent of violating your commands; I renounce my judgments and ask you to bring this crop that I have sown to death.

Luke 11:20-22
20 But if I drive out demons by the finger of God, then the kingdom of God has come to you. 21 "When a **strong man**, fully armed, guards his own house, his possessions are safe. 22 But when **someone stronger** attacks and overpowers him, he takes away the **armor** in which the man trusted and divides up the spoils.
Lord, show me how the strongman has taken my house, my goods and how he is armored. I choose to break agreements with him, to repent and to align with the stronger one, Jesus.

Romans 12:18-19
18 If it is possible, as far as it depends on you, live at peace with everyone. 19 Do not take revenge, my friends, but leave room for God's wrath, for it is written: "It is mine to avenge; I will repay," says the Lord.
Lord, I choose to trust You to avenge every wrong. I choose to love my enemies, take my house back and to enjoy my goods in peace, submitted to the stronger Man.

Matthew 5:21-26
21 "You have heard that it was said to the people long ago, 'Do not murder, and anyone who murders will be **subject to judgment**.' 22 But I tell you that anyone who is angry with his brother will be **subject to judgment**. Again, anyone who says to his brother, 'Raca,' is answerable to the Sanhedrin. But anyone who says, 'You fool!' will be in danger of the **fire of hell**. 23 "Therefore, if you are offering your gift at the altar and there remember that your brother has something against you, 24 leave your gift there in front of the altar. First go and be reconciled to your brother; then come and offer your gift.
25 "Settle matters quickly with your adversary who is taking you to court. Do it while you are still with him on the way, or he may hand you over to the judge, and the judge may **hand you over to the officer**, and you may be **thrown into prison**. 26 I tell you the truth, you will not get out until you **have paid the last penny.**
Lord, I choose to be reconciled and never to experience what these verses mean.

1 Peter 3:7 7- Husbands, in the same way **be considerate** as you live with your wives, and **treat them with respect** as the weaker partner and as heirs with you of the gracious gift of life, so that **nothing will hinder your prayers.**

James 3:16-18
16 For where you have envy **(strife)** and selfish ambition, there you find disorder and every evil practice.
Where there is strife, there is every evil thing. I choose to hate strife.
17 But the **wisdom** that comes from heaven is first of all **pure; then peace-loving, considerate, submissive, full of mercy and good fruit, impartial and sincere**. 18- Peacemakers who sow in peace raise a harvest of righteousness.
Lord, I choose to be "one" rather to have "won".

Matthew 18:19
19 "Again, I tell you that if two of you on earth agree about anything you ask for, it will be done for you by my Father in heaven.
If two can out ten thousand to flight, what can we do, Lord? Praise God.

Ephesians 4:1-3
4:1 As a prisoner for the Lord, then, I urge you **to live a life worthy of the calling you have received.** 2 Be completely humble and gentle; be patient, bearing with one another in love. 3 Make every effort to keep the unity of the Spirit through the bond of peace.

Ephesians 4:26-27
26 "In your **anger** do not sin": Do not let the sun go down while you are still angry, 27- and do not give the devil a foothold.

I have included an anger ladder after hearing it taught by Dr. Ross Campbell on the radio. I use it to measure how far I have gone from appropriate anger to anger with sin.

	ANGER LADDER
-1	Negative, mean, proud, rejecting or condescending looks, judgmental, sarcastic, ungodly comments
-2	Loud irritated tone says, "I'm not on your side." "Don't feel, don't talk, don't ask"
-3	Negative rejecting body language or walking out without a plan to resume talking
-4	Overpowering, threats, separating comments, general condemnations
-5	Interrupting or monopolizing conversations; rebutting without listening to what the other has to say
-6	Calling them names, labeling, stereotyping, bringing up their history and their relatives
-7	Yelling, attacking, cussing, cursing them, any type of verbal abuse or mental cruelty
-8	Public put downs, uncovering them, humiliation, gossip, accusation and slander
-9	Physical abuse, threats of abuse, threatening or abusing their property, abandonment
-10	Passive aggression, any resistant action with intent to punish or to make sorry without owning the intent
-11	Homicidal attempts, homicidal threats, homicide

How did you do? Sometimes, we feel guilty for expressing appropriate anger when anger is a normal emotion to certain circumstances, i.e. intentional violations of our boundaries. The Bible recorded many instances when God became angry (without sin of course) when His law was broken year after year. We can have appropriate anger, fleshly anger or a spirit of anger that is taking over our responses. See our article on Spirit of Anger at online www.CrossWalkLife.com for more clarity.

A – B – C of Assertiveness

Recognizing my Irish temper, renouncing it and casting it out was only half of the solution for me. I wondered how to express my anger with assertiveness rather than being afraid of blurting out explosive sinful reactions. I don't know who originally wrote this model of assertiveness but it has been my favorite for about 25 years. Here is an example of using this acronym in two situations.

A	Admit	I admit that you need more nursery workers
B	But	but I have prayed and asked God about it.
C	Choose	I choose to tell you I can only do it one Sunday.

A	Admit	I admit that you do need 7 days a week coverage
B	But	but I have examined my priorities
C	Choose	I choose to tell you I cannot work 7 days a week.

Once I saw this simple plan for expressing anger without sin, I was free to give a clear and certain answer, without being intimidated, over reacting, without judging their motives, taking offense or offering excuses. They actually appreciated a short answer versus my life story, my excuses or my opinions.

Then Holy Spirit began to convict me of some of my emotions that were "loaded" or that motivate me to answer with "zingers." These emotions were not just feelings; they had ungodly beliefs embedded in them that fueled my anger when people asked too much of me. It was time to pray Liberty Savard's prayer on breaking soul power and to command my soul to bow down to my new spirit that loved to be one with Holy Spirit.

Breaking Soul Power Prayer

Breaking the Power (pg 30, Bridge-Logos, 1995) - Copyrighted material used with permission of author, Rev. Liberty Savard www.libertysavard.com

Bless the Lord, O my soul, with all that is within you. Bless His holy name! Soul, I bind you to your destiny as a fully surrendered and divinely created part of God's Kingdom purposes. I bind myself to the destiny that Christ has made possible for me through divine covenant relationship, a new spiritual family heritage, and a new bloodline. You, soul, will come into alignment with my divine destiny purposes.

Soul, I loose (smash, destroy, rip apart) the wrong beliefs, wrong attitudes, and wrong patterns of thinking you have created to try to control my life. I loose all denial, deception, and discouragement from you. I loose the influences and effects of the word curses you have perceived as "truth". I loose the influences and effects of the wrong agreements and ungodly soul ties you have entered into.

You, soul, were created by God to translate His revelation and understanding to the hurting of this world--you were not created to run my life! You will learn to delight in what God has in store for you. Through a renewed mind, healed emotions, and the courage of a surrendered will, you are going to bring forth answers and new understanding to many. You will cooperate with my regenerated spirit.

Mind, once you turned in circles like a rat caught in a maze; constantly going over and over decisions you had no answers for, yet you felt trapped into making. The unresolved issues you kept trying to bury crawled up out of their soulish graves again and again. Mind, I bind you to the realization of divine interventions occurring all the time in the problems you could never solve before--but now God solves while you sleep.

Emotions, forget how you once reeled between laughter and tears, boldness and fear, hope and despair, affection and anger. You frightened people with tears of neediness and outbursts of anger. You fueled my feelings of rejection, betrayal, and loneliness. You will now receive divine peace, embrace joy and hope, and respond to the Holy Spirit's lifting power when old, negative feelings try to ascend.

Will, forget not the causes and the battles you used to engage in, rigidly implacable and unrelenting in your stands. Unrepentant, unbending, unyielding, unwilling to work with others' ideas, you alienated many from me. You caused much grief with your stubbornness and rebellion to God's ways. But you are learning how to be strong, yet flexible; to be right, yet entreatable; to be bold, yet gentle; to be courageous, yet concerned for others. Only the Holy Spirit can perfectly balance these strengths in me.

Soul, you will surrender the barricades you have erected over the deepest, darkest chambers within me. I loose the self-denial, the self-protectiveness, the self-defense, and the self-centeredness protecting my vulnerabilities that are so needful of God's grace. I loose the lies and all guilt you have tormented me with over things that were not my fault. I loose the deceptions you have hammered me with and have used to cause me to cave in to your control.

Lord, may your truth always be the plumb line to true up my thoughts, feelings, and choices. I want your truth to be the straight edge of my spirit, the guiding light of my life, and the backbone of my soul. Bless the Lord, O my soul, with all that is within you. Forget not His benefits. Remember what He has done for you!

Amen

Control

This chart is based on the work of Chester and Betsy Kylstra, *Restoring the Foundations.* My intention is to provide the resources that you might commonly use to discern your receivers. We need to differentiate between legitimate control (as in a chain of authority) and being officious, taking illegitimate control, without having been given a measure of rule in that person's life.

Direct Control	
Giving commands	Being bossy, even if it is sugar coated
Telling people how to do something (your way)	Using force, physical violence

Overt Control	
Steering conversations	Controlling the finances or checkbook
Insisting on perfection	Controlling the car, people's freedom
Providing money for support, withdrawing it	Deciding where to go on vacations
Refusing to listen or to acknowledge feedback	Deciding how family social time is used

Indirect Control	
Deliberately pleasing someone	Using sex as a reward or payoff
Promoting loyalty as in obligation	Having a headache
Withdrawing, pouting, pity party	Shedding crocodile tears
Being angry, moody, even violent	Accusing, criticizing
Withholding approval	Needing to work
Promoting shame, guilt trips, embarrassing	Using fear, threats, "Jewish Mother"
Getting terribly wounded and hurt	Blaming
"How could you do this to me?"	"Look how much you've hurt me!"
Making excuses	"You don't appreciate all I have done!"
Being passive aggressive, forgetting on purpose	Sabotage by being late

Hidden Control	
Being incapacitated, needing to be first	Withholding information, deception, lies
Playing invalid who needs to be served	Having family idols to measure up to
Alcoholism, addiction, dependence	Unintentional witchcraft control
Paranoid fears, worries	Spells, hexes, intentional witchcraft

Note your methods of control here.

Who me?
I don't use.
Trust me.
Over react?
In denial?
Prove it!

Defensiveness

Defense mechanisms are walls or protective devices that we use to deal with hurts or trauma when we cannot tolerate feeling the pain. Most of these are patterns or automatic reactions to pain, that we chose when we were children. They need to be rethought and updated now that we are more mature. The problem is that being defensive is also a way of resisting Holy Spirit and those He would use to help us get free.

Often, when we find ourselves over reacting to current situations, it is because emotions from past hurts are spilling over our defensive walls into our present reactions. How many of these defense mechanisms do you use? Think about it. Be aware that they could be indicators that your healing is not yet complete. Trust Holy Spirit to convict with gentleness.

1. Rationalizing - I don't over react often, I don't really have a problem.
2. Minimizing - I don't react half as bad as they do.
3. Sublimating - I clean house or exercise when I start to feel the guilt again.
4. Cockiness - I got it made, these other folks are losers.
5. Justifying - If you had a wife/husband/family like mine, you would be angry too.
6. Projecting - You manipulate and say the other person is the one who is upset.
7. Blaming - It's because they make me mad. It is my job stress.
8. Humor - This isn't serious. Life is a joke.
9. Intellectualizing - If I can understand it or analyze it, I have it under control.
10. Lying - I haven't had that many run-ins; I get along with everybody.
11. Manipulation - If you quit complaining, I'll quit drinking/using.
12. Accusing - When you criticize me, it makes me eat even more.
13. Threatening - Get off my back or you will be sorry!
14. Judging - If you just wanted to do _____ right, things wouldn't be so bad.
15. Explaining - Oh, I am not well enough to work anymore because . . .
16. Analyzing - I started using more because of ____, it will slow down later.
17. Arguing - I'm not an alcoholic; I've never gotten a DUI or . . .
18. Defiance - I dare you to prove that I'm cheating!
19. Withdrawing - If I don't do or say anything, they will leave me alone.
20. Shouting - Leave me alone, I don't want to talk about it!
21. Silence –
22. Smiling - Just laugh it off. Nervous smile. Become the office clown.
23. Compliance - I just do and say what they want.
24. Spiritualizing - God doesn't see my bad behavior. I'm forgiven.
25. Fantasizing - They would never treat me the way they did their last spouse.
26. Religiosity - Good Christians don't need counseling. They are already healed.

Did that clear up a few things for you?

This tool is not to be used to "play Holy Spirit," to corner people or to force confessions. We all have unconsciously chosen defenses that we use to try to hide our feelings rather than feel them or heal them. Defensiveness doesn't hide hurts well either. There is no such thing as an unexpressed emotion. They come out sooner or later.

Why do people make appointments to receive prayer ministry and then deny that they have obvious issues? We can be very ambivalent about admitting our fleshly patterns or demonic oppression. Usually, strongholds begin when we try to defend our faults and do not take responsibility for our sinful reactions to wounds. If we continue to try to hide our hurts and don't allow truth into these areas, these hurtful emotions will come out at some point without our permission. Better for us to choose the time and place that we will share those negative feelings in order to prevent them from exploding when our buttons are pushed.

We can choose to be healed quickly, without reliving the trauma, without analysis, without years of counseling, by choosing healing through Issue-Focused Restoration Prayer Ministry. If you or your receiver are ready for our "whole life" 18 hour RPM. Please see our simple sign up site at www.RestorationPrayerMinistry.com.

Some of these items were taken from Dr. John Suler's free handout at
http://www.rider.edu/~suler

INSIGHTS on Self-Deception

Carnality shows: The worst thing about self-deception is that we are the last to know!! Our friends and family can the see the road we took to deceive ourselves, but we cannot. While we may defend our position, they can see that the enemy is using us as a pawn to speak his lies. At the same time, we are distracted from the wonderful plan God has for our life. Our **blind spots**, by definition, are areas that we may never see unless we give our ministers or spiritual advisors permission to speak.

Wake-up Call: How do I am know if I am deceived? Look for the plan of the enemy.

- I don't think I could be the one who is self-deceived, so I will read this for someone else!
- I don't see the enemy battling for my mind. Romans 7:17-18
- Powers of darkness and spiritual wickedness don't attack me. Ephesians 6:12
- My secret thoughts and actions do not hurt anyone. 1 Corinthians 12:25
- If I do not fight Satan he will not destroy me. 1 Peter 5:8
- I don't have imaginations that oppose the knowledge of God. 2 Corinthians 10:5
- I don't think the enemy is trying to corrupt my mind. 2 Corinthians 11:3

Here are some common lies Satan uses to deceive us about demons.

Jesus said He came to set the captives free. We can know God and still have areas of our hearts that have yielded to compromise, especially after seasons of great hurt and disappointment. Demons are opportunists that attack while we are down and give us "an offer we cannot refuse." We begin to think ungodly thoughts which are soon followed by ungodly behavior, which we rationalize, *"under the circumstances."* When our friends try to tell us that we are off course, we defend our right to think this way and misbehave like we do (definition of a stronghold.)

You don't need to be vigilant to look for your adversary the devil.........................1 Peter 5:8
There is no such thing as unclean spirits..Mark 1:23-27
Lust and lies are normal..John 8:44
Christians are always safe and not bothered by demons.......................Ephesians 6:11-12
The Holy Spirit will not allow demons to tempt me.............Matthew 4:1-7, James 1:13
Satan cannot put diseases on the me...Job 2:7
I could never be transformed into a minister of darkness..................2 Corinthians 11:13-15
My disobedience is not because I agree with the prince of the air.................Ephesians 2:2
I can enjoy a little seduction and hypocrisy, can't I?..............................1 Timothy 4:1-2
Fears are just emotions...2 Timothy 1:7
Born again people cannot have evil hearts of unbelief.............................Hebrews 3:13-15
Our church cannot have a spirit of error...1 John 4:6
The devil wouldn't ask me to do good works...Revelation 16:14
I can't stay awake to read the Bible or hear sermons, its hopeless...................Mark 9:25
God made me sick to teach me a lesson..Luke 13:11
If a prophesy comes true then it was from God...Acts 16:16-17

Ministry steps to overcome defensiveness and self-deception.

1. Lord, I confess my sin of trying to defend myself and hiding behind the fig leaves.
2. I confess my sin of choosing self-deception instead of Your Truth, Lord.
3. I forgive those who took advantage of my vulnerability to falsely accuse me.
4. Forgive me for thinking no one knows me better than I do. I choose to listen.
5. Forgive me for resisting conviction about my sinful reactions and behaviors.
6. Forgive me for judging those whom You sent to help and for shooting the messenger.
7. I forgive myself for believing the lies and remaining in Satan's trap.
8. I renounce and break agreement with the ungodly belief that

_____.

9. I choose to receive and believe the godly belief that

_____.

Please see the RPM prayer card under exhibits for additional prayers.

False Identity Statements

Some of the most common issues that you will hear during the interview are statements of false identity. The devil sets us up when we are very little to hear things that damage our identity. Family members who are not aware of this may say things like, "You are bad, you are stupid, you are useless, you are a whore, you are a liar, you are wicked." Satan wants us to believe that we not only did wrong but that we ourselves are defective apart from our actions. He wants to shame us deep down in our identity and cause us to reject what Father God says about us.

For instance, shame, in some ways, is worse than guilt. It is a horrifying sense of "being uniquely and hopelessly flawed." Like rejection, it is very common issue for many of us as we have accepted the lie that "this is who I am," that I am shameful to the core. This is the worst kind of Ungodly Belief, a false belief about our identity.

As you listen to your receiver, ask them to finish the statement, I am _____with all of the negative words that have been said over them. They may also have believed these false identity statements and said them over themselves. As you listen to them describe their issue, make a list of the false identity statements too. These Ungodly Beliefs about our identity are very powerful in blocking us from fulfilling our destiny because they might prevent us from ever basing our significance on who Father God says we are versus on the opinions of others.

When we pray two sentence prayers of agreement to break the power of these false identity statements, we are then free to replace them with God's Truth. Most people need help thinking of what God's Truth is because they have been believing and receiving the lies all their life. Here is a sample of false statements (on the left side) and truths (on the right side) that my receiver and I came up with together. Do not rush the process by handing them this sheet. Teach them to pray this two sentence prayer and listen to Holy Spirit to confirm His Truth about their identity. In one session, you will probably only address a few but this sample list is a good resource to help you. <u>Let each person hear "I am" statements that are unique to them.</u>

Sample Ministry to False Identity Statements

I declare and decree God's truth for at least 40 days. PRAYER:
I renounce and break agreement with the lie that I am _____.
I receive God's Truth that says that I am _____.

IDENTITY STATEMENTS	
Lie - the enemy says I am	**Truth - God says that I am**
Rejected, not chosen	Unconditionally accepted, chosen, welcomed, invited, family
Abused, violated, yelled at	Respected, properly taken care of, protected, addressed
Angry, resentful	Peaceful, at peace, content, assertive, grateful, forgiving, gracious
Not pure, a whore	Pure, holy, full of virtue, a vessel of honor, made whole

Controlled, intimidated	Dependent on God, Holy Spirit, Christ controlled, courageous
Not pleasing	Fully fragrant to God, adequate in Christ, precious, cherished
Doubtful	Hopeful, full of great faith, confident in Christ, believing
Helpless	Protected, empowered, strong, authoritative in Christ
Not worthy, undeserving	Made worthy, valued, God's favorite, deserving in Christ
Fearful, anxious	In peace, loved perfectly, resting in Him, trusting God
A failure, inadequate	More than a conqueror in Christ, a success, more than capable
Lonely, alone	Never alone in Christ, abiding, spending time with God
Not likeable, not valuable	Likeable, attractive, fun, esteemed, consulted, wise
In poverty, unemployable	Blessed and highly favored, rich, a valuable contributor
Not favored	Well favored by God and man, funded, made whole, complete
Misunderstood, not discerned	Well understood, perceived rightly, discerned, transparent
Not protected, vulnerable	Angelically protected, separated, sanctified, safe, concealed
Belittled, criticized, ridiculed	Esteemed, praised, built up, supported, heard, a godly influence
Not honored, dishonorable	Honored, God's precious gem, His Beloved, nurtured, nursed
Not important, tolerated	Very Important, a world changer, ambassador, ordained, anointed
Judged, accused	Totally forgiven, justified, redeemed and transformed, defended
Not appreciated	Highly appreciated, recognized, a glory to God, His voice
A disappointment	An inspiration, successful in Him, His grace and a healing balm
Performing	Resting, releasing Christ to speak and do through me
Not talented	Gifted, an extension of God's creativity, a worshipper
Retarded, insane, crazy	Intellectually gifted, one with the heart and mind of Christ, whole
Stupid, dumb	Body-soul-spirit connected, fair without prejudice or sexism, wise
Not regenerated	Regenerated, a holy nation, partake of a divine nature, redeemed
Trash	Refined like gold, His fruit of His vine, God's valuable asset
Proud, self-promoting	Humble, compassionate, divinely appointed and equipped, strong
Fat	Perfectly and wonderfully made, designed, healthy and purposed
Critical, criticized	Discerning with words of wisdom and knowledge, interceding
Boring and sad	Happy, optimistic, joyful, realistic, inspiring and creative

Fear, Intimidation and Illusions

Is fear sin or just a feeling? An emotion? An illusion? Of the flesh or a spirit?
When Job listened to the spirit of fear, he was exercising negative faith, believing for the worst. Faith always works, whether it is negative faith or positive faith.

Job 3:25-26
25 What I feared has come upon me; what I dreaded has happened to me. 26 I have no peace, no quietness; I have no rest, but only turmoil.

In Job 4:14-15 Job said, "Fear came upon me, and trembling, which made all my bones to shake. Then a spirit passed before my face; the hair of my flesh stood up."

The Bible never calls fear a feeling; it describes fear as a spirit. When fear came to Job, it took his peace, caused him to tremble and shake, gave him goose bumps or maybe a chill. He saw the spirit and heard it questioning him and questioning the truth of God.

In Job 4:16-17, "It stood still, but I could not discern the form thereof: an image *was* before mine eyes, *there was* silence, and I heard a voice, *saying*, Shall mortal man be more just than God? Shall a man be more pure than his maker?"

Nothing has changed for thousands of years. Satan still uses the same old strategies.
1.   He sets us up to agree with his lies instead of God's Truth.
2.   He gains legal access to us by the fruit of our lips, as we agree with the spirit of fear.
3.   He works through the power of intimidation to shut us up or shut us down.
4.   His main power is in the power of illusion and questions like, "What if?"

How is it that we can be so intimidated by fears? The list of fears that we pray over is long and could be longer. What we have learned is that if we begin to believe the lies that the spirit of fear tells us, he just keeps adding fears to the list. If we do not stand up to the spirit of fear, he will take our whole life away.

If we once fail at public speaking or singing, he says we will always fail.
If we are allergic to strawberries, he says we will be allergic to a long list of other foods too.
If we react to chemicals in our environment, he says we will react everywhere we go.
If we are molested by one man, he says we will attract molesters forever and ever.
If we try to resist him, he gives us symptoms that make it appear that he has power over us.
If we agree with him, our bodies will go into "fight or flight," according to our thoughts.

2 Corinthians 10:4-6
4 The weapons we fight with are not the weapons of the world. On the contrary, they have divine power to demolish strongholds. 5 We demolish arguments and every pretension that sets itself up against the knowledge of God, and we take captive every thought to make it obedient to Christ. 6 And we will be ready to punish every act of disobedience, **once your obedience is complete.**
Are you fighting the devil with fear-faith or true faith? Are you quoting scripture in unbelief and doubt? Are you combining positive confessions with disobedience?

I recommend meditating on the Word in order to combat the spirit of fear.

We have divine power to demolish strongholds with spiritual weapons.
Christ inside us, has all power and authority in Heaven and on earth.

Hebrews 11:6
6 And without faith it is impossible to please God, because anyone who comes to him must believe that he exists and that he rewards those who earnestly seek him.
Praying with fear need or faith rest? Praying? Or worrying and complaining?
Is fear unbelief or a feeling? Fear faith asks but doubts that God will do it.

Matthew 6:33-34
33 But seek first his kingdom and his righteousness, and all these things will be given to you as well. 34 Therefore do not worry about tomorrow, for tomorrow will worry about itself. Each day has enough trouble of its own.
Are you settling for second best due to fear? Is the battle lost between your ears?
Are you living in the permissive will of God or fear?

Luke 12:22-23
22 Then Jesus said to his disciples: "Therefore I tell you, do not worry about your life, what you will eat; or about your body, what you will wear."
What is fear projecting onto your future?

Philippians 4:6-7
6 Do not be anxious about anything, but in everything, by prayer and petition, with thanksgiving, present your requests to God. 7 And the peace of God, which transcends all understanding, will guard your hearts and your minds in Christ Jesus.
We repent of stepping out of God's will, way and timing, out of fear, and choose to trust God to have our best interest at heart.

1 Peter 5:6-7
6 Humble yourselves, therefore, under God's mighty hand, that he may lift you up in due time. 7 Cast all your anxiety on him because he cares for you.
God is not a time creature. We repent of a fear of failure and rest in his timing.
Lord, we repent of frustration with Your goals and Your priorities. We loose ourselves of our own agendas and bind ourselves to being conformed to Your image.

Hebrews 4:12-13
12 For the word of God is living and active. Sharper than any double-edged sword, it penetrates even to dividing soul and spirit, joints and marrow; it judges the thoughts and attitudes of the heart. 13 Nothing in all creation is hidden from God's sight. Everything is uncovered and laid bare before the eyes of him to whom we must give account.
We loose ourselves from fear of helplessness and bind ourselves to Your power.

Matthew 25:25-26
25 So I was afraid and went out and hid your talent in the ground. See, here is what belongs to you.' 26 "His master replied, 'You wicked, lazy servant! So you knew that I harvest where I have not sown and gather where I have not scattered seed?
We loose ourselves from being wicked and lazy because of fear of obeying in faith.
Loose us Lord, from a poverty and scarcity mentality; bind us to faith.

1 John 4:18
18 There is no fear in love. But perfect love drives out fear, because fear has to do with punishment. The one who fears is not made perfect in love.
Root: an inability to receive God's love.

Psalm 91:4-5
4 He shall cover you with His feathers, And under His wings you shall take refuge; His truth shall be your shield and buckler. 5 You shall not be afraid of the terror by night, Nor of the arrow that flies by day, …
Animals will give their life to protect their young (or you.)

Ephesians 6:13
13 Therefore put on the full armor of God, so that when the day of evil comes, you may be able to stand your ground, and after you have done everything, to stand.
We repent of taking our armor off and on and choose to keep it on in agreement with our identity, walking it out because faith is who we are.

We Resist Spirits of Intimidation by Declaring Scriptures

2 Timothy 1:7
7 For God did not give us a **spirit of timidity**, but a spirit of power, of love and of self-discipline.
We renounce agreements with a spirit of intimidation that would prevent us from walking out our destiny in Christ.

Revelation 21:8
8 But the **fearful, and unbelieving**, and the abominable, and murderers, and whoremongers, and sorcerers, and idolaters, and all liars, shall have their part in the lake which burneth with fire and brimstone: which is the second death.
In Jesus Name, we loose ourselves from dishonoring God with fear and unbelief and bind ourselves to a holy reverence of You, God, and Your integrity.

Proverbs 29:25
25 Fear of man will prove to be a snare, but whoever trusts in the LORD is kept safe.
We bind ourselves to trust and safety and loose ourselves from fear and a snare.

Psalms 118:6 or Psalms 56:4 or Psalms 56:11
The LORD is with me; I will not be afraid. What can man do to me?
God's faithfulness to me is not limited by other people's choices and behavior.

Proverbs 3:25-26
25 Have no fear of sudden disaster or of the ruin that overtakes the wicked,
26 for the LORD will be your confidence and will keep your foot from being snared.
Lord, forgive us for putting our confidence in our financial plans, money-making schemes, insurance or employment. We are only stewards of each opportunity.

Proverbs 1:33
Ps 23:4
4 Even though I walk through the valley of the shadow of death, I will fear no evil,
for you are with me; your rod and your staff, they comfort me.
We choose to depend on your supernatural protection and undeserved blessing.

Hebrews 2:15
15 and free those who all their lives were held in slavery by their fear of death.
Deliver us Lord, for the bondages we are in because we listened to a spirit of fear.

Deuteronomy 20:8
8 Then the officers shall add, "Is any man afraid or fainthearted? Let him go home so that his brothers will not become disheartened too."
The battle is won by faith, not by the numbers of people who are on our side. There is a transference of spirits of fear if we have open doors to the enemy.

Satan's Power of Illusions

Satan's chief power is to project an illusion on the screen of our mind. He projects a picture of his success in causing us to fail. But most of the time, these things never come to pass. We must speak, "It is written … " as Jesus did when He was tempted for 40 days in the wilderness. (Matthew 4) The washing of the water of the Word cleanses our minds of all of Satan's deceptions.

John 10:10
10 The thief comes only to steal and kill and destroy; I have come that they may have life, and have it to the full.
We choose to fight to keep our joy, our peace and our confidence in God.

2 Timothy 1:6-7
6 Wherefore I put thee in remembrance that thou **stir up the gift of God**, which is in thee by the putting on of my hands. 7 **For God hath not given us the spirit of fear**; but of power, and of love, and of a sound mind.
We repent of being afraid to yield control to the Holy Spirit and to stir up His gifts.

Psalms 91:5-6
5 **You will not fear the terror** of night, nor the arrow that flies by day,
6 **nor the pestilence** that stalks in the darkness, nor the plague that destroys at midday.

Deuteronomy 28:58-61
58 If you do not carefully follow all the words of this law, which are written in this book, and do not revere this glorious and awesome name--the LORD your God-- 59 the LORD will send fearful **plagues** on you and your descendants, **harsh and prolonged disasters**, and **severe and lingering illnesses**. 60 He will bring upon you all the **diseases** of Egypt that you dreaded, and they will cling to you. 61 The LORD will also bring on you every kind of **sickness** and disaster not recorded in this Book of the Law, until you are destroyed.
We repent of idolatry that leaves us vulnerable. We worship You alone, Lord.

Matthew 7:21
21 "Not everyone who says to me, 'Lord, Lord,' will enter the kingdom of heaven, but only he who does the will of my Father who is in heaven.
We bind our hearts to believing and loose ourselves from doubting our salvation.

Proverbs 3:24-26
24 when you lie down, you will not be afraid; when you lie down, your sleep will be sweet. 25 Have no fear of sudden disaster or of the ruin that overtakes the wicked,
26 for the LORD will be your confidence and will keep your foot from being snared.
We loose ourselves from hyper vigilance that prevents sound sleep and we bind our hearts to confidence in the Lord.

Leviticus 26:6-9
6 "'I will grant peace in the land, and you will lie down and no one will make you afraid. I will remove savage beasts from the land, and the sword will not pass through your country. 7 You will pursue your enemies, and they will fall by the sword before you. 8 Five of you will chase a hundred, and a hundred of you will chase ten thousand, and your enemies will fall by the sword before you. 9 "'I will look on you with favor and make you fruitful and increase your numbers, and I will keep my covenant with you.
Caleb and Joshua chose faith and inherited the land with God's unmerited favor.

Mark 4:39-41
39 He got up, rebuked the wind and said to the waves, "Quiet! Be still!" Then the wind died down and it was completely calm.
40 He said to his disciples, "Why are you so afraid? Do you still have no faith?"
41 They were terrified and asked each other, "Who is this? Even the wind and the waves obey him!"
God delivers us of all our distresses, natural, intentional or our own fault. Ps 107

Luke 12:11-12
11 "When you are brought before synagogues, rulers and authorities, do not worry about how you will defend yourselves or what you will say, 12 for the Holy Spirit will teach you at that time what you should say."
We bind our hearts to God's boldness and loose ourselves from fear of speaking.

Luke 21:26
Men's heart failing them for fear, and for looking after those things which are coming on the

earth: for the powers of heaven shall be shaken. 27 And then they shall see the Son of Man coming in a cloud with power and glory.

The Body, Soul, Spirit Connection

1. If our mind listens to fear, the hypothalamus tells the glands and we have a reaction.
2. Our body will develop antibodies as if the allergen was physically offensive.
3. Some illnesses are due to the spirit of fear and do not heal with prescriptions.
4. Many anti-depressants replace Serotonin as it is depleted by reaction to stresses.
5. When we agree with God we do more disease prevention, less disease management.
6. The word says to stand and resist a spirit of fear not to avoid fears.

If fears are your receiver's primary issue, you might use this list to identify and pray over them all. Do not try to judge them or get into a discussion about fears. Just use the time to pray and cast them out.
You can write A if ancestral involvement and S if self-involvement.

A S	A S
Allergies	Fear of Failure
Anxiety / Loss	Fear of Fear
Bewilderment	Fear of Foods
Burden / Less than	Fear of the Future
Darkness / Harassment	Fear of Infirmities
Loneliness / Being alone	Fear of Leaving the house
Mental Torment	Fear of Man
Over-Sensitivity	Fear of Marriage
Panic / Phobia	Fear of Performing
Paranoia / Prejudice	Fear of Punishment
Superstition / Curses	Fear of Rejection
Worry / What if	Fear of Sexual Issues
Fear of Attack	Fear of Singing
Fear of Authorities	Fear of Public Speaking
Fear of Cancer	Fear of Success / Leading
Fear of Death	Fear of Victimization
Fear of Diabetes	Fear of Violence
Fear of Demons	_____
Fear of Evil	_____

Many people are prisoners in their own home due to fear and anxiety regarding leaving the house. The may have multiple chemical sensitivities, environmental illnesses and fears of driving, crowds, passing out, attack, etc. The spirit of fear is behind it all. We lead them to ask forgiveness 5 ways for believing lies and cast the spirits of fear out.

Renouncing Ungodly Beliefs regarding spirits of fear, isolation and withdrawal

1. Father, I forgive anyone that has contributed to these fears. Help me to discern the things that trigger fear in me and show me how to release them fully to You.

2. Lord, I ask others to forgive me for the ways I have affected them as I have believed the lies that have contributed to this fear.

3. Father, I break any agreements with the demonic spirit of anxiety and receive Your promise to give me peace as I keep my mind stayed on You.

4. I forgive myself for allowing this fear to control me and for agreeing with the enemy. I rest in the truth that I am protected by very big Angels, everywhere I go, because You have promised to give your Angels charge over me.

5. Lord, I repent for isolating and withdrawing because of I have agreed with fear.

6. Forgive me for every way I have blamed You, Lord, for my captivity to the spirit of fear.

7. In the Name of Jesus, I cast the demonic spirits of fear to leave and never come back.

8. I choose to believe that in Christ, I have the strength I need to stand up to fear. I know that You love me unconditionally and are a very present help in my time of need. As I walk out of my house, into large open spaces or crowded places, I can take courage and know that I am not alone because I am joined with You. I am one spirit with You; we can never be separated!

Father, help me to use my spiritual authority of Jesus Christ inside me, to overcome fear in every situation. Give me a fresh revelation of Your perfect love for me that casts out ALL fear.

List the ways the spirit of fear has stolen from you.

Healing and Creative Miracles

I have had a lot of questions about divine healing of physical illness and I understand that I am not alone. I began to study the teachings of John G. Lake. Often, I found that I was ambivalent, wanting to believe that "Jesus heals them all" and yet observing the plight of many who seemed to believe in divine healing and yet were not healed on this earth.

Why are only about one out of twenty receiving divine healing in this country, in spite of their faith? Why were 75% healed in some other countries and under the ministry of John G. Lake? Is it simply that they don't have anything else to believe in but divine healing and we actually put our trust in everything but God?

Please understand that I was already commanding spirits of infirmity to go (versus "begging God for healing) before I studied John G. Lake. I saw a woman get out of a wheelchair after thirty-seven years, dance and run. I saw two other women with serious crippling arthritis healed instantly and run up and down the steps with ease. Recently, four out of five of the people I have prayed for with serious illnesses were healed instantly or that week! I have prophesied the divine healing of a man with cancer, commanded the cancer to go and saw him healed that week. His divine healing was documented, before by x-ray and after by cat scan.

I was healed of twenty-four out of twenty-six diagnosed illnesses when I learned how to pray scripture daily. Read Carlotta's Testimony at www.cwlinc.com. The first divine healing that I prayed for was for my dog who needed knee surgery. God healed him that very day and surgery was cancelled.

For myself, I see more people healed instantly when I pray for strangers in the street, the store or somewhere outside the church. Jesus works through each of us in different ways. Some were healed in the parking lot, pet store, the bank, sports arenas, etc. I don't claim to have all the answers. I do know that you definitely don't have to have great faith. In fact, sometimes I think that God heals unbelievers faster. It really isn't about us; it's about Him.

Along with Kathryn Kuhlman and John G. Lake, I ask, **"Why isn't everyone healed?"** If Jesus "healed them all," what is hindering divine healing today? In order to be healed, is it important to repent, to root out the roots and to close open doors to the enemy? What you believe about divine healing. Following is a summary of many of John G. Lake's teachings on divine healing listed below.

Are you ready to let God pinpoint your doubts about divine healing? I was happy to find out that most people who submit results say they agree with most of these teachings.

What do you believe about healing?

☐ God's will is for us to expect to receive divine healing every time.

☐ We are commanded to heal the sick; we do not need a special "leading or unction."

☐ Every believer is already an "heir" of all the authority he needs to minister healing.

☐ All believers can minister healing effectively; some have specialized gifts of healing.

☐ God's desire is to heal all of our diseases just as He forgives all of our sins.

☐ Jesus never asked God to heal anyone, He commanded healing and deliverance.

☐ Jesus healed thousands at a time without requiring them to repent or believe first.

☐ Great faith is not necessary or the key to receiving divine healing from disease.

☐ The disciples did not "intercede" for healing; they commanded infirmity to leave.

☐ Our traditions about healing have hindered us from demonstrating the power of God.

☐ Unconfessed sins may make people sick but they do not prevent divine healing.

☐ Jesus healed them all, regardless of their level of faith, if they wanted to be healed.

☐ Jesus never tried to find the root cause of the illness or the sin that "opened the door."

☐ Jesus was never prevented from healing due to the sin of their ancestors.

☐ Jesus taught the disciples to pray and fast in some cases of healing and deliverance.

☐ We command healing with the power of God impartiality and it flows every time.

☐ We are not to judge who is confessed up, in faith and ready to be healed.

☐ The Baptism of the Holy Spirit is given so that we will minister in the power of God.

☐ We are commanded to lay hands on the sick and pray a prayer of faith (authority.)

☐ The commandment to heal the sick is sufficient without a Rhema word.

☐ Healing may take time to manifest, while creative miracles are usually instant.

☐ Healing for every illness has been provided in our salvation by the Cross of Christ.

☐ The only requirement for a person to receive healing is to want to be healed.

☐ God is an equal opportunity healer and never refuses to heal and deliver.

☐ God will reveal any specific keys to divine healing readily, usually as soon as we ask.

☐ God never causes illness to teach us a lesson; it is never His will for us to be sick.

☐ God is willing to minister healing and creative miracles through any believer.

☐ We are to command the power of God without picking and choosing who is worthy.

☐ We even have authority to cast out the devils that people think they want to keep.

☐ We can receive gifts by the "laying on of hands and impartation" from others.

☐ N.T. believers initiated divine healing and deliverance at will under the anointing.

☐ Signs and wonders follow our belief; we don't wait for a new command every time.

☐ As believers, we can increase our healing gift or anointing by exercising it.

☐ Believers already have 100% of the Holy Spirit -- all that we will ever have.

☐ Christ, in me, is always available to destroy the works of the devil though me.

☐ God will heal through any believer; it is not about us, but about His goodness.

☐ Every believer is God's child, man's servant and the devil's master.

☐ We don't beg God for healing; we proclaim freedom for the captives or prisoners.

☐ There is no one who is so bad that God will not heal them.

- The main hindrance to healing is believing that there are hindrances to healing.

- Because Christ is in me, I already have all the power and anointing that I will need.

- God's anointing abides within me, is always ready to heal and is always on.

- God has healed most of the people that I have ministered divine healing to.

- God never withholds any good thing from me and will heal me every time I ask.

- God will heal every believer -- until He is ready to take them home to Heaven.

- Sickness is the devil's work and Jesus came to destroy the works of the devil.

- We have to maintain our healing with faith, even if we didn't have faith to be healed.

- Returning to sin can enable spirits of infirmity to come back on us.

- We must exercise our authority, refusing to receive spirits of infirmity back again.

Prayer for Divine Healing

Occasionally, Holy Spirit gives directions for intercession or praying through. He may direct us to use ingredients in this prayer and other ways of praying through.

In the Name of Jesus Christ of Nazareth, the Anointed One, we plead the blood of Jesus over _____ and us. We cancel every assignment of the enemy against _____ or us. We place a hedge of protection and a wall of Holy fire around _____, this request, all who will pray, our families, pets, possessions and properties, everyone and everything we care about. We declare that there can be no weapon formed against us, no backlash, no back-up assignments, no hexes, spells, curses or incantations in the Name of Jesus. No other name is higher than the Name of Jesus and every other name will bow to Him.

We command every demonic spirit on _____ or us to leave now in the mighty Name of Jesus and I command them to go to the dry uninhabited places and never come back, in the Name of Lord Sabaoth, Lord of Hosts. We declare that no demon can see or hear what is going on in our homes/offices and we are all in a safe place where only the Holy Spirit of God can affect us. Jesus Christ has given us power over demonic spirits; they are subject to us. (Luke 10:19-20)

We welcome You Holy Spirit and submit ourselves to your strategies to enforce the Word of God for Your precious child. We ask for wisdom knowing You will give it liberally. We believe every promise in the Word and as we declare them, the Holy Spirit will perform them. We partner with You, Spirit of Truth, and release You to fall upon _____, giving _____ comfort, wisdom, knowledge, understanding and Truth to make _____ free. Jesus send Your Word and heal _____.

We come to You Jehovah Rapha, our healer, and ask for a gift of knowledge for the true diagnosis and spirits behind these lingering infirmities. We receive the mind of Jesus Christ to discern the keys to his healing:

1. if any deeper inner healing is needed,
2. if any more repentance is needed or
3. if any more deliverance is needed.

(If you receive a word of knowledge or wisdom regarding a spiritual root, please send us the word for confirmation and for potential corporate agreement. We pray for healing, creative miracles and/or deliverance, as the Holy Spirit leads.)

We pray that ____ will have open eyes to see and ears to hear fresh direction and wisdom from You, Holy Spirit. _____ will know how to be a good steward – body, soul and spirit - and what steps to faith to take. Death and life are in the power of the tongue and we ask that _____ will know what truths and scriptures to proclaim.

Isaiah 57:18-19 18 I have seen his ways and will heal him: I will lead him also, and restore comforts unto him and to his mourners. 19 I create the (praise) fruit of the lips; Peace, peace to him that is far off, and to him that is near, saith the LORD; and I will heal him.

We have steadfast confidence in Your Word and impeccable character, O Lord. We have assurance as we choose to stand in faith, without wavering, knowing that whatever You reveal, You also heal. We have full assurance that we ask according to Your will and our prayer is answered because it is Your will! (Mark 11:22-23) We thank you ahead of time, Lord, that as we agree with You, in the power of this corporate anointing, we move the mountains because whatever we say will be done for him. (1 John 5:14-15)

We continue to pray in the Spirit without ceasing, knowing that the Holy Spirit helps us to pray, overcoming our weakness and interceding with groans that our words cannot express and intercedes in accordance with Father God's will. (Romans 8:26-27) Jesus Christ is the way, the Truth and the Life inside him. His healing, body, soul and spirit, has already been purchased with His atonement.

Lord, we ask You to touch _____ with a creative miracle in the places of ____ spirit, soul and body and that ____ will be better than new. We ask for a new impartation of the perfect love of God that casts out every fear (1 John 4:18) and fills ____ with new revelation of ____ value and identity in the Father's house. We pray that the spirit of honor, glory and blessing will be on ____ tongue. We pray resurrection power to fill ____ with faith, not only for ____ own healing but also with vision for partnering with God for healing for others. We declare that ____ weak places will be made strong and what the enemy has stolen from ____ will be paid back one hundred fold, in this life and in the life to come. (Mark 11:17-31)

We don't beg for healing but command it because it is the children's bread. We unite to renounce every agreement with the spirits of doubt, unbelief and fear and to break their power. We break the power of generational spirits of doubt, unbelief and fear. Teach ____ to swing the Sword of the Spirit with his inherited spiritual power and authority. We say ____ will receive Your forgiveness and healing and that You alone will be ____ source of comfort and power.

He forgives all my sins and heals all my diseases. Psalm 103:3

We command the spirit of infirmity and premature death to leave ____ in the mighty Name of Jesus. We join with ____ to declare, in faith with perseverance, the things ____ does not see, until ____ does see them. We pray that You will restore all that has been lost to the strongholds of fear and infirmity and that ____ will be a mighty warrior of faith. Remove the sorrow and anger and restore Christ-like emotions that the spirit of fear has over-shadowed for so long. We break the power of shame, isolation, hiddenness and denial. As ____ trades in ____ shame, ___ will not be disappointed but will receive a double portion, double honor and joy in ___ inheritance. (Isaiah 50:7, Isaiah 4:4, Isaiah 61:6-7)

We say ____ will not be intimidated by fear but will receive God's perfect love, His power and the mind of Christ. (2 Timothy 1:7) We impart faith and courage, hope and confidence to renounce all fear of the devil, fear of evil and fear of his power to hurt ____. (Luke 10:19) We say that ____ will receive Rhema Words from God and the faith to be obedient to all that God tells ____ to do. ____ will rise up as an overcomer, a mighty warrior who will execute the vengeance of our God on the forces of the enemy. ____ will overcome with the Word of God, the blood of the Lamb and the Word of ____ testimony.

I say what the Father says to say with great boldness of speech. (2 Corinthians 3:11-12)
The Lord is the strength of my life and I am not afraid. (Psalm 27:1)

2 Corinthians 10:4-6 4 For the weapons of our warfare are not carnal but mighty in God for pulling down strongholds, 5 casting down arguments and every high thing that exalts itself against the knowledge of God, bringing every thought into captivity to the obedience of Christ, 6 and being ready to punish all disobedience **when your obedience is fulfilled.**

Jealousy and Envy

<u>Some of the biggest crimes in the Bible, if not history, were motivated by jealousy and envy.</u>

Acts 7:9
9 Because the patriarchs were jealous of Joseph, they sold him as a slave into Egypt. But God was with him.
Some of the greatest crimes have been committed because of jealousy and envy.

Mark 10:29-31
29 "I tell you the truth," Jesus replied, "no one who has left home or brothers or sisters or mother or father or children or fields for me and the gospel 30 will fail to receive a hundred times as much in this present age (homes, brothers, sisters, mothers, children and fields-and with them, persecutions) and in the age to come, eternal life. 31 But many who are first will be last, and the last first."
Lord, I choose to lay it all down on the altar and receive from You in Your time.

Titus 3:2-3
2 to **slander** no one, to be peaceable and considerate, and to show true humility toward all men.
3 At one time we too were **foolish, disobedient, deceived and enslaved** by all kinds of passions and pleasures. We lived in **malice and envy, being hated and hating one another.**
Jealousy motivates us to hate those who have or who are what we want. We submit to You, Oh Lord, and give you all our passions.

Hebrews 13:5-6
5 Keep your lives free from the love of money and be content with what you have, because God has said, "Never will I leave you; never will I forsake you." 6 So we say with confidence, "The Lord is my helper; I will not be afraid. What can man do to me?"
In Christ, I am never to feel inferior, inadequate, insecure, guilty, worried, doubtful or fearful. My significance and self-worth is based on God's truth about me.

2 Timothy 2:23-26
23 Don't have anything to do with **foolish and stupid arguments**, because you know they produce quarrels. 24 And the Lord's servant must not quarrel; instead, he must be **kind to everyone, able to teach, not resentful.** 25 Those who oppose him he must **gently instruct,** in the hope that **God will grant them repentance** leading them to **a knowledge of the truth,** 26 and that they will **come to their senses** and **escape from the trap of the devil,** who has taken them captive to do his will.
Jealousy and envy are behind major competing factions in churches. (God is serious about discerning and dealing with jealousy.) Numbers 5:14, 25

Romans 16:17-18
17 I urge you, brothers, to **watch out** for those who cause divisions and put obstacles in your way that are contrary to the teaching you have learned. **Keep away** from them. 18 For such people are not serving our Lord Christ, but their own appetites. By **smooth talk and flattery they deceive the minds of naive people.**

Job 5:2
2 Resentment kills a fool, and **envy slays the simple**.

Romans 1:29-31
29 They have become filled with every kind of wickedness, evil, greed and depravity. They are full of envy, murder, strife, deceit and malice. They are gossips, 30 slanderers, God-haters, insolent, arrogant and boastful; they invent ways of doing evil; they disobey their parents; 31 they are senseless, faithless, heartless, ruthless.
Jealousy and envy seek to be first, exalting themselves.

Ezekiel 35:11
11 **therefore as surely as I live, declares the Sovereign LORD, I will treat you in accordance with the anger and jealousy you showed** in your hatred of them and I will make myself known among them when I judge you.
We will reap trouble in jealousy and envy, if we sow it. It's God's law.

Philippians 1:15-16
15 It is true that some preach Christ out of envy and rivalry, **but others out of goodwill. 16 The latter do so in love, knowing that I am put here for the defense of the gospel. No one can take my position unless I refuse to take it myself. God has chosen and gifted all of us as He wills.**

1 Timothy 6:4-6
4 he is conceited and understands nothing. **He has an unhealthy interest in controversies and quarrels about words that result in envy,** strife, malicious talk, evil suspicions 5 and constant friction between men of corrupt mind, who have been robbed of the truth and **who think that godliness is a means to financial gain.** 6 But godliness with contentment is great gain.
Lord, help me not to manipulate with "godliness" for financial gain.

Matthew 6:33-34
33 But seek first his kingdom and his righteousness, and all these things will be given to you as well. 34 Therefore do not worry about tomorrow, for tomorrow will worry about itself. Each day has enough trouble of its own.
I choose to be Your bondservant and trust everything I have and hope for to You Lord, for Your use to build Your kingdom, not mine.

Proverbs 14:30
30 A sound heart is the life of the flesh: but envy the rottenness of the bones.
Envy is a spiritual root to unhealthy bones!

Proverbs 16:24
24- Pleasant words are as a honeycomb, sweet to the soul, and health to the bones.

Matthew 5:3
3 Blessed are the poor in spirit, for theirs is the kingdom of heaven.

POP QUIZ: Sometimes, God will give us a pop quiz as a test for our own promotion. His desire is not to tempt us, but to prove our readiness for spiritual promotion. He will reveal to us whether we look at others through eyes of judgment or with His eyes, looking on the heart.

Would you forgive, restore or **even promote someone who:**

1. went on a cruise instead of prophesying to a desperate city

2. went around naked for 3 1/2 years, claiming it was a God thing

3. ate locusts, isolated himself and preached a new gospel

4. had a prostitute for a wife (his house is not in order!)

5. had been delivered of seven demons

6. got rich cheating you and your friends of your tax money

7. who had committed adultery and pre-meditated murder

8. had murdered countless Christians, this year!

9. was an illegitimate, long-haired transient with no experience

10. had been in prison more than any other applicant

11. was a woman "healer" that never graduated from high school

12. had bragged about his loyalty, then betrayed you three times

13. had been married five times and was "living with" someone?

How is your unconditional love doing? Remember that God chooses the weak and the unlikely. Often, the greater the anointing one has, the greater the blind spots. If we judge one who has "failed," we condemn ourselves to do the same. If we bow to public opinion, we may miss the opportunity to support God's anointed with unconditional love when they need it the most.

How can we minister restoration if we have no vision for those who need it? The leaders listed above, rose to greater heights after their "apparent" failure. It takes true humility to forgive. If you had known them, would you: 1. avoid them, 2. tolerate, 3. feel embarrassed, 4. forgive from a distance? or 5. Fully forgive, forgetting the past and actively invest in them, restoring them to a higher place than they were before?

**"If a man is caught in ANY TRESPASS, you who are spiritual,
restore such a one in a spirit of gentleness; each one looking to yourself,
lest you too be tempted." Galatians 6:1**

Breaking the Power of Jealousy and Envy

Lord, we confess our ancestor's sins of jealousy and envy and every way that they taught us to focus on others instead of God. We ask You to sever any cord of jealousy that may have held us since we were born, or ever before we were born.

Lord, we repent of every way that we were jealous and envious of Your plan for someone else and we rebelled against Your plan for us. We repent of every way that we rejected Your choices for us: our appearance, our intellect, our body, our talents, our parents, our siblings, our race, or the economic or social status that You chose for us.

We allow You to take every way that we are envious and bring it to death on the Cross because we cannot do it. We ask You to take every fleshly structure that cooperates with jealous competition and bring the whole structure to death. We repent of judging others who were jealous. We forgive ourselves for agreeing with spirits of jealousy and envy.

We repent for everything we have idolized (image, wealth, spouses, ministry, etc.) We repent for every area that we have been striving and competing for approval and acceptance of man instead of being satisfied with Your free unconditional love, Lord. We repent for basing our worth on the opinions of man instead of Your Word. We repent for wanting pity because You had supposedly shortchanged us.

We repent of competing and comparing or calling it a win when we were able to ace the other person out. We repent of focusing on the material world instead of seeking Your Kingdom first. We repent of defining ourselves or others by the "size" of our gifts and talents. We repent of being jealous of the attention or blessings You have given to others and repent of coveting the favor that You have seen fit to shower on others.

We repent of thinking we have to meet the standards of others in order to be accepted and approved by man. We repent of thinking that someone else's blessing can somehow limit God's faithfulness to us. We repent of believing we are less worthy based on _____ instead of receiving the fact that Jesus made us worthy when He died for us on the Cross. Forgive us for limiting Your ability to bless us God, by our own sinful reactions and for retarding our own growth and then blaming it on _____.

We choose to rejoice in Your choices for ourselves and for others. We trust that there is always enough blessing and favor to go around!

Jezebel Spirits
Review of various teachings by Rick Joyner and John Paul Jackson

The spirit of Jezebel demands recognition of itself even while serving as the enemy of the true prophetic ministry. It opposes preparing the way of the Lord, removes true prophets and seeks to replace them with false prophets. John the Baptist was persecuted by Herod's wife, the personification of Jezebel. The "blind guides" of Jesus' day could look right at John and think he was Beelzebub. Jezebel's prophets were devoted to get the people to put more faith in their sacrifices than God's.

To try to crucify ourselves vs. reckon ourselves crucified with Christ, will result in self-righteousness that has an appearance of wisdom. (Colossians 2:18-23) It keeps all our attention on how well we are doing, is self-seeking and results in our putting confidence in discipline and personal sacrifice. It motivates us to discipline through fear, guilt, pride, ambition and delighting in self-abasement more than Jesus. It will inappropriately exalt angelic revelation, visions, men or women and be inflated by them.

True spiritual maturity will always lead to humility. In AD 56 Paul visited the original Apostles and declared that they "contributed nothing to me" (Galatians 2:6) Six years later, he called himself the "least of the apostles" 1 (Corinthians 15:9) About AD 61, he declared himself to be "the very least of all saints" in Ephesians 3:8. In AD 65, he said he was the "foremost of all sinners" (1 Timothy 1:15) and was glad to have found mercy, the true antidote for the religious spirit. Even true apostles can be growing from pride in their commission toward a place of grace and humility.

When a religious spirit combines with a martyr spirit, it perceives any correction or rejection as persecution for standing for the truth. They will glory more in the death of Christ on the Cross than in His resurrection. They pervert the glory of dying for Jesus and can agree with a suicide spirit, rather than take the challenge to live for Jesus.

Self-help psychology and humanistic psychology attempt to replace the power of the Cross in the church. (Colossians 2:6-8) It is not necessary to analyze the old man but we must take our wounds to the cross for healing, forgiveness and love that will cast out fear. (2 Corinthians 11:3) Ever since the garden, Satan has been tempting us to add something to the simplicity of the Gospel.

Are You a Good Team Player?

The first characteristic of a good leader is that they are a good team player. God always makes and molds the "man" before the ministry. He will require us to work in the vineyard of another before He will give us our own vineyard. He will test our servanthood and our willingness to help build the vision of another. Our character is revealed and molded as we work in relationship with others who have different personality styles, motivations and visions than we do.

Furthermore, He will require us to be accountable to others so "iron can sharpen iron" and our rough edges will be sanded down and polished. While we learn to be flexible, patient, submissive, peaceful, faithful, supportive, joyful, encouraging, respectful etc. we are being transformed into the image of Jesus Christ.

God will even drive us into the wilderness to be tested, like He did Jesus in Matthew 4. We must learn to walk in the Spirit in all situations and to have the heart of a minister with all types of co-workers before we are ready to lead. There is a gold mine of information on team players versus Jezebel spirits in John Paul Jackson's book, *The Veiled Ploy*. I compiled the traits common to a person with a Jezebel spirit (male or female) and created this test. You can ask your receiver to take the test without revealing the purpose.

Do others see you as a good team player?

TEST YOURSELF: Put yourself in the shoes of your family or leadership. If we ask them, would they say that you have these characteristics? Pretend that they were rating your support and place the appropriate number by each line.

0 - never 1- rarely 2 - sometimes 3 - usually 4 - mostly

Make your desires known in the form of a demand or you command them?
Have negative reactions to their new ideas, criticize and complain?
Make them feel disrespected, fearful, hopeless, disillusioned or discouraged?
Feel resentful over past issues when they did not do it your way?
Pull apart from them in a crises rather than pull together?

Become pushy, elevating your insights and spiritual revelation over theirs?
Usurp authority or undermine other people's confidence in their qualifications?
Compare them negatively to your own gifts and abilities?
Don't fit in with or give full support to their vision, demonstrating unfaithfulness?
Often start to dominate with words, your feelings, attitudes or use tears?

Seduce others to separate or divide with your false accusations?
Have sacrificed harmony and unity just to prove your point?
Have become rigid, hard-nosed or unyielding rather than flexible?
Have presented them as unwelcome, mediocre or as a liability?
Become disloyal under stress, causing others to dislike and reject them?

Have to be in the lead or try to manipulate your way into positions?
Shut down communication, pout or withdraw to punish them?
Have unrealistic expectations and exert undue pressure on them to perform?
Undermine other's ability to trust their leadership by your innuendos or gossip?
Cause their progress to be delayed or their contributions to be unheard?

Must have special attention, be catered to or want to be on a pedestal?
Distract the focus of the house from being on Jesus to being on yourself?

Tend to do your part late, half-way or with a less than cheerful attitude?
Have to be thanked, appreciated or rewarded to keep working?
Require coaching and supervision to complete basic job descriptions?

Cause others to doubt the intentions and motivations of the leadership?
Try to control their direction, anointing or compete for righteousness?
Tend to misrepresent their actions and their heart to others?
Emphasize their weaknesses and don't forget their past mistakes?
Focus on your own short-term desires rather than long term (eternal) goals?

—————————————————————

You can subtract all your points from 120 (i.e. 120-40=80) We let you start with 120 to give you the benefit of the doubt.

If you still failed, you are surely sowing seed that you will not want to reap when you are elevated to leadership.

<u>Demonic Oppression and Bondage</u>
1. **confess** my sin of agreeing with demonic spirits of _____ and forgive all who have influenced me to sin.
2. I **repent** for giving place to the demons of _____.
3. **I forgive** myself for the pain and limitations I have allowed the demons to inflict upon me.
4. In the Name of Jesus, I **renounce** and break all agreement with the demons (stronghold) of _____, including all associated demons of _____, _____, _____, _____, _____, _____, etc.
5. I **take authority** over the demons (stronghold) of _____ and command you demons of _____ to leave me/us now based on the finished work of Christ on the Cross and His shed Blood.
6. In the Name of Jesus Christ of Nazareth, the Anointed One, Who has given me spiritual authority, I **command** the demons of _____ to go to the dry uninhabited places and never come back.
7. In its place I choose to **receive God's truth that says** _____.

Any number of other spirits may manifest when you come against a Jezebel spirt. Remember to love the person and come against these demonic spirits. For instance, "self-pity" may claim that the receiver has been misunderstood and falsely accused. An "anti-Christ" spirit may turn against you overtly instead of covertly. Be ready to see this battle through once you stir it up.

Loving Your Neighbor as Yourself

Did you know that Jesus said the "greatest commandment' includes loving your neighbor as yourself?
Luke 10:27 He answered: "'Love the Lord your God with all your heart and with all your soul and with all you strength and with all your mind'; and, 'Love your neighbor as yourself.'" They will know we are Christians by our love? Yes, your ability to LOVE your neighbor is far more important that any gift, talent, skill, calling or resume. Who is your neighbor?

God's plan is for us to love God with our whole heart and to love others and as we love ourselves. His plan is to reconcile us to Himself, to others and to ourselves, in a new oneness. The problem is that most of us have not received Father God's love and do not know how to love ourselves. We measure ourselves and others on a performance basis.

The devil's plan has always been to separate you from others, from God, from yourself and ultimately to destroy your ability to love. He seeks to erode our love by attacking us through others and through our own minds. Usually, how we see God, has been distorted by our perceptions of human father figures around us. The devil's goal is to block us from seeing God's love and seeing ourselves as God sees us. He would take over, establishing a stronghold in our hearts that says we are not loved, not loveable and not able to love others as we should.

Luke 11:21-22
21 "When a strong man, fully armed, guards his own house, his possessions are safe. 22 But when someone stronger attacks and overpowers him, **he takes away the armor** in which the man trusted and divides up the spoils.
We invite you Jesus, to overpower the strongman who has our houses and take away the armor that he convinced us to trust instead of You.

He also speaks through demonic spirits that barrage us with lies about who we are, what people think of us, and lies about what God thinks of us. Doctor Henry Wright, Founder of Be in Health, furnished us with a list of unloving spirits, who are assigned to undermine our self-esteem and our ability to trust in a loving God.

TEST YOURSELF FOR THESE SPIRITS: See if you relate to any of these voices who would prevent you from loving others as you love yourself.

Self-rejection - Says I am the non-person of the family, calls me names, says my opinions and preferences are not important.

Self-hatred - Uses my voice to tell me that I hate myself, then my body/soul/spirit connection reacts with infirmities, auto-immune illnesses and diseases of unknown causes.

Competition - Says I must always compete, win and manipulate for self-promotion. I cannot defer to others easily, as in Matthew 5, 6 and 7.

Self-pride - Causes me to lust for a position, a relationship or material things to complete myself or to maximize my potential.

Selfishness - Makes me hypersensitive to whether I am getting my share (i.e. of the love,) when I want it and how I want it.

Exalted "I" and "I will" - The Devil suggests that I can do it independently, by myself, in my own strength, with my own talents, gifts and resources (Isaiah 14).

Rebellion - I reject God's choices for me: i.e. my IQ, appearance, body, parents, race, birthplace, etc.

Attention getting - I demand attention from people before they even have a chance to offer their love or at least before they can reject me. I am easy prey for counterfeit love.

Excessive talkativeness - Drives me to dominate conversations with my opinions, needs, feelings, knowledge or just chit chat.

Insecurity - Sets me up to be easily offended, to over react, to feel devalued and to take things personally.

Fabricated self - We prematurely create a niche for ourselves and tend to project ourselves as more qualified than we are.

Unworthiness - We fear that we are unworthy of blessing (based on our performance.)

Self-deprecation - We torture ourselves by calling ourselves names, cutting ourselves down (sometimes as humor,) minimize our strengths and maximize our faults.

Self-comparison - Causes me to measure myself negatively in contrast to the progress, blessings, gifts, talents and accomplishments of others.

Self-assertion - I am not just asking for what I need; I demand with pressure, control or manipulation.

Self-deception - I rationalize that sinful reactions, beliefs and behaviors are OK; I defend them when others try to tell me the truth.

Self-questioning - I constantly doubt God's truth about myself, my perceptions, and my abilities. I tend to believe that I will choose unwisely.

Self-indulgence - I am addicted to ineffective coping mechanisms like overspending, binge eating, kleptomania, drug abuse or therapy that "never seems to take effect!"

Self-idolatry - I obsess about my agenda, my needs, my successes and my glory instead of God's purposes and plans.

Perfection - Says that I can only feel good about myself if my performance meets the standards of others, my unreasonably high standards or is perfect (and of course it is not.)

Self-accusation - Refuses to acknowledge the progress or growth in my life; identifies me with my past failures and projects my past onto my future.

Self-condemnation - "I am" a failure, inadequate, inferior, unattractive, to blame and unlovable. I believe that I am shameful because I am basically defective.

Self-bitterness - I keep a record of my failures, withholding forgiveness from myself, and resenting myself for being imperfect.

Unforgiveness toward yourself - False humility tells me that it is more holy not to forgive myself and that I should punish myself.

Need for approval - I try to earn "unconditional love and acceptance" (oxymoron) by meeting the supposed expectations of others.

Not necessary, not needed - I agree with devaluating condescending lies and conclude that I not valuable and that my contributions are not worthwhile.

Self-doubt and unbelief - I disqualify myself, settle for less, believe I am the most unlikely to be chosen and cannot believe that God could love me.

Self-denial - I tend to exclude myself, isolate myself and to suffer vs. asking for what I need

Self-absorption - I obsess on analyzing myself, my interests, my needs, figuring out my own way or ruminating about my issues.

Self-abuse - I blame myself, drive myself with drugs or unrealistic demands, deny basic needs, volunteer for martyrdom, victimize myself, am addicted to self-destructive behaviors.

Self-pity - I accept the identity of a victim, stuck in the past, who is not healed. I insist that I should be pitied rather than believe that I can release my pain to Jesus to heal.

Self-sabotage - I "shoot myself in the foot" because I am afraid to receive promotion, compliments or great opportunities. I disqualify myself when I am afraid of succeeding; I push love away for fear of inevitable rejection.

Self-annihilation or elimination - I have a plan to kill myself, make suicidal gestures or actually attempt suicide.

If you find that these spirits have implanted lies in your mind, you can pray, repent and renounce your agreements with them. First, write the lies that Satan uses to convince you that you are not loved, not loveable or not able to love others. Repent, renounce and replace!

Ungodly Beliefs

1. I *confess* my sin (and if appropriate, my ancestor's sin) of believing the ungodly belief that _____ and for any way I have **blamed you** God.

2. I *forgive* those who contributed to my forming this UGB, including myself.

3. I ask You, Lord, to **forgive me** for living my life by it and for anyway I have judged others, based on this UGB.

4. I *forgive* myself for believing this ungodly belief.

5. I *renounce* and *break* my agreement with this UGB, and the agreement that I have had with deception, the power of darkness, and with demons.

6. I *choose* to accept and **believe** the GB that

_____.

I recognize that I have been believing the lies of the devil and repent.

Demonic Oppression and Bondage

1. **confess** my sin of agreeing with demonic spirits of _____ and forgive all who have influenced me to sin.

2. I **repent** for giving place to the demons of _____.

3. **I forgive** myself for the pain and limitations I have allowed the demons to inflict upon me.

4. In the Name of Jesus, I **renounce** and break all agreement with the demons (stronghold) of _____, including all associated demons of _____, _____, _____, _____, _____, _____, etc.

5. I **take authority** over the demons (stronghold) of _____ and command you demons of _____ to leave me/us now based on the finished work of Christ on the Cross and His shed Blood.

6. In the Name of Jesus Christ of Nazareth, the Anointed One, Who has given me spiritual authority, I **command** the demons of _____ to go to the dry uninhabited places and never come back.

7. In its place I choose to **receive God's truth that says**

_____.

Father, I ask you to fill every empty place in me with Your life and peace. I choose to receive God's truth about me: Because of what Jesus Christ has done for me on the cross, He made me righteous, holy and blameless in His site. (Ephesians 1:4 and Romans 5:18) I agree with God's truth that I am precious, loveable, totally forgiven, unconditionally loved and accepted, completely apart from my performance. I choose to receive all the blessings that I have been afraid to receive. I ask You to restore me to Your purposes and plans. (Romans 8) Amen

Early Wounds that Need Healing

This list is based on insight from <u>Restoring the Christian Family</u> by John and Paula Sandford

Many of us were deeply bruised, even as babies, even before we could talk. Unfortunately, many of our ungodly beliefs today are still based on beliefs that we developed during traumatic times in our childhood. Our view of God has been affected as well.

Ask God if you had any of these pre-natal or childhood wounds:

☐   *I was not planned; I have to prove that I have a right to be here.*

☐   *My mother tried to abort me; each year at that time I feel depressed.*

☐   *I was illegitimate; I am a source of shame and disappointment.*

☐   *Mother and I were abused before I was born; I am a victim.*

☐   *I was untimely and inconvenient; I am a problem.*

☐   *I was born the wrong sex; I must be homosexual.*

☐   *My mother gave me away; people don't keep their commitments to me.*

☐   *I took up finances or love that others needed; I am a burden.*

☐   *I was always in childcare; I don't know how to bond with people.*

☐   *My father didn't care; I don't know my value or true identity.*

☐   *My mother was anxious, insecure and fearful; I have to fix it for her.*

☐   *I was afraid of my father; authorities don't have my best interest at heart.*

☐   *I was potty-trained with abuse; I am uptight, nervous and high-strung.*

☐   *I wasn't allowed to say "No;" I can't set and enforce my boundaries.*

☐   *I was not allowed to be "me;" I am defined by otheer's values and needs.*

☐   *My father abandoned me; I am not valuable or loveable.*

☐   *My parent didn't take care about me; I have to take care of myself.*

☐   *My parent was not affectionate; I can't give and receive affection.*

☐   *I was constantly criticized and misunderstood; I don't belong.*

☐   *My parents bought me with things; I must buy people and their love.*

☐   *I could not live up to my parent's standards; I have to earn acceptance.*

☐   *I wasn't allowed or trusted to make my own choices; I am indecisive.*

☐   *My parent was a perfectionist; I procrastinate if I can't do it perfectly.*

☐   *My parents were horrible; God must not love me like He does other people.*

☐   *My father was simply not there for me; God is not there for me either.*

☐   *My parents didn't listen to me; God doesn't answer my prayers.*

☐   *I was not allowed to share my feelings; it is not OK to be real.*

1 Peter 3:8-10

8 Finally, all of you, live in harmony with one another; be sympathetic, love as brothers, be compassionate and humble. 9 Do not repay evil with evil or insult with insult, but with blessing, because to this you were called so that you may inherit a blessing. 10 For, "Whoever would love life and see good days must keep his tongue from evil and his lips from deceitful speech."

I repent of agreeing with unloving spirits who repay evil with evil, insult or abuse.

Next, I would lead them to pray over the hurts we have already identified. More often than not, Jesus will take over this session if allowed. Remember to wait on the Lord after line one.

Soul/Spirit Hurts

1. I *Ask* You Holy Spirit to reveal the hurt You want to heal today (**Listen/watch** patiently as He tells or shows it to you.)

2. (Be honest with God about how you feel.) Lord, I pour out my heart about the hurt, pain, fear, anger, frustration …

3. I *forgive* _____ (parents, siblings, peers, others) for inflicting this hurt and causing me pain.

4. I ask you to **forgive me,** Lord, for hurting others out of my hurt. I *repent* of this sinful reaction, sinful behavior and my attitude.

5. I *forgive* myself for letting this hurt control me and open doors to strongholds in my life.

6. I **release** this hurt to You, Lord, and I **receive** Your healing touch. Please show me or tell me how You are healing me today. **Listen/watch** as He reveals. (Listen several minutes for Jesus to tell you or show you how He is healing you today.)

7. **Thank you** for redeeming every hurt and taking the pain.

Many times, Holy Spirit will immediately take them from these hurts down to root hurts and disappointments with God. We follow His leading and continue in prayer afterward.

Disappointment with God

Dear God, I **confess** that I have misjudged You and blamed You for things that You did not do. I choose to repent and stop today.

1. I ask You to **forgive me** for my sins against You.

2. I **affirm** that You are good and want only the best for me.

3. I choose to **receive You** as Lord my life and to **believe** You cause all things to work together for good, to mature me so I will be able to rule and reign with You in eternity.

4. I **put the "blame"** where it really belongs, on Satan's kingdom. I choose to stop blaming You, God, and will take responsibility for my own choices under the guidance and control of the Holy Spirit.

5. **Thank You** Lord for new freedom, new ability to trust and a renewed relationship with You. I receive it in the Name of Jesus.

Ask Holy Spirit if other prayers on the RPM prayer card apply here.

Lusts, Love or Codependency?

It was difficult to choose which issues to put in this first manual. I have asked God to tell me which issues are most common to man (or woman.) One of them is lust.

Rather than try to teach on the subject, once again, I will share tools to help our receivers discern themselves rightly and to identify what restoration prayers they need.

Do you spend more time and energy thinking about

LUST	LOVE
Fireworks and butterflies	Building stability
Their outward appearance	Their beautiful soul and spirit
What you can get from them	What you can give to them
Dressing to the nines or tens	Putting on the character of Christ
Overlook serious flaws	Think short and long term
What they want to hear you say	Active listening and being real
Surface chit chat to keep it light	Getting to know their heart
Hiding your weakness or problems	Being accepted as you are
Living for the moment	Living for long term relationship
Putting up your best front	Building a spiritual foundation
Physical attraction and chemistry	Spiritual compatibility
Conditional selfish faithfulness	Unconditional love and commitment
Mostly sex without intimacy	Intimacy and real vulnerability
Getting your needs met	Completing your partner
Skipping the friend stage	Bonding with your life long best friend
Sex, not conversation	Spending quality time sharing
Isolating from their family	Building relationships
The challenge of the "chase"	Learning how to love

Other evidences of lust and unhealthy codependent ways of relating are:
Making commitments based on a feeling of love at first site or infatuation.
Denying your own core values or beliefs in order to be with someone.
Addiction to sex with multiple partners or strangers. Impulsivity.
Ignoring red flags and trusting too much or an inability to trust.
Controlling, manipulating and ignoring good boundaries.
Fear of intimacy or only being involved with people who are emotionally unavailable.
Inability to break off painful relationships for fear of not getting another.
Using sex to deal with other issues like anxiety, depression or shame.
Letting fear of abandonment drive you to an impulsive unhealthy rendezvous.
Choosing partners whom you think need fixing and want your help.
Continuing relationships because "they need me" instead choosing real love.
Using self-deception to convince yourself that you will change them.
Denying the chaotic issues in your own life while you focus on fixing another.
Feeling good about choosing partners who are "beneath you."

See the RPM prayers for the prayer to cast out Demonic Oppression in Exhibits.

Prayers for Deliverance and Renunciation of Sexual Sin. Adapted from Apostle John Eckhardt's book, *Prayers that Rout Demons*

In the Name of Jesus Christ, Son of God, Most high …

I renounce all sexual sin that I have been involved with in the past, including fornication, masturbation, pornography, perversion, fantasy, and adultery in the name of Jesus.

I break all curses of adultery, perversion, fornication, lust, incest, rape, molestation, illegitimacy, harlotry, and polygamy in the name of Jesus.

I command all spirits of lust and perversion to come out of my stomach, genitals, eyes, mind, mouth, hands, and blood in the name of Jesus.

I present my body to the Lord as a living sacrifice (Romans 12:1). My members are the members of Christ. I will not let them be the members of a harlot (1 Corinthians 6:15).

I release the fire of God to burn out all unclean lust from my life in the name of Jesus.

I break all ungodly soul ties with former lovers and sexual partners in the name of Jesus.

I cast out all spirits of loneliness that would drive me to ungodly sexual relationships in the name of Jesus.

I command all spirits of hereditary lusts from my ancestors to come out in the name of Jesus. I command all spirits of witchcraft that work with lust to leave in the name of Jesus.

I take authority over my thoughts and bind all spirits of fantasy and lustful thinking in the name of Jesus.

I cast out all marriage-breaking spirits of lust that would break covenant in the name of Jesus. I cast out and loose myself from any spirit demonic spouses and spirits of incubus and succubus in the name of Jesus.

I cast out all spirits of perversion, including Moabite and Ammonite spirits of lust, in the name of Jesus. I receive the spirit of holiness in my life to walk in sexual purity in the name of Jesus (Romans 1:4).

I loose myself from the spirit of the world, the lust of the flesh, the lust of the eyes, and the pride of life. I overcome the world through the power of the Holy Spirit (1 John 2:16).

I am crucified with Christ. I mortify my members. I do not let sin reign in my body, and I will not obey its lust (Romans 6:6–12).

Prophetic Gifts, Tongues and the Holy Spirit

Want verses on the Holy Spirit?

Operating in individuals? In churches?
In the Old Testament? In the New Testament?
In today's world? How to know the Holy Spirit?
The baptism of the Spirit?

I. Old Testament examples of the Holy Spirit's work.

Numbers 11:25 "Then the LORD came down in the cloud and spoke to him; and He took of the Spirit who was upon him and placed *Him* upon the seventy elders. And when the **Spirit rested upon them,** they **prophesied**. But they did not do it again.' (NASB)

(Compare versions and the literal Hebrew)

Numbers 11:25 "And the LORD came down in a cloud, and spake unto him, and took of the spirit that was upon him, and gave it unto the seventy elders: and it came to pass, that, when the **spirit rested upon them**, they **prophesied**, and did not cease." (KJV) (Correct according to the literal translation)

1 Samuel 10:6 "Then the Spirit of the LORD will come upon you mightily, and you shall **prophesy** with them and be changed into another man."

1 Samuel 10:10 "When they came to the hill there, behold, a group of prophets met him; and the **Spirit of God came upon him mightily**, so that he **prophesied** among them."

II. How does the Holy Spirit manifest and work?

Ephesians 1:13 "In Him, you also, after listening to the message of truth, the gospel of your salvation—having also believed, you were **sealed in Him** with the Holy Spirit of promise,"

John 3:34 "For He whom God has sent **speaks the words of God**; for He gives the **Spirit without measure.**"

Romans 8:14 "For all who are being **led by the Spirit of God**, these are sons of God."

Acts 1:8 "but you will receive power when the Holy Spirit has come upon you; and you shall **be My witnesses** both in Jerusalem, and in all Judea and Samaria, and even to the remotest part of the earth."

1 John 2:27 "As for you, the anointing which you received from Him abides in you, and you have no need for anyone to teach you; but as **His anointing teaches you about all things**, and is true and is not a lie, and just as it has taught you, you abide in Him."

III. Is baptism of the Holy Spirit a scriptural term?

John 1:33 "I did not recognize Him, but He who sent me to baptize in water said to me, 'He upon whom you see the Spirit descending and remaining upon Him, this is the One **[Jesus] who baptizes in the Holy Spirit.' "**

Acts 1:4,5 " Gathering them together, He commanded them not to leave Jerusalem, but to wait for what the Father had promised, 'Which,' *He said*, 'you heard of from Me; for John baptized with water, but you will be **baptized with the Holy Spirit** not many days from now.' "

IV. What is the relationship of Jesus to the Baptism of the Holy Spirit?

John 20:22 "And when He had said this, He breathed on them and said to them, **"Receive the Holy Spirit."**

John 7:38, 39 "He who believes in Me, as the Scripture said, 'From his innermost being will flow rivers of living water.' " [39] But this He spoke of the Spirit, whom those who believed in Him were to receive; for the **Spirit was not yet *given*,** because Jesus was not yet glorified."

V. What is the baptism of the Holy Spirit vs. receiving the Holy Spirit at salvation?

Acts 1:5 "John baptized with water, but **in a few days** you will be baptized with the Holy Spirit."

Acts 1:8 " 'but you will **receive power** when the Holy Spirit has come upon you; and you **shall be My witnesses** both in Jerusalem, and in all Judea and Samaria, and even to the remotest part of the earth.' "

Acts 19:2 "He said to them, 'Did you **receive the Holy Spirit** when you believed?' [had only believed in John] And they said to him, 'No, we have not even heard whether there is a Holy Spirit.' "

Acts 8:15-16 "who came down and prayed for them that they **might receive the Holy Spirit.** For He had **not yet fallen upon any of them**; they had **simply been baptized in the name of the Lord Jesus."**

Acts 2:38-39 "Peter said to them, 'Repent, and each of you be baptized in the name of Jesus Christ for the forgiveness of your sins; and you will **receive the gift of the Holy Spirit.** [39] For the promise is for you and your children and for all who are far off, as many as the Lord our God will call to Himself.' "

Luke 24:49 " 'And behold, I am sending forth the promise of My Father upon you; but you are to stay in the city until you are **clothed with power from on high.'** "

VI. Who may receive the baptism of the Holy Spirit?

Mark 16:17 "These signs will accompany **those who have believed**: in My name they will cast out demons, they will speak with new tongues;"

Acts 2:38-39 38 "Peter said to them, 'Repent, and each of you be baptized in the name of Jesus Christ for the forgiveness of your sins; and you will receive the gift of the Holy Spirit. [39] For the promise is **for you and your children** and for all who are far off, as many as the Lord our God will call to Himself.' "

VII. Evidences

Acts 2:4 "And they were all filled with the Holy Spirit and began to speak with other **tongues**, as the Spirit was giving them utterance."

Acts 10:44-45 44 While Peter was still speaking these words, the Holy Spirit fell upon all those who were listening to the message. 45 All the circumcised believers who came with Peter were amazed, because the gift of the Holy Spirit had been poured out on the Gentiles also. 46 For they were hearing them speaking with **tongues and exalting God**.

Acts 19:6 And when Paul had laid his hands upon them, the Holy Spirit came on them, and they began speaking with **tongues and prophesying**.

Matthew 3:11 "As for me, I baptize you with water for repentance, but He who is coming after me is mightier than I, and I am not fit to remove His sandals; He will baptize you with the Holy Spirit **and fire**."

1 Corinthians 14:15 "What is the outcome then? I will pray with the spirit and I will pray with the mind also; I will **sing with the spirit** and I will sing with the mind also."

Jude 20 "But you, beloved, building yourselves up on your most holy faith, **praying in the Holy Spirit,**"

VIII. How do you receive the Baptism of the Holy Spirit?

Romans 10:17 "So faith comes from hearing, and **hearing by the word of Christ.**"

Galatians 3:2 "This is the only thing I want to find out from you: did you receive the Spirit by the works of the Law, or by **hearing with faith?**"

Luke 11:10, 13b "For everyone who **asks**, receives; and he who **seeks, finds**; and to him who knocks, it will be opened. 13b ... how much more will your heavenly Father give the Holy Spirit to **those who ask** Him?"

IX. Reasons to speak in other Tongues and to Prophesy

Mark 16:17 "These **signs will accompany** those who have believed: in My name they will cast out demons, they will speak with new tongues;"

1 Corinthians 14:4 "One who speaks in a tongue **edifies himself**; but one who prophesies edifies the church."

Ephesians 6:18 "With all **prayer and petition pray at all times in the Spirit**, and with this in view, be on the alert with all perseverance and petition for all the saints,"

1 Corinthians 14:1-5 1 "Pursue love, and desire spiritual gifts, but especially that you may **prophesy**. 2 For he who speaks in a tongue does not speak to men but to God, for no one understands him; however, **in the spirit he speaks mysteries**. 3 But he who prophesies **speaks edification and exhortation and comfort** to men. 4 He who speaks in a tongue edifies himself, but he who **prophesies edifies the church**. 5 I wish you all spoke with tongues, but even more that you prophesied; for **he who prophesies is greater than he who speaks with tongues**, unless indeed he interprets, that the church may receive edification."

1 Corinthians 14:21 "In the Law it is written, 'BY MEN OF STRANGE TONGUES AND BY THE LIPS OF STRANGERS I WILL SPEAK TO THIS PEOPLE, AND EVEN SO THEY WILL NOT LISTEN TO ME,' says the Lord."

Conclusion
Matthew 7:7 "**Ask**, and it will be given to you; **seek**, and you will find; **knock**, and it will be opened to you."

Matthew 5:6 "Blessed are those who **hunger and thirst** for righteousness, for they shall be satisfied."

Prophetic Ministry Guidelines

Seeing (or hearing) is believing! I first received personal prophetic ministry in 1992 and was blown away as Father God spoke to the deepest needs in my heart, in ways that may have sounded general to onlookers but were proof positive to me. I have found that most church people begin to believe in prophecy after they once hear God's heart for them!

Our weekly online radio program, Cross Walk Talk, definitely has more callers when I offer personal prophetic ministry to callers. God is always willing to speak to each one, sharing His heart for each caller. Father God often includes confirmation, exhortation, consolation and impartation. He not only speaks through prophecy but imparts His love, grace, vision and power to accomplish His will. God reads our mail and proves that He hears us.

Some have received vision or direction for their gifts, callings, business, training, mentoring or ministry. Some receive healing for their identity, revelation on who they are in Christ and their important contributions to the family of God. The Lord of Hosts is also hard at work destroying the works of the devil and setting people free. I was grateful for the prophetic ministry guidelines that are used in Christian International churches. See a summary below.

Guidelines: Receiving Personal Prophecy

- Immediately write out your personal prophecy. If your Word was recorded, as you listen to it later, more revelation will come to you than was apparent at first. You want to receive all that God intends. **1Timothy 4:14, 15** states that we should not neglect the gift that is in us by prophecy so we will want to re-visit our prophecy frequently (weekly is recommended). **Proverbs 24:6, Deuteronomy 29:29, James 1:21, 3:17, Matthew 21:21, Psalm 34:2**
- According to **Romans 8:16** we need a witness with the prophecy by the Holy Spirit in us (does it ring true in our own spirit where Holy Spirit abides; so we sense life in it). In conjunction with this is judging and weighing the word of personal prophecy by established Biblical principles (according to the Word of God). Included in establishing our prophecy is discussing our prophecy with our leaders (even if they are the ones who gave the prophecy or it was given in their presence). We will want wise counsel for our victory and safety. **Proverbs 24:6**
- Receive your prophecy with faith, humility, meekness, vision and an open heart. Faith is having confidence that God does have a personal plan for you and only has your best interest at heart. **Hebrews 4:2, Deuteronomy 29:29, James 1:21, 3:17, Matthew 21:21, Psalm 34:2**
- Waging a good warfare with your prophecy is next. 1 Timothy 1:18, 19 We are to declare and decree our prophecy so that we may (v. 19) hold fast to faith. We will need to believe and have faith for our prophecy to come to fruition just as Abraham didn't grow weak in faith as he gave praise and glory to God, fully persuaded that what God had promised (Abraham was the father of many nations) He was able to perform and would deliver.

Romans 4:16-21 So, thanking God and praising Him for the manifestation of the prophecy is also part of our warfare.

- Act upon your prophetic word when you have received confirmation and counsel. Do nothing different unless definitely directed, following all directions to the detail and cooperating with God, neither going ahead of Him nor lagging behind. Examples: **David, 1 Samuel 16:13, Jehu, 2 Kings 9, and Jehoshaphat, 2 Chronicles 20, Matthew 13:18,23**

- Wait patiently upon your prophetic word as timing is very important. **Isaiah 40:31, Psalm 27:14, 37:7, Hosea 12:6, Hebrews 6:11,12** When patience is not applied and when we don't wait on the Lord we may produce an Ishmael like Abraham and Sara (a counterfeit, not of God) or simply negate our prophecy like Saul, who, anointed by the Lord as King ended up losing that position. We must be developed before our ministry is manifested. If our Lord had to be equipped by having human experience for His office as High Priest then we will need to be perfected as well. **Hebrews 2:6-10** Jesus was prepared for 30 years for only 3 years of earthly ministry.

Fulfillment of personal prophecy is always conditional on the receiver's response, such as personal commitment, integrity, steps of obedience, God's timing and other factors such as are impressed upon your spirit by Holy Spirit. We must choose to persevere and not despise our prophecies by staying thankful. **1 Thessalonians 5: 18-20**

Guidelines: Discerning Personal Prophetic Ministry

- All personal prophecy must be judged by proven prophetic principles. We recommend that you consult with mature spiritual leadership regarding your prophetic Word. Often your leadership will be of great help in interpretation.

- Personal prophecy is partial, progressive and conditional. What you will receive will only be part of God's counsel for your life. You must be obedient to the part you have received from God if you are to progress into further revelation. Disobedience can nullify your prophetic word.

- Prophecy does not authenticate character. The absence of rebuke or correction in a prophetic word in no way justifies the character or lifestyle of the individual receiving it. If God fails to mention a particular sin, it doesn't mean that He either doesn't know or doesn't care. Personal prophecy was never given for the purpose of exposing people's sins. We don't judge our "correctness" by personal prophecy, but by the Word of God.

- Be aware of prophetic terminology and tenses. Words such as "now," "today," "soon," "tomorrow," "new," and others may mean something entirely different from what we had imagined. Stay open to God and seek wise counsel. Something prophesied in the present tense may actually refer to something in the future, and vice versa.

- Don't make major decisions based on a prophetic Word. It was never God's intent for you to be led by prophecy alone, but to be "led by the Spirit" (Romans 8:14). Don't neglect God's Word, prayer, wisdom, mature counsel and your inward spiritual witness when making major decisions.

- All revelation is subject to the authority of God's written Word (The Bible). Let the Word of God have the final authority in your life in doctrine, belief, life and conduct.

- Keep a record of your personal prophecies. Don't just read it once and discard it, but use it to strategically focus your prayers for spiritual breakthrough. Use the same principles of Scripture to establish faith for results.

- Never use personal prophecy to justify a personal decision, position or action. This is called spiritual pride and can lead to deception. Be careful that you do not allow your personal desires, wants and aspirations to cloud or influence your judgment and ability to properly interpret and respond to God's Word for your life.

- Don't be too quick to judge a prophetic Word as false. There are many variables that go into making a prophetic Word come to pass. Remember, all prophecy is conditional. Timing, prayer, faith, obedience and preparation are also key issues.

- Things may go completely opposite of what was prophesied to you for a season. After you have received a prophetic Word things may get worse before they get better. Patiently hold fast to the promises of God (Hebrews 6:11, 12).

- Personal prophecy is not limited to confirmation. Some teach that personal prophecy should always be a confirmation; however, there is no biblical basis for such a position. If you hear something that is totally new to you, seek God for further clarity and confirmation. If necessary, shelve it but don't discard it.

- Present-day prophets are not infallible. Even a true prophet is capable of making mistakes or mixing a true Word with error. Just as we should never accept a false prophet because of a true prophecy, we should never reject a true prophet because of a false prophecy. If after careful judgment part or all of your prophetic Word is found to be inaccurate, then bring it to their attention in a spirit of meekness rather than condemnation. Remember Paul's admonition to "Prove (test) all things; hold fast to that which is good" (1 Thessalonians 5: 21).

For more information about the prophetic, see articles on Hearing God in the left site menu at www.CrossWalkLife.com or search our search box for Role of Prophets Today .

What has Father God told you?

Rejection, Whether Real or Imagined

It was when I began to pray scripture strategies in order to tear down my own strongholds that I realized the importance of ministry to tear down the stronghold of rejection. After praying scriptures on eight strongholds for three months, I realized I had been healed of twenty-four diagnoses. It was when I came against the lies of rejection that I realized that God's Truth had healed me. Let me slow down a little on this one and share an article that my alumni wrote.

Are You Rejected or Accepted?

We rely so much on the acceptance of others that we forget that God accepts us *no matter what*. We don't have to do anything to deserve His love because He already loves us perfectly.

A lot of us struggle with rejection. Someone may say something and you automatically think, "They're rejecting me. They don't appreciate me. They don't really love me." Rejection causes us to think we aren't accepted by people and most importantly, by God.

Know who you are in Christ! You are deeply loved and accepted in Christ! Combat lies with the Truth. The devil flees from Truth. Allow your soul to line up with your spirit as you choose to walk in agreement with Jesus. First you have to realize how much He loves you.

You may feel like you aren't accepted. However, wasn't His death enough to pay your debt? Saying you're not accepted implies that His death wasn't enough. You have been redeemed by His works, not yours. You've been *completely* forgiven. Not partially. Completely.

You're accepted because of what Christ did, not what you do. God has chosen us. He desires us. He didn't necessarily *need* us when He created us. He created us because He *wanted* us. He wants you. He loves you. He wouldn't go through all of the pain and suffering of dying on the Cross for nothing. "Let us fix our eyes on Jesus, the author and perfecter of our faith, who for the joy set before Him endured the cross, scorning its shame, and sat down at the right hand of the throne of God." (Hebrews 12:2) You are that joy that He looked forward to. He endured the Cross for *you*.

Jesus "heals the brokenhearted and binds up their wounds." (Psalms 147:3) Satan comes to break our hearts, damage our souls, and wound us. He wants to separate us from Jesus, ourselves and others. As he whispers in our ears, "He doesn't really love you. You have to *work* for His love. You aren't accepted. I mean, come on! Look at you! You do nothing but sin! How could He love you if all you do is hurt Him?" Satan is very good at getting us to believe these are our own thoughts. We start to spiral down into feeling rejected and unloved. Resist the devil, and he will flee!

Anything that we need in order to glorify Christ is within our reach. He makes everything available to us. All His attributes are available to us. He wouldn't wave something in our face, teasing us. He wants us to have it. "…Ask and you will receive, and your joy will be complete." (John 16:24) We have no reason to look at others in envy when we know that everything we need to spread His love is available to us! Why should we think, "God must not love me. That's why He isn't giving me this"? He is faithful. Let your requests be known to Him! He does care about you. We can trust the unchanging perfect character of God.

First we need to check our motivations. Is your motivation to glorify yourself or Christ? Do you want something to make yourself look good? Are you doing good works to express Christ's love or to earn approval, acceptance, and praise from others? Are you defined by the opinions of others? We should desire only to glorify Him, our Creator and Savior of our souls.

When you begin to work wanting only God's approval, you begin to stop worrying whether or not someone *sees* your hard work. When someone doesn't notice, you don't feel unloved and unappreciated because you were doing it for Christ, anyway! Sometimes we work hard to get the acceptance and approval of others. However, even when they tell us they appreciate our hard work, the spirit of rejection still tells us, "They don't know the real you. If they did, they wouldn't be saying that." When we're working to please Him and Him alone, we know we're already accepted! Even when we do a horrible job on something, He still loves us! His love is completely and entirely unconditional. It doesn't matter how bad we mess something up. He wants us to use those events as lessons. You're harder on yourself than He is.

Are you working so hard in order to get closer to Him? Or are you working hard because you're simply doing it out of love for Him? Motives are extremely important. I have to stop and check my motives occasionally when working on a project. If my motive is to please people, the reward isn't as great as it would be if my motive was to show my love for Him.

Christ died on the cross because He loves us. He wasn't trying to please people. If He were, He wouldn't have even ended up on the cross! He would have lived because He would have tried pleasing everyone. Consequently, no one would have been "rubbed the wrong way" and we wouldn't have had a Savior.

When we feel rejected, we aren't happy with our present circumstances. However, 1 Thessalonians 16-18 says, "Be joyful always; pray continually; give thanks in all circumstances, for this is God's will for you in Christ Jesus." God isn't rejecting you when you're going through a difficult time. It isn't His way of saying, "I don't love you." You know He does love you! As was mentioned above, His love is *unconditional.* Nothing you do or say can make Him stop loving you! When you're going through tough times, realize that *joy* is eternal but *happiness* is temporary. Joy comes from the Lord! He will help you through the hard times! Give thanks in *all* circumstances. Use them as stepping blocks to leap higher!

Enter into His rest. He is peace. Battle lies with the Truth. "I AM accepted in Christ! I am worthy because of what Christ did for me! I am fully and unconditionally loved! My worth is not based on my performance! I am secure in Christ and I have everything I need." Realize that the lies are not your thoughts! Break agreement with them. Choose not to agree with them any longer. Demonic spirits will still manifest if you continue to walk in agreement with them. Therefore, it is incredibly important that you don't agree with them.

Also, it is important to realize how badly we hurt others when we say they're not accepted, not good enough, not measuring up, etc. "Accept one another, then, just as Christ accepted you, in order to bring praise to God." (Romans 15:7) Stop agreeing with the enemy about others! And (on another note), when people reject *us,* we don't have to receive it. Know you are accepted in Christ. You don't need their opinions.

When we want to restore relationships, we should first restore our relationship with Him first. Receive His love, then you'll be able to receive love from other people. Our attitude towards God reflects on our attitude towards others.

Dear Jesus,

I know I am accepted because of your Son, Jesus. I'm sorry for ever considering His death as "not enough." I am worthy because of Him. I am loved unconditionally. I am forgiven. Forgive me for agreeing with the Spirit of Rejection. These thoughts of rejection and unworthiness are not from You, Lord. You love me. You want me. Forgive me for also making others feel rejected. Forgive me for working for the approval of others, rather than seeking to glorify You. I lose myself from the Spirit of Rejection and I bind myself to Your acceptance. I command all

spirits of rejection to go to the dry uninhabited places and to never come back! Thank You for always loving me. Fill me with Your Holy Spirit and live through me!
In Jesus' name, Amen.

What are you lacking?

What are 7 things (qualities, gifts, character traits or fruit) that you wish that you could have? People do not step out in their gifts and callings because of fear of rejection, feeling unworthy and intimidated, or because they fear that they do not have everything they need to succeed.

Romans 8:17
Now if we are children, then **we _are_ heirs - heirs of God and co-heirs with Christ,** if indeed we share in his sufferings in order that we may also share in his glory.
Lord, you have already died; we are heirs. We receive our inheritance and all you have promised us now. We are the bride and have joint accounts with Jesus.

Colossians 2:9
For in Him dwelleth all the fullness of the Godhead bodily. 10 And you are complete in Him, which is the head of all principality and power.
Jesus is the all in all and He lives the Christian life through us. We loose our souls from lack, scarcity and need to beg. We bind ourselves to the abundance of Christ inside us.

James 1:8
8 he is a double-minded man, unstable in all he does.
We loose our souls from double-mindedness and bind our soul to being single minded.

Stress = conflict between soul and spirit that destroys our immune system.

Mark 12:30-31
30 Love the Lord your God with all your heart and with all your soul and with all your mind and with all your strength.' 31 The second is this: '**Love your neighbor as yourself.**' There is no commandment greater than these."
We loose ourselves from separation from others, God and myself and rejection. We bind ourselves to the restoration of our souls, renewal of a right spirit and healthy body.

Hebrews 11:6
6 And **without faith it is impossible to please God,** because anyone who comes to him must believe that he exists and that he rewards those who earnestly seek him.
Unbelief motivates people to search for answers in other places, becoming vulnerable to false prophets, divination, mediums, false religion, cults, new age, addictions and the competition of Pharisees. We choose to believe Holy Spirit.

Joel 2:25-26
25 '**I will repay you for the years the locusts have eaten**- the great locust and the young locust, the other locusts and the locust swarm- my great army that I sent among you.
26 **You will have plenty to eat,** until you are full, and you will praise the name of the LORD your God, who has worked wonders for you; never again will my people be shamed.

We loose ourselves from trying to be vindicated, prove our worth or to regain our significance with man. We receive the places and positions that God has for us.

Proverbs 17:22
22- A cheerful heart is good medicine, but a crushed spirit dries up the bones.
In Jesus' name, we release our hurt to Jesus and renounce a victim mentality.

Philippians 4:5-8
5 Let your gentleness be evident to all. The Lord is near. 6 **Do not be anxious** about anything, but in everything, by prayer and petition, with thanksgiving, present your requests to God. 7 And the peace of God, which transcends all understanding, will guard your hearts and your minds in Christ Jesus. 8 Finally, brothers, whatever is true, whatever is noble, whatever is right, whatever is pure, whatever is lovely, whatever is admirable-if anything is excellent or praiseworthy-think about such things.
We loose ourselves from anxiety about our position, promotion, gifting, calling, being known or creating an inheritance for ourselves. We can only start from where we are and we choose to receive God's work in our lives, here and now.

2 Corinthians 1:21-22
21 Now He who establishes us with you in Christ and has anointed us is God, 22 who also has sealed us and given us the Spirit in our hearts as a guarantee.
We loose ourselves from comparing ourselves to others and bind our hearts to God as He establishes, anoints and seals us by His Spirit.

Isaiah 61:3-4
3 and provide for those who grieve in Zion -- to bestow on them a **crown of beauty instead of ashes, the oil of gladness instead of mourning, and a garment of praise** instead of a spirit of despair. They will be **called oaks of righteousness, a planting of the LORD for the display of his splendor.** 4 They will **rebuild the ancient ruins and restore the places long devastated;** they will renew the ruined cities that have been devastated for generations.

Jeremiah 32:27
27 "I am the LORD, the God of all mankind. Is anything too hard for me?
We receive Your kingdom values: our identity is based on agreement and belief. We renounce our agreements with the world's system based on performance.

Philippians 4:7
7 And the peace of God, which transcends all understanding, will guard your hearts and your minds in Christ Jesus.
Peace is based on true identity; anxiety is based on false identity (i.e. I am bitter.) Holy Spirit has all the peace and He lives inside every born again believer. I have it!

Philippians 4:8
8 Finally, brothers, whatever is true, whatever is noble, whatever is right, whatever is pure,

whatever is lovely, whatever is admirable-if anything is excellent or praiseworthy-think about such things.

We loose our souls from seeing others in terms of identity and giving them false identity and bind ourselves in agreement to godly beliefs about others.

Exodus 20:5-6

5 You shall not bow down to them or worship them; for I, the LORD your God, am a jealous God, punishing the children for the sin of the fathers to the **third and fourth generation** of those who hate me, 6 but showing love to a **thousand [generations]** of those who love me and keep my commandments.

As we confess the sins of our ancestors as sin, renounce their idolatry and our own, we find that the key to our well-being lies not in their choices but in our present obedience to God.

Jeremiah 32:18

18 You show love to thousands but bring the punishment for the fathers' sins into the laps of their children after them. O great and powerful God, whose name is the LORD Almighty,

We renounce and break agreement with the sins of abuse, victimization, conditional acceptance, favoritism and every form of rejection that we have practiced.

Hebrews 4:9-11

9 There remains, then, a Sabbath-rest for the people of God; 10 for **anyone who enters God's rest also rests from his own work**, just as God did from his. 11 Let us, therefore, make every effort to enter that rest, so that no one will fall by following their example of disobedience.

We receive Your true gospel, rest from our works and receive Your acceptance.

Genesis 4:5-8

5 but on Cain and his offering he did not look with favor. So Cain was very angry, and his face was downcast. 6 Then the LORD said to Cain, "Why are you angry? Why is your face downcast? 7 If you do what is right, will you not be accepted? But if you do not do what is right, sin is crouching at your door; it desires to have you, ..."

We loose ourselves from the deception of Cain and bind ourselves to obedience.

Hebrews 9:22

22 In fact, the law requires that nearly everything be cleansed with blood, and without the shedding of blood there is no forgiveness.

Thank you, Lord, for forgiveness and acceptance based on Your work at the Cross.

Write down five things God has asked you to do that you aren't doing yet.

Joshua 1:7-8

7 Be strong and very courageous. **Be careful to obey** all the law my servant Moses gave you; do not turn from it to the right or to the left, that you may be successful wherever you go. 8 Do not let this Book of the Law depart from your mouth; meditate on it day and night, so that you may be careful to do everything written in it. Then you will be prosperous and successful.

What 3 things do you need in order to feel much better about yourself?

Romans 10:9-10
9 That if you confess with your mouth, "Jesus is Lord," and believe in your heart that God raised him from the dead, you will be saved. 10 For it is with your **heart** that you believe and are justified, and it is with your **mouth** that you confess and are saved.
Lord, we do choose You as Lord and our source for everything that we need.

Isaiah 53:7
He was oppressed and afflicted, yet he did not open his mouth; he was led like a lamb to the slaughter, and as a sheep before her shearers is silent, so he did not open his mouth.
Jesus, You have experienced every real rejection and demonstrated Your love to us.

Isaiah 54:4-5
4 "Do not be afraid; you will not suffer shame. Do not fear disgrace; you will not be humiliated. You will forget the shame of your youth and remember no more the reproach of your widowhood. 5 For your Maker is your husband-- the LORD Almighty is his name-- the Holy One of Israel is your Redeemer; he is called the God of all the earth.
Lord, we release our trauma and hurt to You. Please heal us, taking the hurt; redeem us, taking the reproach, humiliation and disgrace, leaving us with Your wisdom.

2 Corinthians 5:21
21 God made him who had no sin to be sin for us, so that in him we might become the righteousness of God.
We focus on the righteousness that You gave us more than the rejection of man.

James 5:16
16 Therefore confess your sins to each other and pray for each other so that you may be healed. The prayer of a righteous man is powerful and effective.
We choose to let down our walls, renounce our bitter expectations that we will be rejected, choose to sow acceptance and to receive love and acceptance again.

1 John 4:18
18 There is no fear in love. But perfect love drives out fear, because fear has to do with punishment. The one who fears is not made perfect in love.
Lord, we receive Your perfect love and allow it to perfect us, driving out fear.

Isaiah 54:17 no weapon forged against you will prevail, and you will refute every tongue that accuses you. This is the heritage of the servants of the LORD, and this is their vindication from me," declares the LORD.
We cannot claim this verse and be victims at the same time. Deliver us as victors.

Psalm 139:13-16
13 For you created my inmost being; you knit me together in my mother's womb.
14 I praise you because I am fearfully and wonderfully made; your works are wonderful, I know that full well. 15 My frame was not hidden from you when I was made in the secret place. When I was woven together in the depths of the earth, 16 your eyes saw my unformed body. All the days ordained for me were written in your book before one of them came to be.

We repent of spiritual rebellion i.e. God shortchanged me from birth – appearance, intellect, body, ancestors, status, talents, gender, economic status, etc. etc.

Romans 3:4 Not at all! Let God be true, and every man a liar. As it is written: "So that you may be proved right when you speak and prevail when you judge."
We receive God's choices for us in every area of life, weaknesses and all.

Proverbs 6:16-19
16 There are six things the LORD hates, seven that are detestable to him:
17 haughty eyes, a lying tongue, hands that shed innocent blood,
18 a heart that devises wicked schemes, feet that are quick to rush into evil,
19 a false witness who pours out lies and a man who stirs up dissension among brothers.
We repent of striving with others and trying to build ourselves up at their expense.
We repent of attempting to use Christianity to serve ourselves.

John Wesley's Prayer

I am no longer my own but yours.
Put me to what you will.
Put me to doing, put me to suffering.
Let me be employed for you or laid aside for you,
exalted for you or brought low for you.
Let me be full or let me be empty.
Let me have all things or let me have nothing.
I freely and wholeheartedly yield all things to Your disposal.
And now glorious and blessed Father, Son and Holy Spirit,
You are mine and I am yours.   So be it.
And the covenant now made on earth,
let it be ratified in Heaven.

1 John 1:7-9
 7 But if we walk in the light, as he is in the light, we have fellowship with one another, and the blood of Jesus, his Son, purifies us from all sin. 8 If we claim to be without sin, we deceive ourselves and the truth is not in us. 9 If we confess our sins, he is faithful and just and will forgive us our sins and purify us from all unrighteousness.
We repent of taking our rejection from man and projecting it onto Father God.
We repent of trying to clean our relationships with people and then go to God.
We come to You, Lord, walk in Your light, let You purify us and enjoy good fellowship.

Religious Leaders

One of our most popular radio programs was on wounds from religious leaders. It happens! The question is, "What does God want us to do about it?" What did you do with your deep hurt and disappointment? Did you take them to Jesus and have zero pain left in your heart? On a scale of 0-10, how much pain do these memories have in them? Did you go to them and try to resolve the issues? Did you ask a restoration minister to pray with you? Did you indulge in sinful reactions and behaviors? Did you sow bad seeds that you have been reaping since then? If so, you can pray our eight RPM prayers (see Exhibits) and finally get healing. As you forgive and also ask forgiveness five ways, Jesus will take the pain and leave you with the wisdom. Then what?

Ask God to bless you with a good spiritual father. You can pray for your own father or spiritual father by loosing him from fleshly traits and binding him to the heart of God and to His character. If you have been hurt by an uncaring religious leader, ask God for a good father who is a true spiritual father. If you are afraid to choose one for yourself, the following comparison between a spiritual father and someone who is just a religious leader, may help you to discern a true father and their motivations. These thoughts are taken from the book, "Mentoring and Fathering" by Schultz and Gaborit. (I have not personally met them to know what kind of leaders they are but I can appreciate this.)

A GOOD SPIRITUAL FATHER	A RELIGIOUS LEADER
Encourages you for your own good	Flatters you
Stands with you regardless	Separates from you when you are in trouble
Asks, "What can I do to help you?"	Asks, "What can you do for me?"
Teaches you dependence on God	Keeps you dependent on him
Teaches you Truth from God's Word	Teaches you his doctrinal bias
Has the heart of a true worshipper of God	"Attends" or sends you to a worship service
Is happy when you succeed more than he	Is threatened when you succeed more than he
Has the 'team' concept of service	Has a 'golfer caddy' idea of your service
Makes you feel comfortable / protected	Threatens to expose you or attack you
Helps, wanting nothing in return	Expects something for helping you
Willing to admit his weaknesses	Will not admit weakness or mistakes
Is interested in what you are doing	Only talks about what he is doing / his vision
Finds time to be available to you	Is too busy to spend quality time
Will bless you when you are led to leave	Will cut you off if you are led to move on
Prays for you without ceasing	Will pray if you ask them
Willingly imparts spiritual gifts	Doesn't want to lose 'spiritual' advantage
Sees potential gifts, talents & callings in you	Only sees you as you are now
Trusts you to step out (with room to fail)	Will not release you for fear of your failure
Isn't afraid to discipline or correct you	Will either avoid correction or will over react
Has a heart to restore the broken	Withdraws from high maintenance children
Will pay a debt they do not owe	Will hold your debts over your head
Will fellowship with other fathers	Will hide from accountability to his peers
Moves toward the current move of God	Will wed you to his institution / past moves

TESTIMONY FROM A LOVELY FELLOW MINISTER OVERSEAS

Many years ago, I was involved in a small intercessory group of ladies praying for the church we attended. After a few months, to our surprise, the Lord started to show us some serious matters involving the worship team. It was quite scary for us as the Lord was quite adamant that there was sin going on, which we personally did not know about (or even wished to know about!) Each week, I would ring the Pastor after our meetings and just let him know that our intentions were good and I told him everything the Lord was showing us. However, this time it was different. I did not have the courage or gumption to tell him something about the church musicians for fear of its repercussions, so I wrote to him about it instead. I never heard a word from him for 2 months, so was very worried I had 'crossed a line'.

Finally, I got word to come in and see him. He had his assistant pastor there and proceeded to give me a telling off I shall never forget; how I was delusional and totally wrong in my assumptions of the music/worship team. I reminded him that the Lord had revealed it to the three of us women, not just me - but to no avail. I was devastated as he put me down and humiliated me as I sat there on my own with no defense. I went home, cried and went to bed. Eventually, after a few months, because I felt progressively ostracized, I left the church and went into deep depression. To my surprise (which shouldn't have been the case) two of the music team members produced illegitimate children within a year. A few years later, the Pastor was dismissed for having an affair.

In my heart, I said at that time, I would never do this again and the Lord said to me one day when I was doing RPM homework, "I want you to not only trust me again with words I give you, but I also want you to be confident in your own authority again." I know this is true as I was like a tortoise that pulled back in after I received this rebuke and have feared stepping out again.

When I was growing up, I was never allowed to approach authority figures because of the fear of authority instilled in me by my parents, so I had some work to do regarding this matter. I asked forgiveness using the 5-way prayer to deal with this matter, which had become a cycle in my life:

1. I asked the Lord to forgive me for not forgiving my parents or this Pastor in leadership who did not receive the word of the Lord as I had portrayed it to him;

2. I asked the Lord's forgiveness for judging my parents for not allowing me to speak up, causing fear to reside in my heart, and also forgive this Pastor for his response towards me, which hurt me deeply;

3. I asked the Lord's forgiveness for not wishing to step out in authority again, thus relinquishing my God-given gift, which was my reaction to this episode;

4. I asked the Lord's forgiveness for doubting and blaming God for what I saw as Him 'setting me up' for failure, which was erroneous of course; and

5. I asked the Lord's forgiveness for not forgiving myself all these years, living in regret for stepping out.

Without realizing it, I had developed bitter root expectations about this kind of ministry and authority the Lord had given me and one ungodly belief I formed was that "If the Lord asks me to deliver a word of warning again, He is quite capable of finding someone of greater standing and in a better position than I to deliver it".

My new godly belief is: "Because the Lord has worked His authority within me, it is my privilege to be His mouth piece and it is His desire to take responsibility for the responses of those it is given to, not mine".

Since I prayed the above 5-way prayer, forgiving and asking for forgiveness, I have had the privilege of being in a fellowship where there is very godly leadership who cherish and honour me, and can also address differences between us in a constructive and loving way. I have broken the cycle of fear of authority, thanks to the above prayer and the faithfulness of the Lord to place me where He would have me exercise a prophetic ministry for His glory.

Religious Spirits

My notes from <u>Epic Battles of the Last Days</u> by Rick Joyner

Loving God with our whole heart and our neighbor as our self will enable us to obey all the "do nots" of the Bible and overcome most of the evil in our hearts. Satan's strategy is to get us focused on evil, knowing we will become like the evil we behold. As we focus on the Lord and His glory, we will be changed into His image. When the light reveals sin in our life, do we turn to the Tree of Good and Evil or the Tree of Life?

The religious spirit seeks to substitute religious activity for the power of the Holy Spirit in the believer's life. (2 Timothy 3:5) The religious spirit is the leaven of the Pharisees in that it does not add substance but inflates. (Matthew 16:6) Satan knows that if he can inflate our service with pride God will not inhabit it.

To the degree that we are free of Satan's deception, we will be free to preach the true gospel. The strategy of the religious spirit is to keep the Pharisees (and us) more focused on the wrong in others than the need for our own correction.

The great deception is that the religious spirit is based on zeal (for the wrong reasons). It seeks to have us serve in order to gain approval rather than because we have received approval through the cross of Jesus. It bases relationship with God on personal discipline rather than the sacrifice of Christ; it is usually motivated by fear or pride or both.

Any attempt to make our own atonement for sin will surely result in pride. It will emphasize our cross more than the Cross of Jesus. One is God-centered and the other is self-centered in the most destructive way -- to circumvent the Cross. (1 Samuel 3:13-14, 2:17)

Its idealism is one of the most deceptive disguises, as it appears to have the highest standards, but is a deadly enemy of true revelation and grace. It will cause us to impose standards on others above what God requires for them. Idealists look for the perfect church and cannot come alongside the "Helper" to serve in more "lowly" works.

Perfectionistic pride sees everything as black or white, rather than grace that sets people free. Religious spirits point out all the problems but offer no solutions. Maturity has a vision of making it to the top but never condemns people who are still climbing; it allows the imperfect to minister. (James 3:2) The combination of fear and pride will cause us deep anguish and remorse over our failures, drive us to attempts to make more sacrifices, and then flip to feeling superior, being unteachable and unable to receive reproof.

It deals in counterfeit discernment motivated, by suspicion and fear and is rooted in rejection, territorial preservation or insecurity. **** **When someone submits a judgment or criticism about someone, we should disregard it unless we know they truly love that person.**

Paul warns about those who minister out of a religious spirit, bringing a yoke of legalism on the church. (2 Corinthians 11:13-15) They bring truths as a servant of righteousness, but use them to tear down and divide. Some set impossible unbiblical standards for others. He may appear to be protecting the sheep, but is really declaring himself to be better than they are. True grace is found somewhere between faultfinding and unsanctified mercy (that even approves of things God disapproves of); either extreme can be a religious spirit.

Warning Signs of the Religious Spirit adapted from a sermon by Jack Deere

1. Will see his primary mission as tearing down what he believes is wrong.

2. Will be unable to accept rebuke, especially from those "less spiritual than himself."

3. Will have a philosophy that will not listen to men, but "only to God."

4. Will be inclined to see more of what is wrong than what is right.

5. Will be subject to an overwhelming guilt (can never meet God's standards.)

6. Will keep score in his spiritual life.

7. Will believe that he has been appointed to fix everyone else.

8. Will have a style that is bossy, overbearing and intolerant of other's failures.

9. Will believe that he is closer to God and his ministry is more pleasing than others.

10. Will take pride in his maturity, discipline in comparison to others.

11. Will believe that he is on the cutting edge of what God is doing.

12. Will have a mechanical prayer life.

13. Will do things in order to be noticed by men.

14. Will be overly repulsed by emotionalism.

15. Will use emotionalism as a substitute for the work of the Holy Spirit.

16. Will be encouraged when his ministry looks better than others.

17. Will glory more in what God has done in the past than in the present.

18. Will be suspicious of or oppose new movements, churches, etc.

19. Will have the tendency to reject spiritual manifestations that he does not understand.

20. Will overreact to carnality in the church.

21. Will overreact to immaturity in the church.

22. Will base evidence of God's approval on supernatural manifestations.

23. Will be unable to join anything that he does not deem as perfect or near perfect.

24. Will be overly paranoid of the religious spirit.

25. Will glory in anything but the Cross of Christ, what He has accomplished and who He is. (James 3:17-18, 1 Thessalonians 5:21, 2 Corinthians 13:5, Galatians 6:1)

LORD, HELP US DISCERN IF RELIGIOUS SPIRITS OPERATE THROUGH US

1 Samuel 15:23
23 For **rebellion** is like the sin of divination, and **arrogance** like the evil of idolatry. Because you have rejected the word of the LORD, he has rejected you as king.

1 Samuel 22:17
17 Then the king ordered the guards at his side: "Turn and kill the priests of the LORD, because they too have sided with David. They knew he was fleeing, yet they did not tell me." But the **king's officials were not willing to raise a hand to strike the priests of the LORD.**

Revelation 12:11
11 They overcame him by the blood of the Lamb and by the word of their testimony; they did not love their lives so much as to shrink from death.

1 Corinthians 15:57-58
57 But thanks be to God! He gives us the victory through our Lord Jesus Christ. 58 Therefore, my dear brothers, stand firm. Let nothing move you. **Always give yourselves fully to the work of the Lord,** because you know that your labor in the Lord is not in vain.

Romans 8:37-39
37 No, in all these things **we are more than conquerors through him who loved us**. 38 For I am convinced that neither death nor life, neither angels nor demons, neither the present nor the future, nor any powers, 39 neither height nor depth, nor anything else in all creation, will be able to separate us from the love of God that is in Christ Jesus our Lord.

2 Corinthians 2:14
14 But thanks be to God, who always leads us in triumphal procession **in Christ and through us spreads everywhere the fragrance of the knowledge of him**.

Jude 10-16
10 Yet these men speak abusively against whatever they do not understand; and what things they do understand by instinct, like unreasoning animals-these are the very things that destroy them … 16 These men are grumblers and faultfinders; they follow their own evil desires; they boast about themselves and flatter others for their own advantage.

2 Timothy 3:5
5 … having a form of godliness but denying its power. Have nothing to do with them.

Matthew 16:6
6 "Be careful," Jesus said to them. "Be on your guard against the yeast of the Pharisees and Sadducees."

James 3:2
2 We all stumble in many ways. If anyone is never at fault in what he says, he is a perfect man, able to keep his whole body in check.

2 Corinthians 11:13-15
13 For such men are false apostles, deceitful workmen, masquerading as apostles of Christ. 14 And no wonder, for Satan himself masquerades as an angel of light. 15 It is not surprising, then, if his servants masquerade as servants of righteousness. Their end will be what their actions deserve.

Colossians 2:18-23
18 Do not let anyone who delights in false humility and the worship of angels disqualify you for the prize. Such a person goes into great detail about what he has seen, and his unspiritual mind puffs him up with idle notions. **19 He has lost connection with the Head, from whom the whole body, supported and held together by its ligaments and sinews, grows as God causes it to grow.** 20 Since you died with Christ to the basic principles of this world, why, as though you still belonged to it, do you submit to its rules: 21 "Do not handle! Do not taste! Do not touch!"? 22 These are all destined to perish with use, because they are based on human commands and teachings. 23 Such regulations indeed have an appearance of wisdom, with their self-imposed worship, their false humility and their harsh treatment of the body, but they lack any value in restraining sensual indulgence.

Colossians 2:6-9
6 So then, just as you received Christ Jesus as Lord, continue to live in Him, 7 rooted and built up in him, strengthened in the faith as you were taught, and overflowing with thankfulness. 8 See to it that no one takes you captive through hollow and deceptive philosophy, which depends on human tradition and the basic principles of this world rather than on Christ. 9 For in Christ all the fullness of the Deity lives in bodily form.

2 Corinthians 11:3
3 But I am afraid that **just as Eve was deceived by the serpent's cunning, your minds may somehow be led astray from your sincere and pure devotion to Christ.**

James 3:17-18
17 But the wisdom that comes from heaven is first of all pure; then peace loving, considerate, submissive, full of mercy and good fruit, impartial and sincere. 18 Peacemakers who sow in peace raise a harvest of righteousness.

1 Thessalonians 5:21
21 Test everything. Hold on to the good.

2 Corinthians 13:5
5 Examine yourselves to see whether you are in the faith; test yourselves. Do you not realize that Christ Jesus is in you-unless, of course, you fail the test?

Galatians 6:1-2
6:1 Brothers, if someone is caught in a sin, you who are spiritual should **restore him gently.** But watch yourself, or you also may be tempted. 2 Carry each other's burdens, **and in this way you**

will fulfill the law of Christ.

Hebrews 7:25
25 Therefore he is able to save completely those who come to God through him, because he always lives to intercede for them.

Romans 11:8
8 as it is written: **"God gave them a spirit of stupor**, eyes so that they could not see and ears so that they could not hear, to this very day."

1 Timothy 4:1
4:1 The Spirit clearly says that in later times some will **abandon the faith** and follow deceiving spirits and things taught by demons.

2 Timothy 3:1-5
3:1 But mark this: There will be terrible times in the last days. 2 People will be lovers of themselves, lovers of money, boastful, proud, abusive, disobedient to their parents, ungrateful, unholy, 3 without love, unforgiving, slanderous, without self-control, brutal, not lovers of the good, 4 treacherous, rash, conceited, lovers of pleasure rather than lovers of God- 5 **having a form of godliness but denying its power. Have nothing to do with them.**

Matthew 16:6
6 "Be careful," Jesus said to them. **"Be on your guard against the yeast of the Pharisees and Sadducees."**

Ephesians 5:10
10 **and find out what pleases the Lord.**

Matthew 15:3
3 Jesus replied, "And why do you break the command of God **for the sake of your tradition?"**

Mark 7:8-9
8 You have let go of the commands of God and are holding on to the traditions of men."
9 And he said to them: "You have a fine way of **setting aside the commands of God in order to observe your own traditions!"**

Luke 18:11-14
11 The Pharisee stood up and prayed about himself: **'God, I thank you that I am not like other men**-robbers, evildoers, adulterers-or even like this tax collector. 12 I fast twice a week and give a tenth of all I get.' 13 "But the tax collector stood at a distance. He would not even look up to heaven, but beat his breast and said, 'God, have mercy on me, a sinner.'
14 "I tell you that this man, rather than the other, went home justified before God. For everyone who exalts himself will be humbled, and he who humbles himself will be exalted."

Now before the conviction of God is forgotten, write down your ungodly beliefs and pray the Ungodly Belief Prayer to break the power of them. (See Exhibits)

Taking Offense – "The Bait of Satan" by John Bevere
This is a very helpful book review written by one of our alumni.
This book is a fresh look at one of Satan's oldest and most common traps.

If only I had read this book ten years ago! How much deception could I have possibly avoided? How many pity parties would have been left unattended! Explanatory and convicting, the experience of reading it was truly bittersweet. It actually felt very autobiographical. If only churches could institute required reading lists!

Inherent in the definition of *deception* is that you do not know it is being done to you. Satan is commonly known as the "master of deception", and less commonly recognized for his mastery in his use of *skandalon.* What a painful reality this is.

Blindness and self-centeredness result from taking up an offense. As we focus on the faults of others to the exclusion of self-evaluation, much fruit results, but not fruits of righteousness. The enemy means it for separation, hurt, anger, strife, jealousy etc., yet the Lord desires us to see <u>our</u> true condition. God allows the *fire* of hurtful, difficult experiences to burn off our dross and purify our gold.

After an offense many of us become inward and guarded, unconditional love becomes impossible because we will not risk being hurt. Our love grows cold. The walls we erect for our protection from further hurt become our prison instead. Doubt and unbelief begin to prevail. Doubts about God's goodness arise as we filter everything through hurts of the past and experiences of rejection. Believing God becomes harder and harder. We become unable to function in our calling, incapable of reaching our full potential because of wounds and offenses.

When we see flaws in leaders we judge and criticize, then we run away from the difficulty. Our enemy has garnered another success in uprooting us from the place of God's planting. Eventually we become isolated, escaping the test. Conflict is temporarily avoided, relationships are severed instead of reconciled, character development is derailed and the cycle begins all over again.

What a comfort to know it was God who put David under Saul and Samuel under Eli. God allows our sifting for our good. The test – shall we become like our offenders? Shall we assume God's prerogative in judging and correcting our offender? What a comfort that "we are not ignorant of Satan's devices."

Dear Lord, may I learn obedience through my hardships and acknowledging my sin. Grant me humility and selflessness that pursues peace with all men. Help me, God, to fulfill my ministry of reconciliation before You. As You have forgiven me, may I forgive also and allow You the place of Judge, Defender and Avenger. Please heal my heart and fill it with a fervent love for others. Enable me, Father, to walk in mature love and may I love with the same intensity after their sin and frailties have come to light. For this is how <u>You love me.</u>

TRUST! The #1 healing ingredient needed today

Satan's number one strategy is to wound us from day one so that we are less able to trust God. **An inability to trust God is the grandfather root to every sin.** Basic trust is the ability to hold our heart open to God, others and ourselves. Basic trust is an absolute must for those who would minister to hurting people who are not yet healed and free. Isn't that almost everyone?

Basic Trust Test: Most of the time ...

- I can easily hold my heart open to others to communicate heart to heart.
- I readily let people know me and I share who am; I am OK as a person.
- I have a strong resilient spirit with plenty of bounce back after I am hurt.
- I have the courage to venture out to take risks with minimal anxiety.
- I am flexible to shift gears and to flex without getting all frustrated.
- I have strength of spirit and can make good decisions readily.
- I would rather have intimate friendships than settle for casual acquaintances.
- I am comfortable to give and receive appropriate affectionate touch.
- I meet God spirit to spirit rather than just know Him with my mind.
- I am confident that I am totally forgiven because Christ died for me.
- I have strong relationships with my leaders whom I trust to mentor me.
- I have strength to stand alone and to say 'no' as well as 'yes' to others.
- When God tells me 'no' I still know that He has my best interest at heart.
- I trust God to do 'greater works' through me in His supernatural power.
- I have trusting relationships without domination, control and manipulation.
- I easily say 'no' to possessive smothering friends who try to run my life.
- I firmly choose God's moral values rather than give in to peer pressure.
- My internal godly beliefs are more important to me than following traditions.
- I am accountable allowing my authorities to teach me better life skills.
- My significance is based on God's Truth vs. what people think and say.
- I know that I am loved and accepted even when I do not perform well.
- I mostly have mature relationships based on mutual trust and respect.
- I trust myself to hear God and to make important decisions with confidence.
- I am no longer controlled by my parents but I am open to their counsel.

⌐ I am able to 'let go' when people I care about insist on making bad choices.

⌐ I am responsible to others but not responsible for other people's choices.

⌐ I was taught valuable skills to deal with life's adult issues without fear.

⌐ Teens who are included in decision making learn how to make decisions.

⌐ I am able to admit my mistakes without fear of rejection or shame.

⌐ I am strong enough to give 'gifts of trust' to those who have let me down.

⌐ I can give more 'space' to significant others even when it hurts me to 'let go.'

⌐ When God asks me to do something new, I trust Him to enable me to do it.

⌐ God always answers my prayers, provides for me and is there for me.

Prayer to restore basic trust

Lord, my life was built on a shaky foundation. I don't trust as I should—not You, not Your people, not even my own family. Instead of growing up believing in affection and warmth, I grew up thinking life was cold and hard, that I had to take care of myself because no one else would. In refusing to reach out to others, I closed my heart.

But this is not the way You meant Your children to live. This is no life at all. I want Your healing touch to minister to my imprisoned spirit so I no longer approach people with cynicism and distrust. Take my hand and walk with me back to my childhood and show me where that basic trust should have been built into my life.

I forgive my parents fully for not modeling good examples. They didn't teach me to trust and my home life was not as accepting as it could have been. I was wrong to judge them. But now, because of Your love for me, I can let go of that regret and be a better person for it.

I forgive any others who may have wounded me, whether in ignorance or innocence or even purposely. Those actions and words hurt me deeply, but through the finished work of Christ on the cross, all is released and I hold no one in debt.

For my own responsibility, I forgive myself for damaging the emotions of others by my lack of confidence in them, for my false belief that they would only let me down. By my actions and my words, I let them down instead.

I admit I even blamed You, Lord, for allowing others to hurt me. Help me to see Your faithfulness, bind up my wounded spirit, and teach me to trust You, no matter what happens. Heal me, Father, that I may be able to point others, who also need healing, to You.

Please forgive me for closing my heart to You and Your world. I was so lost in self-preservation, so bent on protecting myself from being hurt, that I would not or could not place my heart in anyone's hands, not even Yours. I'm beginning to understand just how trustworthy You are. You loved me all the time I was pushing You away.

In the past, I stubbornly determined not to trust. Now I choose to give and receive trust by the mighty power of the risen Christ within me. Give me the courage to reach out in confidence to others, proving myself a trustworthy friend. Help me to grow steady in faith, with an optimistic outlook on life, based on Your sure and constant love. Give me discernment to perceive those who are truly honest and dependable and protect me from people who are not. Teach me to lean on You, Lord, assured of Your faithfulness and reliability, so that I can face life's difficulties with confidence and hope because of You. Amen

Visions and Open Spiritual Eyes

Do YOU believe:

☐ It is good to ask God to open your spiritual eyes and ears to see the spiritual realm?

☐ Jesus will appear to people in the form of an angel and hold a conversation?

☐ God will speak to unbelievers and give them prophetic warnings to avoid sin?

☐ God will open your eyes to see angelic help in an open vision?

☐ Your prayers may be answered with a prophetic angelic visitation?

☐ God will instruct your unbelieving employer or competitor not to harm you?

☐ You should pray for national leaders to have open visions and to promote believers?

☐ God wants to give us favor and new direction even while we are sound asleep?

☐ God still speaks to us in the midst of supernatural phenomena in natural objects?

☐ God will reveal Himself through nature like the glory of the Lord appeared in a cloud?

☐ God will give us revelations of His will and way in God-dreams or open visions?

☐ Animals are sometimes more able to see into the spiritual realms than people are?

☐ We should repent of a fear that it is ungodly to have open visions from God?

☐ We can choose to have our prophetic spiritual eyes and spiritual ears opened?

☐ God will send warrior angels to help us fight a battle or to fight on our behalf?

☐ God will speak correction to our national leaders when their plan is not from God?

☐ God will take you up in the Spirit to see what is happening in another area?

☐ God will give us knowledge, skill, learning, wisdom and understanding in visions?

☐ Secrets and future events are sometimes revealed by God in prophetic visions?

☐ Meanings of events are given to individuals who ask God for interpretation?

☐ Angels are sometimes sent to touch or heal those who are open to a visitation?

☐ We are commanded to be still and to watch to see what God will say to us?

☐ We are commanded to write our dreams down when we sense they are from God?

☐ God is pouring His Spirit out on all flesh and all can see prophetic dreams and visions?

☐ Divine connections are orchestrated by God through prophetic dreams and visions?

☐ God will correct our false doctrine or theology though dreams and open visions?

☐ We can receive an impartation of Godly boldness as God visits us in the night?

☐ We can choose to be "in the Spirit" and receive prophetic revelations?

☐ God will foretell future events in prophetic visitations or open visions?

☐ God is still a talking God and all "His sheep" can hear His voice if they will?

Please Open Our Spiritual Eyes, Lord!

From Genesis to Revelation, God has spoken to people through dreams and visions! But from the very beginning Satan has tried to make us afraid of using our spiritual eyes, hoping to make us too paranoid to want them opened. He has counterfeited God's visions with demonic visions, in hopes that we will fear seeing into the spiritual realm and will quench the Holy Spirit when He speaks to us through dreams and visions.

In the beginning, Satan had a great fear that Adam and Eve would have spiritual eyes to see the truth, so he perverted the truth, in hopes of making them afraid to see with open spiritual eyes. Genesis 3:5 For God doth know that in the day ye eat thereof, then your <u>eyes shall be opened</u>, and ye shall be as gods, knowing good and evil.

In Restoration Prayer Ministry, you learn to see God better with spiritual eyes. God wants us to hunger and thirst to see Him. The pure in heart will see God! Isn't it about time we quit letting Satan steal from us? God chooses to speak and bless with visions. Genesis 15:1 After these things the word of the LORD came unto Abram in a vision, saying, <u>Fear not</u>, Abram: I am thy shield, and thy exceeding great reward.

Let us pray to have our spiritual eyes opened. The Lord Himself appeared to open the eyes of Abraham. Genesis 18:1 And the LORD <u>appeared unto him</u> in the plains of Mamre: and he sat in the tent door in the heat of the day

Pray for others to see God also. God chose to warn unbelievers with visions. Genesis 20:3 But God came to Abimelech in a <u>dream by night</u>, and said to him, Behold, thou art but a dead man, for the woman which thou hast taken; for she is a man's wife.

Pray for help and open eyes to see it. God wants to open our eyes to see His help for us. Genesis 21:19 And God <u>opened her eyes</u>, and she saw a well of water; and she went, and filled the bottle with water, and gave the lad drink.

God will bridge heaven and earth to initiate a covenant in our sleep. Genesis 28:12 And he dreamed, and behold a ladder set up on the earth, and the top of it <u>reached to heaven</u>: and behold the angels of God ascending and descending on it.

God will come to warn our competitors not to harm us. Genesis 31:24 And God came to Laban the Syrian <u>in a dream</u> by night, and said unto him, Take heed that thou speak not to Jacob either good or bad.

God may want to reveal our destiny to us privately. Genesis 37:5 And Joseph dreamed a dream, and he <u>told it</u> his brethren: and they hated him yet the more.

God will give us His interpretation of a God dream. Genesis 40:5 And they dreamed a dream both of them, each man his dream in one night, each man according to <u>the interpretation</u> of his dream, the butler and the baker of the king of Egypt, which were bound in the prison.

God wants to warn our leaders and make a way for our promotion. Genesis 41:1 And it came to pass at the end of two full years, that Pharaoh dreamed: and, behold, he stood by the river.

God wants to give us favor and new direction in visions of the night. Genesis 46:2 And God spoke unto Israel in the visions of the night, and said, Jacob, Jacob. And he said, Here am I.

God will appear to us in the midst of natural things. Exodus 3:2 And the angel of the LORD appeared unto him in a flame of fire out of the midst of a bush: and he looked, and, behold, the bush burned with fire, and the bush was not consumed.

God wants us to see His glory. Exodus 16:10 And it came to pass, as Aaron spoke unto the whole congregation of the children of Israel, that they looked toward the wilderness, and, behold, the glory of the LORD appeared in the cloud.

God wants to visit His people. Exodus 24:16-17 And the glory of the LORD abode upon mount Sinai, and the cloud covered it six days: and the seventh day he called unto Moses out of the midst of the cloud. 17 And the sight of the glory of the LORD was like devouring fire on the top of the mount in the eyes of the children of Israel.

God will make Himself known to us in visions and dreams. Numbers 12:6 And he said, Hear now my words: If there be a prophet among you, I the LORD will make myself known unto him in a vision, and will speak unto him in a dream.

God will open our donkey's eyes and our eyes! Numbers 22:31 Then the LORD opened the eyes of Balaam, and he saw the angel of the LORD standing in the way, and his sword drawn in his hand: and he bowed down his head, and fell flat on his face.

God wants us to choose to lift up our eyes and allow the Spirit of the Lord to come upon us. Numbers 24:2-3 And Balaam lifted up his eyes, and he saw Israel abiding in his tents according to their tribes; and the spirit of God came upon him. 3 And he took up his parable, and said, Balaam the son of Beor hath said, and the man whose eyes are open hath said:

God will use a trance to open our spiritual eyes. Numbers 24:4 He hath said, which heard the words of God, which saw the vision of the Almighty, falling into a trance, but having his eyes open:

God wants us to lift our eyes up and to interact with His warrior angels. Joshua 5:13 And it came to pass, when Joshua was by Jericho, that he lifted up his eyes and looked, and, behold, there stood a man over against him with his sword drawn in his hand: and Joshua went unto him, and said unto him, Art thou for us, or for our adversaries?

God wants us to see our angel who is ready to help. Judges 6:12-13 And the angel of the LORD <u>appeared</u> unto him, and said unto him, The LORD is with thee, thou mighty man of valour.

God wants to give national leaders instructions. 2 Samuel 7:4-5 And it came to pass that night, that the word of the LORD came unto Nathan, saying, 5 Go and <u>tell my servant David</u>, Thus saith the LORD, Shalt thou build me an house for me to dwell in?

The Holy Spirit will take us up to other places in visions. Ezekiel 11:24 Afterwards the spirit <u>took me up</u>, and brought me in a vision by the Spirit of God into Chaldea, to them of the captivity. So the vision that I had seen went up from me

God will give us knowledge, skill, learning, wisdom and understanding in visions and dreams. Daniel 1:17 As for these four children, <u>God gave</u> them knowledge and skill in all learning and wisdom: and Daniel had understanding in all visions and dreams.

God will hear our prayer and reveal the secret in a night visions. Daniel 2:19 Then was the <u>secret revealed</u> unto Daniel in a night vision. Then Daniel blessed the God of heaven.

God will give us visions and we are to seek for the meaning. Daniel 8:15 And it came to pass, when I, even I Daniel, had seen the vision, and <u>sought for the meaning</u>, then, behold, there stood before me as the appearance of a man.

Angels are sent to touch us in visions. Daniel 9:21 Yea, whiles I was speaking in prayer, even the man Gabriel, whom I had seen in the vision at the beginning, being caused to fly swiftly, <u>touched me</u> about the time of the evening oblation.

We are to watch to see what God will say to us. Habakkuk 2:1 I will stand upon my watch, and set me upon the tower, and will <u>watch to see</u> what he will say unto me, and what I shall answer when I am reproved.

We are to have pen and paper ready to write our dreams and visions. Habakkuk 2:2 And the LORD answered me, and said, <u>Write the vision</u>, and make it plain upon tables, that he may run that readeth it.

God's desire is to abundantly pour out His Spirit with dreams, visions and prophesy on all flesh. Joel 2:28 And it shall come to pass afterward, that I will <u>pour out my spirit</u> upon all flesh; and your sons and your daughters shall prophesy, your old men shall dream dreams, your young men shall see visions:

God will interact with us about healing and prophetic words through use of visions. Acts 9:10 And there was a certain disciple at Damascus, named Ananias; and to him said the Lord in a vision, Ananias. And <u>he said</u>, Behold, I am here, Lord.

God will use visions to connect us with unbelievers. Acts 10:33 He saw in a vision evidently about the ninth hour of the day an angel of <u>God coming in to him</u>, and saying unto him, Cornelius.

God will set up divine appointments through visions. Acts 10:17,19 Now while Peter doubted in himself what this vision which he had seen should mean, behold, the men which were sent from Cornelius had made inquiry for Simon's house, and stood before the gate. 19 While Peter thought on the vision, the Spirit said unto him, Behold, three men seek thee.

God will correct our doctrines and theology in visions. Acts 11:5 I was in the city of Joppa praying: and in a trance I saw a vision, A certain vessel descend, as it had been a great sheet, let down from heaven by four corners; and it came even to me:

God will direct our ministry outreach through visions. Acts 16:9 And a vision appeared to Paul in the night; There stood a man of Macedonia, and prayed him, saying, Come over into Macedonia, and help us.

God will give us boldness and confidence to speak. Acts 18:9 Then spoke the Lord to Paul in the night by a vision, Be not afraid, but speak, and hold not thy peace.

God is ready to reveal the future when we are in the Spirit. Revelation 1:10 I was in the Spirit on the Lord's day, and heard behind me a great voice, as of a trumpet

God will enable us to look and behold the Spiritual realm! Revelation 4:1-2 After this I looked, and, behold, a door was opened in heaven: and the first voice which I heard was as it were of a trumpet talking with me; which said, Come up hither, and I will show thee things which must be hereafter. 2 And immediately I was in the spirit: and, behold, a throne was set in heaven, and one sat on the throne.

From Genesis to Revelation, God has spoken to people through dreams and visions! We can choose to invite God's Spirit to speak to us in any way that He chooses. God has not limited us to know Him only with our minds and the written logos Word of God. **God, the same yesterday, today and forever!** Agreeing with God's Truth is very important but we need to repent and ask forgiveness 5 ways for blocking His Truth and not using our eyes for spiritual vision.

Ungodly Beliefs
1. I *confess* my sin (and if appropriate, my ancestor's sin) of believing the ungodly belief that _____ and for any way I have **blamed you** God.
2. I *forgive* those who contributed to my forming this UGB, including myself.
3. I ask You, Lord, to **forgive me** for living my life by it and for anyway I have judged others, based on this UGB.
4. I *forgive* myself for believing this ungodly belief and blocking spiritual vision.
5. I *renounce* and **break** my agreement with this UGB, and the agreement that I have had with deception, the power of darkness, and with demons.
6. I *choose* to accept and **believe** the GB that _____.

Voices: God's, Satan's or My Own?

A radio listener transcribed my message about my own search to learn to hear God.
Dr. Mark Virkler asked me to teach on his four keys to hearing God's voice.

Men and woman throughout the Bible heard the voice of God and saw visions. There is a deep hunger within each of us to know and experience the voice of God. There is a desire to have communion with God on a daily basis to hear God speak to our heart.

I would like to thank you for allowing me to share my aggressive search to learn how to hear the voice of God. The world inundates us with opportunities to access the spiritual realm, and contact spirits. The world talks about having "spirit guides" of our own. These New Age influences have caused many Christians to shrink back from their heritage, and not hear the voice of God. Remember, it was the privilege of Adam and Eve to walk with God in the cool of the evening.

Jesus said, "My sheep can hear my voice." In Acts 2:17, we are told that in the last days we would not only dream dreams, and see visions, but we will be able to hear him. My prayer to God is if anybody can have this communion, I want it.
Romans 7:1-6 is seldom preached, but I believe it shares the key to having an intimate relationship with God that is FRUITFUL.

[Romans 7:1] Know ye not, brethren, (for I speak to them that know the law,) how that the law hath dominion over a man as long as he liveth?
[Romans 7:2] For the woman which hath an husband is bound by the law to her husband so long as he liveth; but if the husband be dead, she is loosed from the law of her husband.
[Romans 7:3] So then if, while her husband liveth, she be married to another man, she shall be called an adulteress: but if her husband be dead, she is free from that law; so that she is no adulteress, though she be married to another man.
[Romans 7:4] Wherefore, my brethren, ye also are become dead to the law by the body of Christ; that ye should be married to another, even to him who is raised from the dead, that we should bring forth fruit unto God.
[Romans 7:5] For when we were in the flesh, the motions of sins, which were by the law, did work in our members to bring forth fruit unto death.
[Romans 7:6] But now we are delivered from the law, that being dead wherein we were held; that we should serve in newness of spirit, and not in the oldness of the letter.

This is a manner of expressing that when we are no longer married to our ability to keep the law, then we are **free to marry Jesus, as a matter of speaking.** When we are free to marry Jesus, we are free to come into a union or oneness with Him. It is only in the union where fruit is formed and something is birthed.

So how do I hear God? How do I know if it God speaking to me? Someone suggested, "If you think it is God, ask if it is the Lord." How many think it might be a problem if I have never heard the voice of God to hear the answer? If Jesus is within me, then I should be able to hear Him! In fact, Jesus said, "I only do what I see the Father doing. I only say what I hear the Father saying." So if Jesus is inside me, then I ought to be able to hear what the Father wants to say.

I had a passion to learn how to worship Him, like the woman at the well. She wanted to worship in spirit and in truth. She did not get bogged down in NOT having a relationship with God. She just wanted to know how to have a relationship.

In Habakkuk, we find four steps that are key to hearing God's voice and seeing Him in vision.

[Habakkuk 2:1] I will stand upon my watch, and set me upon the tower, and will watch to see what he will say unto me, and what I shall answer when I am reproved. [Habakkuk 2:2] And the Lord answered me, and said, Write the vision, and make it plain upon tables, that he may run that readeth it.

This verse is amazing to me. Notice the verse says **I will watch to see, not listen to hear**. This means the prophet could see what was said, and he could hold on to the vision long enough to write it, and RUN with it. Certainly Daniel the prophet, and John the Revelator did also.

One of the most important things to keep in mind is that we receive like a little child. How do we become like a little child?

1. Renounce any fear of hearing the voice of God, and of Satan's power to confuse me. Sometimes we may think the power of Satan is stronger. Even though we ask God for something Biblical, sometimes we are fearful that Satan can bring confusion and deception.
2. Would you like to denounce fear with me? Would you like to denounce the fear of hearing the voice of God? The word says if we ask our earthly father for a fish, he would not give us something that would hurt us. How much more will our Heavenly Father give good things to those who ask Him! Whatever I ask in faith believing, I can believe and I already have what I say!
3. Would you like to live with the well of the spirit springing up within? John 4:4 tells me it is a spring that wells up within me.

Have you experienced that flow with the Holy Spirit of God? We live in the cognitive ability of our mind. We must repent of living out of what our natural ears and eyes can sense. We must submit our eyes and ears to God. Romans 6 tells us we must yield all our members unto God. We are servants to whomever we submit our members to.

The words of John the Apostle tells us that the Word of God (the Rhema word) is Life, and that life is the Light of men. If I have the Life of Christ, I am free to tune into the flow of the Rhema Word of God.

All of God's sheep can hear the voice of God, not just the gifted ones. Even non-Christians can hear the voice of God. The Bible is full of stories of people who had no covenant with God, yet they heard the voice of God.

I would like to share **four spiritual keys for hearing the voice of God.**

1. **God's voice in our hearts sounds like the flow of spontaneous thoughts.** Therefore, when I tune to God, I tune to spontaneity.
2. **I must learn to still my own thoughts** and emotions so I can sense God's flow of thoughts and emotions within me. Be still before God.
3. **I fix the eyes of my heart upon Jesus,** seeing in the spirit the dreams and visions of Almighty God. Watch what God will speak to you.
4. **Journaling** our prayers and God's answers, provides a great freedom in hearing God's voice. Record the vision.

These keys will not only work for me, but for you as well. Practice all of these keys, not just one or two. These keys are found in Habakkuk 2:1-2.

[Habakkuk 2:1] I will stand upon my watch, and set me upon the tower, and will watch to see what he will say unto me, and what I shall answer when I am reproved. [Habakkuk 2:2] And the Lord answered me, and said, Write the vision, and make it plain upon tables, that he may run that readeth it.

Habakkuk knew the sound of God's voice. Elijah knew the sound of God's voice and described it as a still small voice. I have always listened to that still small voice, but I was not sure I had heard it. Passages like this describe the voice of God and reaffirm they were hearing God's voice. They were sure enough that they wrote it down. They were able to make decisions and run with it.

For most of us, the voice of God comes as a still small spontaneous thought, vision, feeling or an impression. It is not a booming bass voice. It is not audible. At least it is not heard with human ears. We must learn to discern what is the voice of God, what is our voice, and what is the voice of the enemy.

Ever pictured someone's face and felt impressed to pray for them? The thought just popped in your mind? Did you hear the Lord say to pray for a particular person? We generally acknowledge instances like that in casual conversation. We might say, "I felt like God wanted me to pray for that person." That is an example of hearing God's voice.

What does the voice of God sound like? It is an inner still small voice. It is spontaneous. It suddenly pops into your awareness. You were not trying to figure it out. Many times you were not even thinking about praying for someone, and suddenly a thought or picture comes to your mind.

The best way we can describe it is **a still small voice or a spontaneous thought or**

picture. Many times I receive thoughts, impressions or feelings that I would not normally experience. Many times when you hear the Holy Spirit, He is encouraging you to be more loving and kind, wise or more unselfish than you might choose. You know that is not your voice, it is the voice of God. The voice of God is noble.

The definition of the Hebrew word *pagá,* which is the word for intercession, is *a chance encounter or intersection.* When a thought of intercession lights upon us, we experience the voice of God! A thought intersects with our thought process. Therefore, when I tune into God, I tune into a God-encounter.

I must learn to still my own thoughts and emotions so I can sense God's flow of thoughts and emotions within me. Be still before God.

I will climb to the lookout tower. **[Habakkuk 2:1-2]** That is an expression of being still. If Habakkuk was going to hear the voice of God, he would have to still his mind, will and emotions. He would have to tune in to those spontaneous thoughts in a quiet place. He had to still his own mind, and he had to do it early in the morning before his mind was crammed with the pressures of the day.

Some Jewish Rabbis set their clock for exactly 2 hours before dawn because they believe they can hear God the best in the early morning. They believe there is more revelation in that two hour window. That is a helpful hint, but not required.

[Psalm 46:10] Be still, and know that I am God:

You have to be still to know that He is God. I want to know God and have a relationship with God. There is a spontaneous flow in the Spirit when we know that we are connecting with God. I want living water. **I want fresh bread. If anybody can have it, I want it too!**

I must quiet my mind and command it to submit to the Spirit. There are many ways to quiet yourself. One way is to connect with God through worship in song.

When we still our thoughts and emotions, we can enter into His divine flow – into the river of God. That river wells up within us! Worship songs help me to position my heart toward my Creator, and see what He has to say, and to see what He wants me to see. If my thoughts come spontaneously in a higher and nobler way than I would normally think, then I believe my prayer has been answered.

I asked the Lord to speak to me or show me what He would have me to know. I have believed. I have bound other spirits and no other spirit can affect me or speak to me.

Now if you are like me, as soon as I sit down to pray many other thoughts crowd in to distract me. I think of all the things I could be doing with that time. Many of those things are needful things which should be done. I have learned to keep a pencil and paper available so I can write these things down in order to acknowledge them. Once I have given proper attention to that thought, I can dismiss it.

If I have thoughts of unworthiness, guilt or shame, I repent.
I address the unworthiness or shame by telling my spirit the truth that God says about me.

I am forgiven, and totally accepted.
I am accepted apart from my performance.
I have been given a new future. I am free from my past.
I am not only loved, but God has made me loveable in him.
I receive the washing of the Word if I study the Word, and the Word sustains me.

As I incubate the Word of God in my spirit, I am able to hear God and come into agreement with Him. Then I fix my gaze on Jesus. When I fix my gaze on Jesus, I am tuning my heart to His divine frequency.
Turn your eyes upon Jesus,
Look full into his wonderful face,
And the things of earth shall grow strangely dim
In the light of his glory and grace.

When I connect to His glory and grace, the distractions do become dim. I find that I am actually conversant with the King of Kings. It is dialogue with Christ who is inside me.

[1 Corinthians 6:17] But he that is joined unto the Lord is one spirit.

[John 15:5] I am the vine, ye are the branches: He that abideth in me, and I in him, the same bringeth forth much fruit: for without me ye can do nothing.

[John 17:21] That they all may be one; as thou, Father, art in me, and I in thee, that they also may be one in us: that the world may believe that thou hast sent me.
[John 17:22] And the glory which thou gavest me I have given them; that they may be one, even as we are one:
[John 17:23] I in them, and thou in me, that they may be made perfect in one; and that the world may know that thou hast sent me, and hast loved them, as thou hast loved me.

Are we experiencing being one with the Father? If we cannot see or hear God, how can that be oneness? If you become still and focus on Jesus, you will receive the pure word of God. You will not get a stone instead of a fish. However, if you are not still, you might receive an echo of your own thoughts. If you are not focused on Jesus, you may have an impure flow.

But if you focus on Jesus, still your thoughts and watch to see what God might say, you will hear from God. You will hear that God is giving you the desire of your heart. You will sense the intuitive flow when you become still before God and fix your eyes upon Him.

As I pray, I fix the eyes of my heart upon Jesus, seeing vision in the Holy Spirit.
Watch what God will speak to you.

We have already alluded to this principle. It is interesting to notice that Habakkuk recorded the vision. Furthermore, Habakkuk started looking for the vision as he prayed. He went into prayer expecting vision. He went into prayer expecting to hear. Habakkuk went to a special place, and expected to see and hear God. He determined to open the eyes of his heart and the ears of his spirit. He decided to look into the spiritual realm and to see what God wanted to show him.

Have you ever thought about opening your eyes to look for vision or opening your ears to hear God? Have you submitted your eyes and ears to God? God put us here in order to have communion with us.

How do we start? Look. Habakkuk said he was going to look to see what God might say to him. Daniel saw visions in his mind. Not only did he look, but he kept looking.

[Daniel 7:1] In the first year of Belshazzar king of Babylon Daniel had a dream and visions of his head upon his bed: then he wrote the dream, and told the sum of the matters.
[Daniel 7:7] After this I saw in the night visions . . .
[Daniel 7:9] I beheld till the thrones were cast down . . .
[Daniel 7:11] I beheld then . . .

[Daniel 7:13] I saw in the night visions, and, behold, one like the Son of man came with the clouds of heaven, and came to the Ancient of days, and they brought him near before him.

I also see the same pattern in the Book of Revelation where John saw visions. He looked. He kept looking, and he wrote them down. So now when I pray, I am starting to watch to see what he will speak to me. I will do what the Father says to do in vision, and say what the Father says to say. John "saw or looked" at least 34 times and "heard" at least 14 times, not counting phrase like "He said to me"

The name of Jesus is Emanuel, meaning God with us. Why is He with us? He is with us so we can receive the divine spontaneous flow of thoughts. He is present within us. The Psalmist said, "Be still, and know that I am God." God is willing and able to communicate with us.

As we surrender our ears and eyes, we watch to see what God wants us to see. Instead of running in panic or doubt, we believe that whatever we see is from God. Doubt is an effective weapon of Satan. **But can we believe that God answers prayer and whatever we see next is from Him?**

If we believe what we see is from the Holy One, we can record it. We can run with it. But do not run with it unless we submit the record to those who have spiritual oversight for us so they may confirm it is from God, or if we need to pray about it some more, or that it is not God at all. God continually revealed Himself in the Bible to His covenant people by dreams and visions. Why would He not do the same for us?

In Acts 2:1-4, God confirmed at Pentecost that the people could expect to receive dreams and visions from God. Jesus of Nazareth demonstrated that it was possible to live with an on-going conversation with God – seeing and hearing what the Father wanted done. Jesus said we would have that ability as well. He said He did nothing on His own initiative, and we do not have to either. He said He did what He saw the Father doing. We can do the same. God is ready and willing to show us and tell us what He wants done. Christ is in us, and is able to do it.

It is Christ in me, the hope of glory. It is by the power and presence <u>OF</u> the Risen Christ that we live the Christian life. It is His power and His faith according to Galatians 2:20. Christ in YOU, is the mystery of the Gospel. Colossians 1:27

Journaling, the writing out of our prayers and God's answers, provides a great freedom in hearing God's voice. Record the vision.
Whenever we write something it imprints it upon our mind. It is more likely to go into our recall memory. It is also better to write it by hand than to type it, but that is not a requirement. God told the prophet in Habakkuk 2:2 to write the vision, and record it on tablets. But the question is, "Has it ever occurred to you to write your prayers?"

That is not quite the same as Habakkuk was doing. He was writing whole conversations with God. Try this: write out the scripture passages you feel God has put upon your heart, and what it means to you. Then write out your response.
You will find many examples of journaling in the Bible. The Psalms exist because of David's habit of journaling. He poured out his heart to God. Sometimes he poured out ungodly thoughts to God, but he always came back to agreement with God.

There is a quality which comes with this practice which helps to escalate the process. It helps us to come into agreement and fellowship with God. It helps us to have a pure heart much more quickly. It is a *facilitator* to help us tune into the spontaneous flow of the Holy Spirit, His guidance and His will for our lives.

Write in faith! Do not quench it because that will shut off the flow. You can share or test it later with a spiritual person, but do not be quick to share it with everybody. Some things are meant to be kept close to your heart and pondered.

When you doubt, you will hinder the Spirit of God. Doubt will shut you off from the flow. But come in faith! This is Biblical. There are strong examples in the Bible. Choose. Choose to continue to look into the vision actively, and continue to listen.

Do not take yourself too seriously. Do not be tense or anxious. Enter into the rest. Stay in the flow. Believe that God has initiated the flow of the Spirit. Write your questions for God. Listen and look for the answers, and you will begin to receive those answers. Those spontaneous thoughts will come as fast as or faster than you can record them.

I challenge you to do all four steps. Doing one or two steps has not worked well in the past, and probably will not in the future. Pray in faith believing that God is the rewarder of those who diligently seek Him. You can journal and stay in faith for an extended period of time. You can test it later. You should have people in place who are willing and able to test those things. They can let you know whether they believe it is from God, or do not believe it is from God, or you need to pray about it longer.

Are you ready to step into the river of God?
Are you ready to yield your ears and eyes to God?
Are you ready to tune into the flow of spontaneous thoughts and visions?
Are you ready to watch to see what God will say to you?
Are you willing to submit to what God might say to you?

****

I encourage you to read the New Testament all the way through if you have not already done so. Make a habit of staying in the Word! You should know the biblical foundations and boundaries. Make sure you have a mentor in the area of hearing God who has a biblical foundation as well.

Witchcraft in the Church
My notes from <u>Epic Battles of the Last Days</u> by Rick Joyner

NOTE: Since January of 2000, a large percentage of my prayer receivers have been survivors of witchcraft influences. **Witches usually make every effort to remain hidden,** but infiltrators want to be in your church, prayer groups, leadership teams and children's church. Whether they are practicing indirect witchcraft, covert witchcraft, "manipulation and control" or actual overt witchcraft, you will have to own your spiritual power and authority to set the captives free. It is important to teach the sheep how to begin the day by praying protection prayers.

The spirit of witchcraft is dedicated to dilute, subjugate and destroy Christianity. Many Christians are suffering because they do not know how to discern and overcome these attacks. **We must not be ignorant of his devices (2 Corinthians 2:11).** We can only be defeated if we are ignorant or passive, without armor and are not vigilant to stand and prevail.

Witchcraft is "counterfeit spiritual authority. It is using a demonic spirit to dominate, manipulate or control others." It is using emotional pressure to manipulate others, soul power to recruit them, scheming, using pressure points, worldly sales techniques, and other ways of manipulating us to trust our own influence instead of God. Any authority or influence we gain by our own efforts will be a stumbling block to us and our ability to trust God to establish us in His time. (1 Peter 5:6) Few things breed insecurity faster than trying to maintain a position that we have gained prematurely through counterfeit spiritual authority. No matter how noble our goals are, power gained by witchcraft is doomed to failure. The flesh wars against the spirit no matter how good it looks.

Much that is called discernment in the church today, is really suspicion rooted in fear and territorial or self-preservation spirits rather than the Holy Spirit. True spiritual discernment is rooted in love that is not naive but accurate by the Spirit. (1 Corinthians13) Unhealed wounds, unforgiveness, bitterness, insecurity and the kingdom of self all confuse and neutralize true spiritual discernment. In order to walk in true discernment, we must come to a level of mature true love that does not take offense, retaliate, reject others or insist on proving ourselves.

The fear of man leads to witchcraft, as we begin to fear man and circumstances more than God. Those who have gained influence by self-effort will fear anyone who walks in God's true anointing. As manipulation and control increase their dominance, so will paranoia and an irrational desire to drive out or destroy anyone who threatens their control. Those who receive their security from men, will eventually end up like Saul, in the witch's house. (1 Samuel 15:23) He took sides against the true priests of the Lord, persecuting them and killing some.

<u>1 Samuel 22:17</u> And the king said unto the footmen that stood about him, "Turn, and slay the priests of the LORD; because their hand also is with David, and because they knew when he fled, and did not shew it to me. But the servants of the king would not put forth their hand to fall upon the priests of the LORD. 18 And the king said to Doeg, Turn thou, and fall upon the priests. And Doeg the Edomite turned, and he fell upon the priests, and slew on that day fourscore and five persons that did wear a linen ephod."

Spiritual authority is a dangerous occupation. If we are wise like David, we will not seek or accept a position of authority until we are certain that it is the Lord giving it. Satan offered to Jesus and all of us, authority over kingdoms if we will bow down to him. He offers a shortcut around the path of servanthood to quick and easy promotion.

True spiritual authority is more of a burden than an honor. On the few occasions that David did not inquire of the Lord before a decision, the consequences were devastating. Remember that presumption can kill us. Words of knowledge and power are great, but words of wisdom are needed in order to use them properly. Prominence before humility will also ensure failure. False prophets will use their gifts and the people, for themselves -- rather than give themselves for the people.

Those in leadership must remember that they will be the primary target of charismatic witchcraft. They may fall for subtle forms of manipulation because they cannot be straightforward enough. They may begin to gain influence or control by looking super-spiritual through false prophecies, dreams and visions. They may begin to bring leadership to the point of despising prophecy altogether. They may begin to think that the leadership are the ones in rebellion rather than them. How is it that we are still overcome by evil? It is because we are seduced with deception more often than we are confronted by demons in obvious power. Pride after a victory can leave a breach in our armor. **** Our first defense against witchcraft is a humility that knows that we stand only by God's grace.

The Stinger

The attacks of witchcraft usually come in series of stings that attack in the weak area left behind by the previous sting. Often they come in the following order: discouragement, confusion, depression, loss of vision, disorientation, withdrawal, despair, and defeat. This can happen quickly or slowly and in many ways; through cults, the New Age, deceived Christians praying against us, gossip, manipulation, jealousy, etc. We can fall prey if we agree with the control spirit or if we resist by departing from the fruit of the Spirit. As we bless those who curse us, the power of manipulation and control is broken. We must overcome evil with good.

Discouragement - for no reason may be due to witchcraft. When things seem insurmountable, even when they actually are not, you may be under attack.

Confusion - may cause us to lose our clarity regarding our calling and weak our resolve. This compounds the discouragement, making us more vulnerable.

Depression - is the unshakable dread that is usually accompanied by poor spiritual discipline that leads to a poor defense or offense.

Loss of Vision - means we begin to doubt that we are called in the first place. We can only hold our course if we know where we are going and that we are called.

<u>Disorientation</u> - is the combination of all three and now we cannot even read the compass. We begin to not trust in the scriptures to speak to us, the Lord's voice or the most anointed.

<u>Withdrawal</u> - we retreat from our purpose in ministry, the fellowship and often our family and friends.

<u>Despair</u> - and withdrawal from the battle lead quickly to hopelessness and we are easily taken out by the enemy.

Without hope even the most healthy deteriorate and die. With hope, men and women have **lived long past the point when a normal body would have quit.**

<u>Defeat</u> - comes as we fall further and further behind; then we are picked off more easily. The strategy of the Amalekites was to pick off the stragglers and those who don't want to fight.

In <u>Revelation 12:11</u> we see the road to victory. We take our stand on what Jesus has already done on the cross, the word of our testimony and the Sword of the Spirit, and an utter commitment to follow Jesus regardless of the price. *** To the degree that we remain in self-centeredness and self-effort we are vulnerable to the enemy. Dead men cannot be offended, tempted, fearful, depressed or looking for the easy way out. When we see Satan, we are going to marvel at the pitiful nature of the one who caused so much trouble. This is our finest hour. (Isaiah 60:1-2)

Resisting the Spirit of Witchcraft

- We must take captive every thought of discouragement and put up our faith shield!

- As good soldiers we can speak confusion to the plans of the enemy.

- Conquer depression with increased discipline in prayer, the Word, fellowship etc.

- Review every way God called you and the revelation of your vision in detail.

- "Fly" through disorientation by focusing on the "instrument panel" or the word of God.

- Withdrawal from the front line is dangerous; the front line has fewer casualties.

- Return to the body and get help solving or resolving the problems. (1 Corinthians 15:57, Romans 8:37, 2 Corinthians 2:14)

WARNING: Those who give themselves to the study of and become authorities on the nature of evil, usually become darkened and evil themselves. Cult watchers often release a more foul spirit in the church than the cult they are watching. They become paranoid, divisive, faultfinding, and damage the church with their suspicions and slander, as if they were proven facts. Jude warned that these are being reserved for the "black darkness" in which many of them have already begun to live. (Jude 10-16)

Why Restoration Teams?

I believe God is allowing the body of Christ to come to the place where we will have to rise to our calling to minister restoration. Do you believe that believers can be taught, trained and equipped to have a significant part in restoring individuals, small groups, churches, cities and nations? Who will minister restoration prayers to the great harvest?

Do you believe you can be a part of a new generation of restoration ministers? If you had an opportunity to be trained to be on a restoration team or to train up restoration teams, would you be interested? For many believers, this is radical thinking. The Bible says that if you have Christ in you, you have everything you need for life and godliness. Christ in you has all you need to fulfill your destiny but most people may not know how to release this life-changing power. Believers have His unlimited power within to be all He has called them to be. He has made unique deposits into each believer's life and has been preparing us for a unique gifting, a unique calling and a unique anointing.

I believe that most Pastors and Priests would be interested in training up restoration teams if they saw this manual. Why? Because they are accountable for how their members minister and they need a protocol and guidelines to define what a restoration team does. With the manual in hand, they can define what tools are to be used:

1. Clear definitions of what each issue is about
2. Approved prayers asking forgiveness five ways
3. Scripture prayer strategies to define "biblical"
4. Helpful handouts and self-tests
5. Relevant books, articles and teachings

Do you share my vision of churches raising up restoration teams who will minister to the great harvest of new believers, prodigals and even the fallen? God has already given revelation and spiritual insights that enable believers to partner with Him to heal the broken hearted and minister freedom to the captives. The big question is how to equip members to minister healing, freedom, activation in the spiritual gifts and to be demonstrations His love and power.

Manual Two and Manual Three

Restoration Prayer Ministry Manual Two will provide you with insights, scriptures, resources, tools and prayers for ministry to more complex issues that are common in prayer ministry. It will have advanced teaching and ministry helps. It is necessary to master the ministry guidelines in Manual One before you study the complex issues in Manual Two. If you sense a call to begin a Restoration Prayer Ministry of your own, you will appreciate the forms and advanced resources in Manual Two.

Manual Three will include insights, resources, tools and prayers for more advanced issues. It is absolutely critical that you have received our 18 hour Restoration Prayer Ministry yourself before you attempt the advanced ministry in Manual Three. It will be a priceless asset to those who have studied to show themselves approved and prepared by applying the insights in Manual One and Two.

Part 4: Exhibits and Opportunities

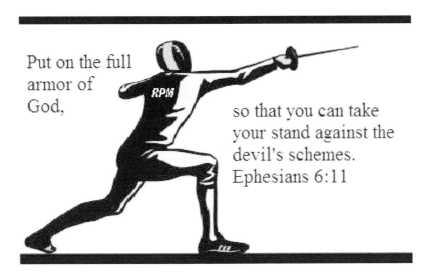

Put on the full armor of God, so that you can take your stand against the devil's schemes. Ephesians 6:11

Cross Walk Prayer

Dear Lord Jesus,

I have a negative pattern in my life, that is not Godly and I cannot get rid of it by myself. I know that a bad fruit has a bad root. I don't want this pattern of _____ any longer. I don't want to reap this in my own life or in the people around me. Please show me the spiritual root of it and how to deal with my part of this problem (even if I am only 10% of the problem.)

Did I sow this and now I am reaping it, more and later?   Galatians 6:7-10
Did I dishonor my parents or authorities in this area?   Ephesians 6:1-3
Did I judge someone and now I draw that thing to me?   Matthew 7:1, Romans 2:1-4
Did a bitter expectation spring up in me, defiling others?   Hebrews 12:14-15
Did I make an inner vow in not to be like them?   James 5:12, Matthew 5:37

1. **I RECOGNIZE** that the reason this problem of _____ is now a pattern in my own life, is because of my sinful reaction of (dishonor, judgment, sowing the sin myself, inner vows or bitter root expectation.) The fruit is that I am reaping similar problems in others and myself according to the LAW of sowing and reaping. I am reaping this crop because of my sinful reactions to their sin. I am reaping from the sinful seed that I have sown - not from what they have sown.

2. **I REPENT** and ask forgiveness 5 ways. Please forgive me:

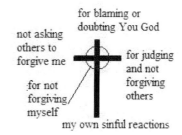

   1. for not asking others to forgive me
   2. for judging others and not forgiving others
   3. for sowing my own sin / sinful reactions
   4. for blaming or doubting you God
   5. and for not forgiving myself

3. **I RENOUNCE** my sin of dishonor, judgment, sowing the sin myself, bitter root expectations or fleshly inner vows. I choose to forgive them, releasing them to you, the Judge of all the earth.

4. **RELEASE** me from reaping this crop that is now mine to reap because of my sinful reactions to others.

5. **I RECKON** dead on the cross all flesh that identifies with this reaction and all automatic reactions that I have developed with it. I ask you Jesus, to bring it to death, because I cannot. Create in me a pure heart that agrees with your responses.

6. **RESURRECT** your likeness into every area that you have brought to death.

7. **RESTORE** all the years that the locusts have eaten while I was disobedient.

8. I RECLAIM **all the spiritual blessings that my family and I have missed.**

9. REWARD **us for generations to come, as we sow true discernment, grace and mercy. Thank you Lord for the forgiveness you have provided for us on the cross and all the blessings that we are free to walk in now. We believe you for them! Amen**

Circles Diagram

Body, Soul and Spirit diagrams adapted from "Exchanged Life" by Charles Solomon

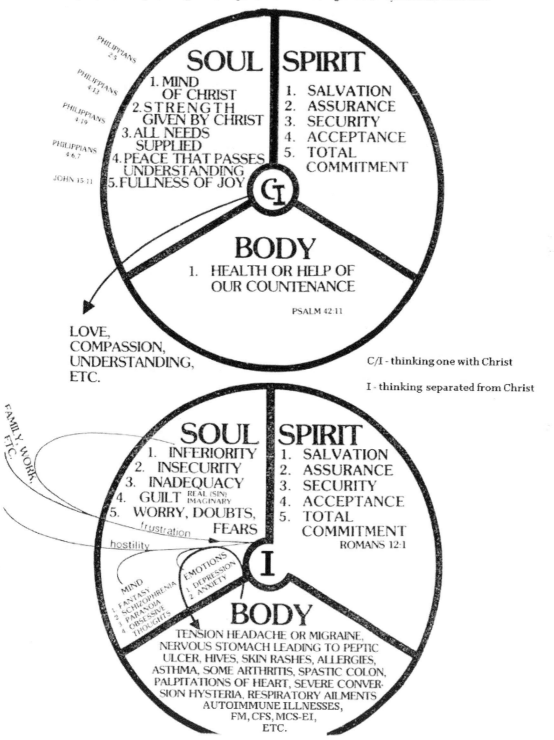

Probably one of the biggest challenges we have is to understand the love of God. Don't ask me, "Why does God love us? He is love and He does. Let's pray and ask Father God to expand our hearts so we can receive our Father's Love Letter, His love and His unconditional acceptance. It is truly more humble to receive God's love than it is to refuse it. Pray that you will be able to run into His arms with abandon, when you begin to see Him waiting for you. You will find incredible peace sitting in His lap.

Love Letter
Adapted from the Father's Love Letter - free downloads at www.fathersloveletter.com

You may not know me, but I know everything about you. Psalm 139:1
I know when you sit down and when you rise up. Psalm 139:2
I am familiar with all your ways. Psalm 139:3
Even the very hairs on your head are numbered. Matthew 10:29-31
For you were made in My image. Genesis 1:27
In Me you live and move and have your being. Acts 17:28
For you are My offspring. Acts 17:28
I knew you before you were conceived. Jeremiah 1:4-5
I chose you when I planned creation. Ephesians 1:11-12
You were not a mistake, all your days are written in My book. Psalm 139:15-16
I determined the exact time of your birth and where you would live. Acts 17:26
You are fearfully and wonderfully made. Psalm 139:14
I knit you together in your mother's womb. Psalm 139:13
And brought you forth on the day you were born. Psalm 71:6
I have been misrepresented by those who don't know Me. John 8:41-44
I am not distant and angry, but the complete expression of love. 1 John 4:16
And it is my desire to lavish my love on you. 1 John 3:1
Simply because you are my child and I am your father. 1 John 3:1
I offer you more than your earthly father ever could. Matthew 7:11
For I am the perfect father. Matthew 5:48
Every good gift that you receive comes from My hand. James 1:17
For I am your provider and I meet all your needs. Matthew 6:31-33
My plan for your future has always been filled with hope. Jeremiah 29:11
Because I love you with an everlasting love. Jeremiah 31:3
My thoughts of you are countless as the sand on the seashore. Ps 139:17-18
And I rejoice over you with singing. Zephaniah 3:17
I will never stop doing good to you. Jeremiah 32:40
For you are My treasured possession. Exodus 19:5
I desire to establish you with all My heart and all My soul. Jeremiah 32:41
And I want to show you great and marvelous things. Jeremiah 33:3
If you seek Me with all your heart, you will find Me. Deuteronomy 4:29
Delight in Me and I will give you the desires of your heart. Psalm 37:4
For it is I who gave you those desires. Philippians 2:13
I am able to do more for you than you could possibly imagine. Ephesians 3:20
For I am your greatest encourager. 2 Thessalonians 2:16-17
I am also the Father who comforts you in all your troubles. 2 Corinthians 1:3-4

When you are brokenhearted, I am close to you. Psalm 34:18
As a shepherd carries a lamb, I have carried you close to My heart. Isaiah 40:11
One day I will wipe away every tear from your eyes. Revelation 21:3-4
And I'll take away all the pain you have suffered on this earth. Revelation 21:3-4
I am your Father and I love you even as I love My son, Jesus. John 17:23
For in Jesus, My love for you is revealed. John 17:26
He is the exact representation of My being. Hebrews 1:3
He came to demonstrate that I am for you, not against you. Romans 8:31
And to tell you that I am not counting your sins. 2 Corinthians 5:18-19
Jesus died so that you and I could be reconciled. 2 Corinthians 5:18-19
His death was the ultimate expression of My love for you. 1 John 4:10
I gave up everything I loved that I might gain your love. Romans 8:31-32
If you receive the gift of My son Jesus, you receive Me. 1 John 2:23
And nothing will ever separate you from My love again. Romans 8:38-39
Come home and I'll throw the biggest party heaven has ever seen. Luke 15:7
I have always been Father, and will always be Father. Ephesians 3:14-15
My question is, "Will you be my child?" John 1:12-13
I am waiting for you. Luke 15:11-32

Love, Your Dad, Almighty God

A PROTECTION PRAYER FOR EVERY DAY

We plead the Blood of Jesus over us, our loved ones, pets, possessions and property, everything and everybody we care about. In the Name of Jesus Christ, Son of God Most High, we bind all evil spirits within or around us and cancel every assignment of the enemy against us or them! In the Name of Jesus Christ of Nazareth, Son of God Most High, we command all demonic spirits to go to the dry, uninhabited places and never come back!

We take the Sword of the Spirit and in the Name of Jesus, we cancel and break all witchcraft practices and prayers, curses, hexes, spells, circles, triangles, incantations, any mind binding or mind control actions taken against us and our loved ones! In Jesus Name, we cancel every assignment of area covens, familiar spirits, watchers, interjects and astral spirits! We place a wall of fire and a hedge of protection around us that no spirit can astral project over and if they attack us on purpose, their human hosts will be literally burned. We bless them that continue to try to curse us and bless them with knowledge that the love and power of Jesus Christ is stronger.

In the Name of Jesus Christ the Anointed One of the Most High God, only the Holy Spirit can affect us and no other spirit can see or hear what is happening on our properties or any of our communications. In the Name of Jesus Christ of Nazareth, we bind and crush every evil source of every evil activity and loose the Spirit of Truth on those who practice it, that they may come to know Jesus Christ is Lord and Master of ALL!

PROTECTION PRAYER AS WE MINISTER

In the Name of Jesus, we trust You Lord, to undo all assignments of the enemy and all knowledge of who we are, what we are doing, our sessions and the work of Holy Spirit. We trust You to hide us in a place that is safe from attacks from demonic spirits and to establish genuine trust between us and our prayer receivers. We believe for Your discernment to know Your prayer strategies to destroy the works of the enemy.

We ask You, God Most High, to rebuke or bind any being from realms of darkness, making them deaf, dumb and mute, cancelling all their plans for backlash, back up forces, back up curses or retaliation of any kind. We call every part of our own hearts to come into alignment with Father God's Truth so they can receive healing and freedom.

We swing the Sword of the Spirit, pray in the Spirit, speak the will of Almighty God and call holy warrior angels of God to fight against the enemy (principalities, powers, rulers and wickedness in high places Eph 6:12) with swords of fire! We ask You Lord, to rebuke all cosmic interference from the second heavens and even from outside of time.

In the Name of Jesus Christ, the Anointed One, we ask you Oh Lord, to dismantle spiritual structures of hierarchies of darkness, mind control and programming, as you see fit, in Your will, way and timing. We release Your mighty angels to execute Your will and empower them as we speak Your Word. We thank you for making us, and Your ministry through us, invisible to enemy forces and making a way for believers to "step out" of captivity into true freedom in Jesus Christ, our blessed Lord and Savior. We choose to believe You are transforming us and making us one with You and rest in Your supernatural power.

We trust You to cleanse us from any doubts, worries, fears, demonic attachments or transferences, to purify our hearts, making us true expressions of your heart, in Your love and power, so we can serve You, wholly given to You. Amen

Sins of the Fathers and Resulting Curses

1. I *confess* the sin (iniquity) of my ancestors, my parents, and my own sin, of ___.
2. I *forgive* and *release* them for passing these sins on to me and the resulting curses. (Can add a new specific.)
3. I ask You to *forgive* me, Lord, for this sin, for yielding to it, to the resulting curses and for doubting You God.
4. I *repent* of this sin and for judging them.
5. I *forgive* myself for participating in this sin.
6. I *renounce* the sin and resulting curses of ___, and break the power of it and all resulting curses through the redemptive work of Christ on the Cross and His shed Blood.
7. I *receive* God's freedom from the sin and from the resulting curses. In their place I **receive** ___.

Ungodly Beliefs

1. I *confess* my sin (and if appropriate, my ancestor's sin) of believing the ungodly belief that **blamed you God**.
2. I *forgive* those who contributed to my forming this UGB, including myself.
3. I ask You, Lord, to **forgive me** for living my life by it and for anyway I have judged others, based on this UGB.
4. I *forgive* myself for believing this ungodly belief.
5. I *renounce* and *break* my agreement with this UGB, and the agreement that I have had with deception, the power of darkness, and with demons.
6. I *choose* to accept and **believe** the GB that ___.

Word Curses

1. I **forgive** those who cursed me with the spoken word (and if appropriate) including myself, by saying ___.
2. I **repent** for receiving this curse and judging myself.
3. I ask You to **forgive me**, Lord, for giving it place in my life. ___.
4. I **renounce** and break the legal rights/power of this curse in my life based on the shed Blood of Jesus and His finished work on the Cross.
5. I **release** all related fleshly structures to You and ask You to bring them to death on the Cross.
6. I **cancel** all judgments and all work of all demons associated with this curse by the power of the Blood and the Cross of Christ.
7. I **receive** God's Truth that says I am ___.

Ungodly Soul Ties

1. I **confess** all emotional and spiritual ungodly soul ties and agreements with ___.
2. I **forgive** ___ for their part in my ungodly Soul Ties.
3. I **ask for forgiveness**, Lord, for my sin resulting in ungodly Soul Ties.
4. I **renounce** and break all ungodly Soul Ties. I release myself and ___ to be all that we were created to be.
5. In the Name of Jesus, I **cancel** the assignments of all demons associated with these Ties.

Disappointment with God

Dear God, I **confess** that I have misjudged You and blamed You for things that You did not do. I choose to repent and stop today.

1. I ask You to **forgive me** for my sins against You.
2. I **affirm** that You are good and want only the best for me.
3. I choose to **receive you** as Lord my life and to **believe** you cause all things to work together for good, to mature me so I will be able to rule and reign with You in eternity.
4. I **put the "blame"** where it really belongs, on Satan's kingdom. I choose to stop blaming You, God, and will take responsibility for my own choices under the guidance and control of the Holy Spirit.
5. **Thank You** Lord for new freedom, new ability to trust and a renewed relationship with You. I receive it in the Name of Jesus.

Soul/Spirit Hurts

1. I *Ask* You Holy Spirit to reveal the hurt You want to heal today **(Listen/watch** patiently as He tells or shows it to you.)
2. (Be honest with God about how you feel.) Lord, I pour out my heart about the hurt, pain, fear, anger, frustration …
3. I *forgive* ___ (parents, siblings, peers, others) for inflicting this hurt and causing me pain.
4. I ask you to **forgive me**, Lord, for hurting others out of my hurt. I *repent* of this sinful reaction, sinful behavior and my attitude.
5. I *forgive* myself for letting this hurt control me and open doors to strongholds in my life.
6. I **release** this hurt to You, Lord, and I **receive** Your healing touch. **(Listen/watch** as He does. Allow Jesus time to tell you or show you how He is healing you.)
7. **Thank you** for redeeming every hurt and taking the pain.

Spiritual Roots and Suppressed Memories

1. Lord please **tell me or show me** the hidden memory that contains the starting point of my issue/problem. Reveal how this memory and the spiritual root or deception has affected my life. (**Share** what the Lord reveals _____)

2. Lord, show me the areas of my life that this hurt has damaged: _____)

3. **Show me or tell me** the lies or deceptions buried in this memory. (**Share** the lies or deceptions _____)

4. **I turn my eyes** on You Jesus and invite You to show me or tell me how you are healing my hurts. (Share _____)

5. Lord Jesus, **I ask you** to take all the hurts and lies and replace them with your Truth about myself, about others and about You.

6. I choose to **believe and receive** Your Truth.

7. (**Measure** the pain now: 0 = gone and 10 = very painful.)

8. (**Give thanks** if the pain is gone. If not, ask Jesus to show what healing is still needed and pray this prayer again.)

Demonic Oppression and Bondage

1. **confess** my sin of agreeing with the demonic spirits of _____ and forgive all who have influenced me to sin.

2. **I repent** for giving place to the demons of _____ .

3. **I forgive** myself for the pain and limitations I have allowed the demons to inflict upon me.

4. In the Name of Jesus, **I renounce** and break all agreement with the demons (stronghold) of _____ , including all associated demons of _____ , etc.

5. **I take authority** over the demons (stronghold) of _____ , and command you demons of _____ to leave me/us now based on the finished work of Christ on the Cross and His shed Blood.

6. In the Name of Jesus Christ of Nazareth, the Anointed One, Who has given me spiritual authority, **I command** the demons of _____ to go to the dry uninhabited places and never come back.

7. In its place I choose to **receive** _____ .

Lord Jesus, I receive You as my Savior and Lord. I ask you to take control of my life in every way. Fill me with Your Holy Spirit and His power, anointing and fruit. I choose to receive the gifts of the Spirit and to yield my life to You for Your glory and your purposes. Amen

* See the Cross Walk Prayer for a maintenance prayer.

Restoration Prayer Ministry Card
provided by Cross Walk Life, Inc.

Take the helmet of Salvation and the Sword of the Spirit, which is the Word of God. And pray in the Spirit ...
Ephesians 6:17-18

Confess your sins to one another, and pray for one another, that you may be healed. James 5:16

For additional copies of this card, please contact Cross Walk Life, Inc.
128 Prophets Pkwy, Santa Rosa Beach, FL 32459
Web sites: www.cwlinc.com , www.NowFaith.TV and www.RestorationPrayerMinistry.com

Opportunities

18 Hour Restoration Prayer Ministry Works Better

You can't heal your heart with your head; you can't heal spiritual problems with analysis. What we do is not talking it to death, rewriting history or behavior modification. God has shown us how to offer an integrated ministry, including His revelations given to many ministries. Restoration Prayer Ministry is **over 18 hours of integrated ministry,** praying over issues from your whole life. We offer follow-up appointments and mentoring. Our alumni can continue a growing lifestyle with a godly strategy for mentoring, training, activations, ongoing education and residential internships.

We begin with a strong start in cooperation with the supernatural power of God. We take a 6 hour history of the patterns and blockages in your spirit, soul and body. We hear God's voice for the **root symptoms and causes** and His strategies.

We partner with God to break the power of long standing **destructive patterns.**

1. We renounce the **deceptions and ungodly beliefs** blocking your true identity.
2. We break the power of **word curses, bitterroot judgments and expectations.**
3. We invite Holy Spirit to heal **hurts and memories** that have been suppressed.
4. We minister **lasting deliverance** from bondages and spiritual oppression.
5. We bring alignment of your **identity, personal purpose and the power** of God.

Restoration Prayer Ministry is NOT a one-time fix; it's a life style of growing in freedom. Once you are healed and free, you will be ready for mentoring and training. You may come in person or make appointments by phone or free Skype.com or ooVoo.com.

First steps to apply: Go to http://www.restorationprayerministry.com/restoration.html

- Read the 4 articles about RPM
- 10 page application and costs
- Request a phone interview
- Agree on appointment times
- Make reservations by donating
- Sign and send the 10 page application
- Read *Biblical Healing and Deliverance* by Chester and Betsy Kylstra
- Prepare your heart in prayer

I am usually booked 1-2 months ahead of time. Be sure to call ASAP!

Mentoring opportunities

We are delighted to offer mentoring by phone, Internet, Skype, ooVoo.com or in person at your site or ours. Mentoring is important for those who are called to the ministry, business, education, media, government, arts, marketplace ministry, and everyone who is called to include ministry in their business and outreaches.

Our purpose is to provide a place for you to receive unconditional love, wisdom and insight so that you will develop such an intimate relationship with God, that you can be transformed and impart His restoration and transformation to others, who will be able to better fulfill their callings, with adequate healing, freedom mentoring and training.

We are available to be a Christian mentor for you or your ministry teams, on site at your ministry or with mentoring for ministry internships here at Cross Walk Life. If you have ministers or team candidates who are called and gifted to minister, we are available to train them, if they meet the pre-requisites. See our requirements for mentoring and internships on our main mentoring pages at **www.CrossWalkLife.com**

Most people begin mentoring with follow up appointments after receiving RPM. They continue to submit issues and ungodly beliefs for healing and deliverance. They learn to tear down personal strongholds using our audio course and manual on CD. As they begin attending NowFaith.TV, they send in a paragraph of testimony homework after viewing each video and I reply in writing or in phone appointments. They participate in our conversations and testify on Facebook and on Cross Walk Talk Radio, our online talk show. You can host a seminar or webinar for your small group or teams whether they are small or large.

We are happy to offer MEGA Weekend training and activations for your teams. See the form to apply to be a training host on our main seminar page.

Your 8 step mentoring plan:

- **Restoration Prayer Ministry** - Six three hour sessions to get healed and free and to identify your mentoring plan
- **Mentoring follow-up appointments** - learn to use your new tools as a lifestyle of overcoming
- **Tearing Down Personal Strongholds** course and manual on computer CD
- **Resources** - Courses and whole seminars on CDs, DVDs and as downloads
- **NowFaith.TV Video Training School Online** - Interactive mentoring using videos, audios, articles, prayers, emails and appointments
- **Participate on Facebook** and our live call in program **Cross Walk Talk Radio** online
- **Seminars and webinars** - Host your own or attend a MEGA Weekend or sizzling Saturday of training and activation.
- **Internships** - Requirements and applications for 1-2 or 3-6 months of residential internship

Join NowFaith.TV Training School - Online - Any time
Videos, audios, articles, prayers
Live ministry demonstrations
Hot Cutting Edge Interviews
Whole video training seminars
Pastoral Prayer and Counseling
Earn a Certificate of Attendance

TO ENROLL: Go to www.NowFaith.TV and click JOIN

1. Read our NowFaith.TV Covenant
2. Introduce yourself to us
3. Be a blessed contributing member
4. Fill out the interests questionnaire
5. **Click Schools - Ministry archives**

REQUIRED READING TO EARN A CERTIFICATE OF ATTENDANCE

FIRST SEMESTER:

Transformation of the Inner Man semester one. (Can order as a used book.) *Biblical Healing and Deliverance* learn know how to minister restoration.

SECOND AND THIRD SEMESTER:

Healing Women's Emotions (Every minister will minister to women. *The Bait of Satan* is a must for all Christians to maintain their own freedom. *Breaking Intimidation* key to walking the walk in faith, free of intimidation. *Search for Significance* with workbook for renouncing ungodly beliefs.

HOMEWORK: The homework, for each class is to email a testimony of Holy Spirit's work in your life after you prayed the prayer for that class. Your testimony must be less than one page and include a balance of your ISSUE BEFORE, the PRAYER you prayed and the RESULTS after you prayed. Credit will only be given for a testimony of how God worked in YOUR OWN LIFE and the result.

MINISTRY TRIPS: We are invited to hold seminars for other ministries. Please contact us if you would like to go, can pay your own way (travel, room and board) and assist our ministry team every day, serving us and our host ministry or business.

SEMINARS: We would like to do seminars in your area. Please contact us to schedule a seminar. We are a para-church ministry and hope to be of service to you by offering healing, mentoring and training to your existing local teams or potential teams.

LEARN MORE AT **http://www.restorationprayerministry.com/schools.html**

Resources, Downloads, CDs and DVDs

Visit our online store for a great selection of downloads
http://crosswalklife.com/Download_Store_CWL.html

Tearing Down Strongholds for 40 Days

Jesus demonstrated the key to victory: a 40 day prayer strategy based on scripture. <u>The key is for each person to pray for healing, deliverance and revival in himself for 40 days</u>. We could have instant worldwide revival if every person confessed what sins they had sown, instead of focusing on the person through whom they are reaping!! Please pass this on!

Here is an example of a scripture prayer strategy similar to what Jesus demonstrated in Matthew 4. It is not short; it is 40 days' worth of praying! Please note that it is appropriate, not selfish, to pray down ungodly mindsets and strongholds in yourself first.

1. He drew a circle around Himself and submitted His own heart to God first.
2. He addressed the enemy directly rather than being tricked into fighting people.
3. He used scripture rather than "reason" to fight the enemy.
4. He dealt with the temptations and the mindsets that the enemy offered Him first.
5. He fasted and prayed scripture for <u>40 days</u> (and His results were perfect.)
6. He prayed scripture that related to very specific strongholds.
7. He prayed using His delegated authority along with fasting, and trusted God with the results.

----

40 Day Prayer Strategy

Jesus demonstrated the 40 day Prayer Strategy to tear down strongholds, when He was driven into the wilderness to be tempted. He responded to every mindset that the enemy offered Him with, "It is written ....." Even though He was sinless, He still had to choose to agree with God's truth about Him for 40 days in order to defeat all fragments of the devil's mind sets!

When we are empty of strongholds, then we are finally able to be truly filled with God's Holy Spirit and to be healed people - healing people.

We need to "defrag" our minds (like computers) from every fragment of old and current mental strongholds. Programming in Truth will replace every "program" of agreements with the lies that have been spoken over us. When our obedience is complete, we will be able to take revenge on the devil according to 2 Corinthians 10:4-6. Do you 10-4?

A STRONGHOLD IS a mindset impregnated with hopelessness, which causes us to accept as unchangeable, situations and beliefs that we know are contrary to God's truth about us and all that concerns us.
PRAYER of commitment to pray for 40 days:

Father God, I renounce the deceptions, lies and guilt that have tormented me. In your name, Lord, I strip away every stronghold or mindset in my soul that blocks God's truth. I choose to believe your Word and to submit to truth, in balance, and with my whole heart. I break agreement with all my ancestor's sins. I release all my hurts to your healing and justice. We will covenant together to take the Word of God, resist lies and embrace truth, like Jesus did, for 40 days. We will swing the Sword of the Spirit until we have victory in our own lives and the beam is out of our own eye!

WE WILL UNITE OUR PRAYERS to agree with God's truth rather than our negative mindsets. We will persevere for our hope is in God's Word to us, which will not fail. In the name of Jesus, we loose ourselves from contending with the Word and bind ourselves to God's will, way and timing.

Romans 12:2
2 Do not conform any longer to the pattern of this world, but be transformed by the renewing of your mind. Then you will be able to test and approve what God's will is--his good, pleasing and perfect will.
2 Corinthians 10:4-5
4 The weapons we fight with are not the weapons of the world. On the contrary, they have divine power to demolish strongholds.
5 We demolish arguments and every pretension that sets itself up against the knowledge of God, and we take captive every thought to make it obedient to Christ.
Ephesians 6:11-12
11 Put on the full armor of God so that you can take your stand against the devil's schemes.
12 For our struggle is not against flesh and blood, but against the rulers, against the authorities, against the powers of this dark world and against the spiritual forces of evil in the heavenly realms.
Philippians 1:9-11
9 And this is my prayer: that your love may abound more and more in knowledge and depth of insight,
10 so that you may be able to discern what is best and may be pure and blameless until the day of Christ,
11 filled with the fruit of righteousness that comes through Jesus Christ--to the glory and praise of God.

WE UNITE OUR PRAYERS to loose ourselves from every form of selfish independence and every strategy of the enemy to separate us from others, from God and even from ourselves. We bind ourselves to the unity of the Spirit of God in our homes, churches and in our city. It is written in the Word of God:

Matthew 18:18-20
18 I tell you the truth, whatever you bind on earth will be bound in heaven, and whatever you loose on earth will be loosed in heaven. 19   Again, I tell you that if two of you on earth agree about anything you ask for, it will be done for you by my Father in heaven. 20   For   where two or three come together in my name, there am I with them."
Psalm 133:1

1 How good and pleasant it is when brothers live together in unity!

Proverbs 3:5-7

5 Trust in the LORD with all your heart and lean not on your own understanding;

6 in all your ways acknowledge him, and he will make your paths straight.

7 Do not be wise in your own eyes; fear the LORD and shun evil.

Proverbs 3: 13-18

13 Blessed is the man who finds wisdom, the man who gains understanding,

14 For she is more profitable than silver and yields better returns than gold.

15 She is more precious than rubies; nothing you desire can compare with her.

16 Long life is in her right hand; in her left hand are riches and honor.

17 Her ways are pleasant ways, and all her paths are peace.

18 She is a tree of life to those who embrace her; those who lay hold of her will be blessed.

Proverbs 6:16-19

16 There are six things the LORD hates, seven that are detestable to him:

17 haughty eyes, a lying tongue, hands that shed innocent blood,

18 a heart that devises wicked schemes, feet that are quick to rush into evil,

19 a false witness who pours out lies and a man who stirs up dissension among brothers.

Proverbs 31:11-12, 26-31

10 A wife of noble character who can find? She is worth far more than rubies.

11 Her husband has full confidence in her and lacks nothing of value.

12 She brings him good, not harm, all the days of her life.

26 She speaks with wisdom, and faithful instruction is on her tongue.

27 She watches over the affairs of her household and does not eat the bread of idleness.

28 Her children arise and call her blessed; her husband also, and he praises her:

29 Many women do noble things, but you surpass them all."

30 Charm is deceptive, and beauty is fleeting; but a woman who fears the LORD is to be praised.

31 Give her the reward she has earned, and let her works bring her praise at the city gate.

Ephesians 5:21-27

21 Submit to one another out of reverence for Christ.

22 Wives, submit to your husbands as to the Lord.

23 For the husband is the head of the wife as Christ is the head of the church, his body, of which he is the Savior. 24 Now as the church submits to Christ, so also wives should submit to their husbands in everything.

25 Husbands, love your wives, just as Christ loved the church and gave himself up for her

26 to make her holy, cleansing her by the washing with water through the word,

27 and to present her to himself as a radiant church, without stain or wrinkle or any other blemish, but holy and blameless.

Genesis 2:18

18 The LORD God said, "It is not good for the man to be alone. I will make a helper suitable for him."

Isaiah 32:17

17 The fruit of righteousness will be peace; the effect of righteousness will be quietness and confidence forever.

WE UNITE OUR PRAYERS, to loose ourselves from the effects of the guilt, shame, hurt, trauma and hopelessness that devils have brought into our lives. In the Name of Jesus

Christ, as the bride of Christ, we bind ourselves to Christ our healer, who redeems every experience, removes the pain and makes our weak places strong for His glory.

Isaiah 54:4-5, 14

4 Do not be afraid; you will not suffer shame. Do not fear disgrace; you will not be humiliated. You will forget the shame of your youth and remember no more the reproach of your widowhood.

5 For your Maker is your husband-- the LORD Almighty is his name-- the Holy One of Israel is your Redeemer; he is called the God of all the earth.

14 In righteousness you will be established: Tyranny will be far from you; you will have nothing to fear. Terror will be far removed; it will not come near you.

Isaiah 61:1-4

1 The Spirit of the Sovereign LORD is on me, because the LORD has anointed me to preach good news to the poor. He has sent me to bind up the brokenhearted, to proclaim freedom for the captives and release from darkness for the prisoners,

2 to proclaim the year of the LORD's favor and the day of vengeance of our God, to comfort all who mourn,

3 and provide for those who grieve in Zion-- to bestow on them a crown of beauty instead of ashes, the oil of gladness instead of mourning, and a garment of praise instead of a spirit of despair. They will be called oaks of righteousness, a planting of the LORD for the display of his splendor.

4 They will rebuild the ancient ruins and restore the places long devastated; they will renew the ruined cities that have been devastated for generations.

Isaiah 61:7

7 Instead of your shame, you will have a double portion and instead humiliation they will shout for joy over their portion. Therefore they will possess a double portion in their land, everlasting joy will be theirs.

Joel 2:25-32

25 I will repay you for the years the locusts have eaten-- the great locust and the young locust, the other locusts and the locust swarm -- my great army that I sent among you.

26 You will have plenty to eat, until you are full, and you will praise the name of the LORD your God, who has worked wonders for you; never again will my people be shamed.

27 Then you will know that I am in Israel, that I am the LORD your God, and that there is no other; never again will my people be shamed.

28 And afterward, I will pour out my Spirit on all people. Your sons and daughters will prophesy, your old men will dream dreams, your young men will see visions.

29 Even on my servants, both men and women, I will pour out my Spirit in those days.

30 I will show wonders in the heavens and on the earth, blood and fire and billows of smoke.

31 The sun will be turned to darkness and the moon to blood before the coming of the great and dreadful day of the LORD.

32 And everyone who calls on the name of the LORD will be saved; for on Mount Zion and in Jerusalem there will be deliverance, as the LORD has said, among the survivors whom the LORD calls.

1 John 1:9

9 If we confess our sins, He is faithful and just to forgive our sins and to CLEANSE US FROM ALL UNRIGHTEOUSNESS.

Romans 8:28

28 And we know that God causes all things to work together for good for those that love God, to those who are called according to HIS purposes.

SATAN, WE UNITE OUR PRAYERS to loose ourselves from hopelessness and helplessness and to bind ourselves to God's plans, purposes and VISION for our lives with new faith and commitment.

Jeremiah 32:27

27 "I am the LORD, the God of all mankind. Is anything too hard for me?"

1 Corinthians 1:21-22

21 Now He who established us with you in Christ and anointed us is God, 22 Who also sealed us and gave us the Spirit in our hearts as a pledge.

Jeremiah 33:3

2 This is what the LORD says, he who made the earth, the LORD who formed it and established it--the LORD is his name:

3 Call to me and I will answer you and tell you great and unsearchable things you do not know.

Habakkuk 2:1-2

1 I will stand at my watch and station myself on the ramparts; I will look to see what he will say to me, and what answer I am to give to this complaint.

2 Then the LORD replied: "Write down the revelation and make it plain on tablets so that a herald may run with it.

Romans 5:5

5 and hope does not disappoint us, because God has poured out his love into our hearts by the Holy Spirit, whom he has given us.

WE UNITE OUR PRAYERS to bind ourselves to the love of God, His humility and to be expressions of His heart. We loose ourselves from fleshly concerns, fears and carnal jealousy and envy that divides.

Mark 12:30-31

30 Love the Lord your God with all your heart and with all your soul and with all your mind and with all your strength.'

31 The second is this: `Love your neighbor as yourself.' There is no commandment greater than these."

Matthew 5:8-11

8 Blessed are the pure in heart, for they will see God.

9 Blessed are the peacemakers, for they will be called sons of God.

10 Blessed are those who are persecuted because of righteousness, for theirs is the kingdom of heaven.

11 Blessed are you when people insult you, persecute you and falsely say all kinds of evil against you because of me.

Matthew 5:25-26

25 Settle matters quickly with your adversary who is taking you to court. Do it while you are still with him on the way, or he may hand you over to the judge, and the judge may hand you over to the officer, and you may be thrown into prison.

Matthew 7:3
3 Why do you look at the speck of sawdust in your brother's eye and pay no attention to the plank in your own eye?
Mark 10:42-45
42 Jesus called them together and said, "You know that those who are regarded as rulers of the Gentiles lord it over them, and their high officials exercise authority over them.
43 Not so with you. Instead, whoever wants to become great among you must be your servant,
44 and whoever wants to be first must be slave of all.
45 For even the Son of Man did not come to be served, but to serve, and to give his life as a ransom for many."
John 8:15
15 You judge by human standards; I pass judgment on no one.
Romans 8:1-2
1 Therefore, there is now no condemnation for those who are in Christ Jesus,
2 because through Christ Jesus the law of the Spirit of life set me free from the law of sin and death.
Romans 8:15-17
15 For you did not receive a spirit that makes you a slave again to fear, but you received the Spirit of sonship. And by him we cry, "Abba, Father."
16 The Spirit himself testifies with our spirit that we are God's children.
17 Now if we are children, then we are heirs--heirs of God and co-heirs with Christ, if indeed we share in his sufferings in order that we may also share in his glory.

LORD, WE BIND OURSELVES to Godly motives, to speaking in love, with patience and kindness in every sentence... To speak with humility, without rudeness, self-centeredness or anger... We loose our wrong reactions to offenses. We repent of and loose any right to keep a record of wrongs... We loose ourselves from rejoicing in the other's weaknesses and bind ourselves to rejoicing with them and in the truth. Our words will protect and express our trust in others and show that we believe in them.

Romans 12:9-12
9 Love must be sincere. Hate what is evil; cling to what is good.
10 Be devoted to one another in brotherly love. Honor one another above yourselves.
11 Never be lacking in zeal, but keep your spiritual fervor, serving the Lord.
12 Be joyful in hope, patient in affliction, faithful in prayer.
Romans 15:1
1 We who are strong ought to bear with the failings of the weak and not to please ourselves.
Romans 15:5-7
5 May the God who gives endurance and encouragement give you a spirit of unity among yourselves as you follow Christ Jesus,
6 so that with one heart and mouth you may glorify the God and Father of our Lord Jesus Christ.
7 Accept one another, then, just as Christ accepted you, in order to bring praise to God.
1 Corinthians 9:26-27
26 Therefore I do not run like a man running aimlessly; I do not fight like a man beating the air.
27 No, I beat my body and make it my slave so that after I have preached to others, I myself

will not be disqualified for the prize.
1 Cor 10:13
1 Corinthians 10:13
13 No temptation has seized you except what is common to man. And God is faithful; he will not let you be tempted beyond what you can bear. But when you are tempted, he will also provide a way out so that you can stand up under it.
Galatians 5:22-24
22 But the fruit of the Spirit is love, joy, peace, patience, kindness, goodness, faithfulness,
23 gentleness and self-control. Against such things there is no law.
24 Those who belong to Christ Jesus have crucified the flesh with its passions and desires.
Ephesians 4:14-15
14 Then we will no longer be infants, tossed back and forth by the waves, and blown here and there by every wind of teaching and by the cunning and craftiness of men in their deceitful scheming.
15 Instead, speaking the truth in love, we will in all things grow up into him who is the Head, that is, Christ.
Philippians 2:1-8
1 If you have any encouragement from being united with Christ, if any comfort from his love, if any fellowship with the Spirit, if any tenderness and compassion,
2 then make my joy complete by being like-minded, having the same love, being one in spirit and purpose.
3 Do nothing out of selfish ambition or vain conceit, but in humility consider others better than yourselves.
4 Each of you should look not only to your own interests, but also to the interests of others.
5 Your attitude should be the same as that of Christ Jesus:
6 Who, being in very nature God, did not consider equality with God something to be grasped,
7 but made himself nothing, taking the very nature of a servant, being made in human likeness.
8 And being found in appearance as a man, he humbled himself and became obedient to death-- even death on a cross!

IN JESUS' NAME, we loose ourselves from strongholds of unforgiveness, distrust, fear and anger rooted in the victim spirit, painful memories, fear of closeness, and our "rights." We bind ourselves to mercy and grace, trust, and forgiving as Jesus did, paying the price.

Ephesians 4:30-32
30 And do not grieve the Holy Spirit of God, with whom you were sealed for the day of redemption.
31 Get rid of all bitterness, rage and anger, brawling and slander, along with every form of malice.
32 Be kind and compassionate to one another, forgiving each other, just as in Christ God forgave   you
Ephesians 4:26-27
26 In your anger do not sin": Do not let the sun go down while you are still angry,
27 and do not give the devil a foothold.
Philippians 2:12-13

12   Therefore, my dear friends, as you have always obeyed--not only in my presence, but now much more in my absence--continue to work out your salvation with fear and trembling,

13   for it is God who works in you to will and to act according to his good purpose.

Colossians 3:14-15

14 And over all these virtues put on love, which binds them all together in perfect unity.

15 Let the peace of Christ rule in your hearts, since as members of one body you were called to peace. And be thankful.

1 Peter 2:20-25

20 But how is it to your credit if you receive a beating for doing wrong and endure it? But if you suffer for doing good and you endure it, this is commendable before God.

21 To this you were called, because Christ suffered for you, leaving you an example that you should follow in his steps.

22 "He committed no sin, and no deceit was found in his mouth."

23 When they hurled their insults at him, he did not retaliate; when he suffered, he made no threats. Instead, he entrusted himself to him who judges justly.

24 He himself bore our sins in his body on the tree, so that we might die to sins and live for righteousness; by his wounds you have been healed.

25 For you were like sheep going astray, but now you have returned to the Shepherd and Overseer of your souls.

IN JESUS' NAME, we loose ourselves from the strongholds of control, manipulation and self-indulgence rooted in fears of hurt, interdependence, bonding and in not giving others value. We bind ourselves to Your servant heart out of faith, love and peace.

Hebrews 11:6

6 And without faith it is impossible to please God, because anyone who comes to him must believe that he exists and that he rewards those who earnestly seek him.

Hebrews 12:14-15

14 Make every effort to live in peace with all men and to be holy; without holiness no one will see the Lord.

15 See to it that no one misses the grace of God and that no bitter root grows up to cause trouble and defile many.

James 1:8

8 A double minded man is unstable in all his ways.

James 1:12

12 Blessed is the man who perseveres under trial, because when he has stood the test, he will receive the crown of life that God has promised to those who love him.

James 3:17-18

17 But the wisdom that comes from heaven is first of all pure; then peace-loving, considerate, submissive, full of mercy and good fruit, impartial and sincere.

18 Peacemakers who sow in peace raise a harvest of righteousness.

James 5:16

16 Therefore confess your sins to each other and pray for each other so that you may be healed. The prayer of a righteous man is powerful and effective.

IN JESUS' NAME, we loose ourselves from the strongholds of protection behind false securities, confusing the issues and every facade we use to protect our flesh. We bind ourselves to the love of Jesus, integrity, truth, His joyful strength and genuine motives.

Hebrews 4:12-13
12 For the word of God is living and active. Sharper than any double-edged sword, it penetrates even to dividing soul and spirit, joints and marrow; it judges the thoughts and attitudes of the heart.
13 Nothing in all creation is hidden from God's sight. Every creature is uncovered and laid bare before the eyes of him to whom we must give account.

1 Peter 3:7
7 Husbands, in the same way be considerate as you live with your wives, and treat them with respect as the weaker partner and as heirs with you of the gracious gift of life, so that nothing will hinder your prayers.

1 John 1:6-10
6 If we claim to have fellowship with him yet walk in the darkness, we lie and do not live by the truth.
7 But if we walk in the light, as he is in the light, we have fellowship with one another, and the blood of Jesus, his Son, purifies us from all sin.
8 If we claim to be without sin, we deceive ourselves and the truth is not in us.
9 If we confess our sins, he is faithful and just and will forgive us our sins and purify us from all unrighteousness.
10 If we claim we have not sinned, we make him out to be a liar and his word has no place in our lives.

Philippians 4:5-8
5 Let your gentleness be evident to all. The Lord is near.
6 Do not be anxious about anything, but in everything, by prayer and petition, with thanksgiving, present your requests to God.
7 And the peace of God, which transcends all understanding, will guard your hearts and your minds in Christ Jesus.
8 Finally, brothers, whatever is true, whatever is noble, whatever is right, whatever is pure, whatever is lovely, whatever is admirable--if anything is excellent or praiseworthy--think about such things.

1 John 4:18-19
18 There is no fear in love. But perfect love drives out fear, because fear has to do with punishment. The one who fears is not made perfect in love.
19 We love because he first loved us.

Be Blessed as you pray in corporate agreement for 40 days, Carlotta

If you like scripture prayer strategies, see our archives at
www.CrossWalkLife.com

Bibliography

Bevere, John. (1973). *Breaking the Power of Intimidation.* Lake Mary, FL. Charisma House.

Campbell, Ross. (1982) Anger Ladder. Radio program.

Deere, Jack. Religious Spirits. Cassette tape. (n.d.)

John G. Lake. (2003). *The John G. Lake Sermons.* Dallas Texas. Christ for the Nations.

John & Paula Sandford. (1979). *Restoring the Christian Family.* Tulsa, OK. Victory House.

John & Paula Sandford. (1982). *Transformation of the Inner Man.* Tulsa, OK. Victory House, Inc.

Joyner, R. (1997). *Epic battles of the last days.* New Kensington, Pa. Whitaker House

Kylstra, C., & Kylstra, B. (2005). *Biblical healing and deliverance: A guide to experiencing freedom from sins of the past, destruction beliefs, emotional and spiritual pain curses and oppression.* Grand Rapids, Mich.: Chosen.

Kylstra, C., & Kylstra, B. (1994) *Restoring the Foundations.* Santa Rosa Beach, FL. Proclaiming His Word Publications.

Kylstra, C., & Kylstra, B. (2002) *Restoring the Foundations Issue-Focused Ministry.* Santa Rosa Beach, FL. Proclaiming His Word Publications.

Savard, Liberty. (1995) *Breaking the Power* (pg 30, Bridge-Logos. Copyrighted material used here by permission of author.

Savard, Liberty. (1993) *Shattering Your Strongholds.* North Brunswick, NJ. Bridge Logos.

Schultz, Steve and Gaborit, Chris. (1996) *Mentoring & Fathering.* Santa Rosa Beach, FL. Christian International Ministries.

Solomon, Charles. The Exchanged Life Seminar.

Wright, H. (2000). *A More Excellent Way.* Thomaston, GA. Pleasant Valley Publications.